William Findley

History Of The Insurrection In The Four Western Counties Of

Pennsylvania

William Findley

History Of The Insurrection In The Four Western Counties Of Pennsylvania

ISBN/EAN: 9783741117190

Manufactured in Europe, USA, Canada, Australia, Japa

Cover: Foto ©ninafisch / pixelio.de

Manufactured and distributed by brebook publishing software
(www.brebook.com)

William Findley

History Of The Insurrection In The Four Western Counties Of Pennsylvania

HISTORY

OF THE

INSURRECTION,

IN THE

FOUR WESTERN COUNTIES

OF

PENNSYLVANIA:

IN THE YEAR M.DCC.XCIV.

WITH A RECITAL OF THE CIRCUMSTANCES SPECI-
ALLY CONNECTED THEREWITH:

AND AN

HISTORICAL REVIEW OF THE PREVIOUS SITUATION OF THE COUNTRY.

———————

BY WILLIAM FINDLEY,

MEMBER OF THE HOUSE OF REPRESENTATIVES OF THE UNITED STATES.

———————

PHILADELPHIA:

PRINTED BY SAMUEL HARRISON SMITH,
No. 118, CHESNUT-STREET.

M.DCC.XCVI.

PREFACE.

PERHAPS there is no nation on the earth, that has in fo fhort a period experienced fuch various and interefting fcenes as the people of the United States. Compofed as they are of individual adventurers from different nations, or the defcendants of fuch, and bringing with them the various habits and languages of the nations to which they had refpectively belonged, braving the horrors of the wildernefs, and combating unaided with favage tribes, they affociated together in fmall dependent republics, and always admitted the emigrants from other nations to a participation of their privileges, and emigrants of different nations and languages attached themfelves to the fociety and foil, and foon learned to embrace the country as if it had been their native land. The colonies adapted their laws to their own fituation and circumftances, and all of them preferved a love of liberty and equality in their focial order. Though the feeds of jealoufy were artfully fown among them by the power on whom they were dependent, yet watchful againft thofe infidious arts, they united to vindicate their rights againft the aggreffions of that very power, whofe authority they were accuftomed to acknowledge, and by their exertions finally triumphed over it, till they affumed a rank and ftation among the independent nations of the earth. They not only formed conftitutions and laws, for the internal police of their respective states, but for the government of the whole, in a national capacity, and changed and revised not only their laws, but the forms and powers of their government, without an appeal to arms, and without the effects of those changes operating any sensible alteration in the circumstances of the people, nd thus exhibited a spectacle, new and interesting in the history of human events.

The citizens, being thus collected from various nations, or from such different parts of the same nation as had little correspondence with each other, and their character being influenced by a continual succession of emigrants, they seem to have formed a character peculiar to themselves, and in some respects [distinct from that of other nations. Indeed though they emigrated from different nations, they were generally of the same rank in society. None of the privileged orders of Europe visited the colonies, except as governors of provinces, when the government of a province became, by the industry of the planters, an object sufficient for the support of a lord, whose ancestors had dissipated the family estate, or who enjoyed a noble title without a patrimony. Privileged orders never made a part of the mass in the colonial settlements, and the settlers derive their dignity and importance, through the natural and honourable channels of prudence and industry.

Perhaps no part of the American character is more prominent than that of mildness of temper ; even their mobs and riots are accompanied with less ferocity, and marked with fewer instances of bloodshed, than those of any other nation. Even during that period at the commencement of the revolution, when the regular governments gave way to what in the language of law was called a government of mobs, or committees acting according to discretion, and under peculiar circumstances of irritation, occasioned by the opposition of the adherents to the old government, yet the public peace was preserved and property secured, and the severities towards the opposers of the revolution were more mild than has been exhibited by any other nation in similar circumstances.

During a tedious war, in which the citizens generally were at one time or other perfonally engaged, there was an unavoidable relaxation of morals, and of the execution of the laws, yet notwithstanding this circumstance, the weaknefs of the general government, and the preffure of an accumulating debt, which neceffarily occafioned oppreffive taxes on the people, and difcontent among the creditors, I fay thefe imperious circumstances were fo well borne during the continuance of the confederation, that there was no fymptom of an infurrection, except in one inftance in the ftate of Maffachu-fetts. Though this infurrection is acknowledged to have been excited by very oppreffive taxes, and to have been long premeditated and well digefted, and occafioned confiderable alarm for fome time, yet it was finally fettled almoft without bloodfhed, or occafioning any lafting confufion. That under fo great a change as was made by the revifion of the federal government, and the new extenfion of its fifcal powers to internal objects of taxation, and the operation of thefe powers on fubjects, and in modes, againft which the people in moft of the ftates had the ftrongeft prepoffeffions, it being only known to them by the odium of its name, and that odium having been ftrongly fanctioned by the firft Congrefs, and the law, from not having provided for extending the judicial authority of the federal government, being ill calculated for the convenient protection of the fifcal officers, or citizens aggrieved by their means, I fay that, under fuch circumftances, violent oppofition fhould have been given but in one diftant furvey, affords a further proof of the mildnefs of the American character, and of a prevailing love of order and refpect for the authority of the laws; and if even this inftance was unpremeditated and defultory, and might have been eafily prevented by a proper and feafonable application of the means provided by law, and if when all the circumftances are taken into view, and proper allowances made for the indifcretions of thofe who took a temporary lead in the exceffes, and for the ufual appearances of human nature in a ftate of extreme agitation ; I fay, when all thefe circumftances are confidered maturely, and proper allowances made, I apprehend the infurrection in the weftern counties of Pennfylvania will not form a very ftrong exception to the mildnefs of the American character.

Having been an early actor in, and an attentive obferver of, the American revolution and its confequences, and having been under early apprehenfions, that the introduction of the excife fyftem without competent arrangements for the prompt execution of it would put the American character to a new teft, and thefe apprehenfions being excited by the deep rooted prejudices which I knew to have always exifted againft it in the weftern country, where providence had ordered my lot, I was anxious to procure a repeal of the law, or, that not appearing to be then attainable, to have it fo modified as to give the leaft poffible caufe of irritation. I was attentive, as far as I had an opportunity to imprefs the people with whom I correfponded, with a fenfe of the danger of riots, and to advife thofe intrufted with the execution of the laws to purfue fuch meafures as might feafonably difcourage a difpofition to violent oppofition; but my advice to this purpofe not being taken, I fat down in folemn filence, to wait the event. And unfortunately, that event happened which my fears had in fome meafure anticipated, and which I had for fome time fufpected was defired by fome, who appear to have been much better acquainted, than I was, with the difpofition that led to the infurrection, and were poffeffed of the means of preventing it. I was more fortunate, however, in my private correfpondents ; for, with one lonely exception, they were all uniformly friends of order.

Such an extraordinary event happening fo near to the place of my refidence, and among a people who then formed a part of my immediate conftituents, and fuddenly fpreading its influence over a confiderable extent of country, and involving not only the actors, but thofe who endeavoured to quench the fpreading flame, and even fuch as ftudied to act the part of heutral obfervers, in anxiety and dread, and determining thofe who adminiftered the government to have recourfe to the phyfical power of the nation, feemed to me a proper fubject for hiftorical inveftigation.

I conceived, that a record of the infurrection, and of the circumftances which led to it, and the events connected with it, might be of ufe, to teach the citizens in other places, and perhaps in future times, the danger of fmall beginnings in making oppofition to eftablifhed laws, and of connecting their refpect to the government, with the prejudices they may entertain againft perfons in office, or even with their prepoffeffions againft particular laws. It may alfo teach the lovers of order, the impropriety of affecting a neutrality of conduct, in the time of civil convulfion. They will difcover, that if a fpirit of diforder is permitted to prevail, no character or intereft in fociety will be fecured from its effects. And that if government is reduced to the neceffity of extraordinary efforts, even the innocent may not always be fecure from hardfhips in the refult.

A knowledge of thefe events may be of ufe even to thofe who are intrufted with the adminiftration of the government, if fuch a crifis fhould ever again happen, or rather for the falutary purpofe of guarding againft fuch emergencies.

If a record of cafes in the practice of medicine is of ufe for the prevention or cure of difeafes in the animal fyftem, certainly a knowledge of the difeafes which fometimes fhake the political frame may be of future advantage, for preventing or correcting fuch events. This is the more neceffary in fuch a government as ours, the ftability and profperity of which depend fo much on the confidence of the citizens at large.

I had many reafons for wifhing this work to have been performed by fome other hand. To write impartially of tranfactions, wherein fo many living characters are concerned, is not a very defirable work, and can fcarcely fail of being cenfured by fome. However, being confcious that I am not in-

b

fluenced by hopes or fears, and being at a time, and in a situation of life, that leaves me little to dread or hope, from the frowns or favours of party, or of men in power, I have studied impartiality in the characters. I have delineated, and the facts which I have stated; and I have sought after truth with the utmost solicitude. Indeed, I have declined introducing such persons by name, especially, where there was any thing disagreeable attached to their character, as were not already rendered very prominent in these transactions.

A history of the western insurrection is also necessary, to correct wrong information that is gone abroad concerning it. Indeed, the citizens of the United States, having no authentic channels, through which to derive information concerning it, can form their opinion only from desultory and unconnected reports, and if there are any, who through prejudice or any other motive, have studiously misrepresented some material circumstances respecting it, or injured the characters of any of the agents engaged one way or other in it, the necessity that there should be some responsible standard for correcting such mistakes, whether they are wilful or inadvertent, is the greater.

I was soon convinced of the necessity of such a work, and early turned my attention towards making preparations for it, but delayed the execution in hopes, that some other person would undertake it; but finding that no person engaged in it, on a plan sufficiently extensive, I resumed the task, but suppressed a number of incidents, which, though they were interesting in themselves, were not essential to the understanding of the general subject, the retaining of which would have swelled the work too much. Many more of these than I intended to insert are to be found related in a very entertaining manner, in a work written by Mr. Brackenridge, which being, however, chiefly confined to what fell under his own observation, is not sufficiently extensive in its plan to supersede the necessity of this work. In some few instances, the facts are differently ftated. In feveral inftances, I have myfelf had occafion to correct the information on which I firft depended.

No part of thefe tranfactions have been more mifreprefented, than the conferences of the commiffioners from the fecond Parkifon ferry meeting, with the Préfident of the United States, at Carlifle, and this feems to have been done with a criminal defign. Aware, that fome mifreprefentations might be made (though not of the extent to which they have been carried), Mr. Redick and myfelf were attentive in keeping the difcourfes in memory, and had frequently, both feparately, and together, repeated the fubftance of them, but particularly, thofe delivered at the meeting convened at Parkifon's ferry to receive the report of our miffion. I wrote out the fubftance of the difcourfes delivered in the various conferences with the Prefident, and fent them to Mr. Redick for his correction, before I inferted them in this work. Though the Prefident expreffed himfelf more largely than is here inferted, yet we only ftudied to preferve the fcope and as nearly in his own language as we could.

However neceffary it was for my own vindication, to introduce my own name and character fo much in the latter part of this work, I would not have troubled the reader with it, if my conduct, and the conduct of fome of my friends, had not been evidently mifreprefented, with a view to caft an odium on Republican principles.

CONTENTS.

(xv)

H I S T O R Y

INSURRECTION, &c.

C H A P. I.

IF the numerous difficulties encountered
and hardſhips ſuſtained, by the people inhabiting the
weſtern counties of Pennſylvania, were to be minutely related, and their behaviour under them fairly ſtated, their conduct generally would be entitled to a
much greater proportion of approbation than blame,
and their ſufferings would have a powerful claim on the
ſympathy of their fellow citizens. But it is not my
intention to give a hiſtory of the peculiar circumſtances, with which the firſt ſettlement and progreſs of
that country was accompanied. A very ſuperficial

ſketch of it, however, will be neceſſary to the right un-
derſtanding of the circumſtances which influenced thoſe
diſorders, which in the year 1794 roſe to ſuch a height
as to be denominated an Inſurrection.

As ſoon as General Boquet had eſtabliſhed peace
with the Indians north-weſt of the Ohio, in the year
1766, a number of people commenced a ſettlement
on the lands adjacent to Redſtone creek, which emp-
ties into the Monongahela river, about forty miles a-
bove its junction with the Allegany at Pittſburgh.

The boundary line not being then run between
Pennſylvania and Virginia, and the land not having
been purchaſed from the Indians, no legal title could
be obtained for land, but it was well known that both
provinces had always admitted the right of pre-emption
to thoſe who had ſettled and improved on the land,
previous to warrants having iſſued for it to any other
perſons.

The proprietary of Pennſylvania having, in the
year 1768, purchaſed the country from the Indians
as far weſt as the Allegany and Ohio rivers, opened an
office for the ſale of thoſe lands on the 3d of April 1769.
When the office was opened he made proclamation,
and inſtructed his ſurveyors to reſpect the lands of actual ſettlers who had improved to the value of five
pounds, and not to ſurvey them on warrants (or locations) of a date poſterior to the ſettlements, except to
thoſe by whom the ſettlements were made.

Favoured by this indulgence, which however was
uſual in both provinces, few of thoſe who lived
adjacent to the Monongahela, and had already occupied the lands, applied to the office for locations or

warrants. They were not certain to which province the foil belonged, and probably had a fecret wifh that it fhould belong to Virginia; becaufe in that cafe it would coft them but about one fourteenth part of the price for which land was fold in Pennfylvania, and men eafily believe according to their wifhes.

In or about the year 1774, governor Lord Dunmore opened feveral offices for the fale of land within the bounds of what are now called the four weftern counties of Pennfylvania. The warrants were granted on paying two fhillings and fix-pence fees: The purchafe money was trifling, being only ten fhillings per hundred acres, and even that was not demanded. This was an effectual inducement to apply to Dunmore's agents in preference to the Pennfylvania landoffice; the land being the property of the king was at the difpofal of the governor, who alfo procured a court of Virginia to be extended to the Ohio, and in a fhort time two county courts were held fouth of the Monongahela, and one north of it at Redftone old fort, all of them within the territory fince afcertained to belong to Pennfylvania. Lord Dunmore alfo commenced an unprovoked war againft the Indians then at peace, and led out an expedition againft their towns, in defence of which a fevere battle was fought at the mouth of the great Kenhawa; in which, though the Indians were defeated, the white people loft a number of men.

From the firft fettlement of this territory the inhabitants had fuffered by occafional predatory excurfions of the Indians, but there had been no general war with them. It was well underftood that the defign of the Britifh governor was to embroil the colonies with each other, and to produce a general Indian war, in order to turn their attention from the rapid progrefs of Britifh encroachments, or weaken their confidence in each other, and oblige them to exhauft their ftrength in an Indian war. Though he failed in the firft, he was too fuccefsful in the laft ; for his wanton attack on the Indians laid the foundation for that favage enmity which they difplayed in their ceafelefs depredations committed on the weftern frontiers during the whole courfe of the revolutionary war, and which probably is not yet extinguifhed.

The governor of Pennfylvania having opened the land-office in April 1769, feveral thoufands of locations were applied for on the firft day. The greateft number of thefe was taken for land laying north of the Monongahela, in what yet continues to be Weftmoreland county, to the greater part of which the claim of Virginia was never fuppofed to extend, and great numbers made actual fettlements in that country without any office rights. This fettlement was very rapidly extended under Pennfylvania, as far north as Crooked creek, above forty miles north of the Monongahela, and the firft fettlers were generally a more fober, orderly people, than commonly happens in the firft fettlement of new countries. A great proportion of them were farmer's fons, or farmers themfelves, with rifing families, who emigrated from the old counties, and who were generally acquainted with each other.

The legiflature erected all the country weft of the Laurel-hill into a county by the name of Weftmoreland, but did not fix a permanent feat of juflice, on account of the unfettled ftate of the country. The courts were provifionally held at Hanna's-town, about three miles north of Greenfburgh, the prefent county town. This county was erected fome years previous to the extenfion of the Virginia courts into that country.

After the Virginia courts were erected a ftrange ftate of fociety was produced, in that part of Weftmoreland county which now forms the counties of Wafhington and Fayette, and that part of Allegany which lies fouth of the Monongahela. Juftices of the peace, who were then judges of the court in both ftates, held commiffions under, and executed the laws of, their refpective ftates, in fuch a manner as that magiftrates, militia officers, &c. exercifed their authority over the people in the fame fettlement, according as they made their election of fubmitting to the one or the other. Many fubmitted alternately to the one or the other, as it comported with their intereft or their caprice, and it is reafonable to believe that by many neither was well fubmitted to. This relaxed ftate of fociety encouraged a greater number of ungovernable people to fettle among them than otherwife would have done.

When the boundary line was amicably fettled towards the end of the Britifh war, a number of thofe who had imbibed the greateft prejudice againft the laws of Pennfylvania, together with thofe who were offended at the high price, which thofe who had always adhered to Pennfylvania were obliged to pay for their land, projected a plan for erecting a new ftate.

By the terms of fettling the boundary every perfon was to hold his land on the terms under which he had firſt fettled. The new ſtate ſcheme being made trea- ſonable by a law of Pennſylvania, was no further at- tempted, but many of thoſe who had ſtrong prejudi- ces againſt the government of Pennſylvania, ſold their plantations, and gave place to others.

During the whole time of the war with Britain, and for ſome time after it ceaſed, the country was cru- elly waſted by perpetual ſavage depredations. The fron- tier was equally expoſed on all ſides, round the whole extent of the country, except perhaps a few miles on the eaſt, near Youghiogany river. The whole of what is now Weſtmoreland and Allegany counties, except a very few townſhips, was either actually laid waſte, or the inhabitants obliged to ſhelter themſelves in forts. The then county town of Weſtmoreland was attacked in the time of court, and though the records were pre- ſerved, yet the town, with moſt of the property it contained, was burnt; a number were alſo killed and taken priſoners. The Indians were ſo numerous as to afford juſt ground to apprehend that they would deſtroy the other ſtations, where people were collected, and a detached party did kill ſeveral at the next ſta- tion; however the firing, which was continued in platoons againſt the fort all that day, was ſo loud as to be heard diſtinctly at eight or nine miles diſtance. This, with the alarm given by thoſe who eſcaped from the court, put the people in the interior part of the country on their guard. At this time it was uſual with the Indians to attack thoſe ſettlements in great force, accompanied by the militia of Canada.

But though the northern frontier of this country was thus perpetually harraffed, thofe in the more fouthwardly fettlements were by no means exempted from their fhare of the general diftrefs. Scarcely a neighbourhood in that whole extent of country, where favage cruelty could not be diftinctly traced by the deftruction of property and the blood of the inhabitants. The competition between the two rival governments, by preventing their union and fyftem, greatly weakened their exertions in the common defence, and it was near the clofe of the war, before any accommodation was likely to take place by arrangements being made for an amicable adjuftment of the boundary line.

Though this ftate of fociety was extremely difagreeable, and naturally invited to the difplay of an ungovernable difpofition, and in fact prevented proper meafures for promoting the education of youth, and while it continued difcouraged minifters of the gofpel from fettling in the country, yet it muft be acknowledged, that notwithftanding the party animofity, the controverfy was conducted with a milder fpirit than has been ufually difcovered in fimilar fituations. Though there were fome inftances of oppofition to the execution of the laws of the interfering ftates, yet there were no outrageous riots, no lives loft, no deftruction of property. One perfon indeed loft his life at Pittfburgh in a party quarrel, but it was a private quarrel, not a riot. On the whole, crimes do not appear to have been more frequent there than in places where fuch circumftances did not exift. I went to refide in the weftern country about the time this con-

troverfy was near the conclufion, and obferved a
good deal of heat and animofity, but no violence, nor
traces of it.

How different was this from other contefts of the
fame nature. The bloodfhed and violence committed
in the controverfy about the boundary line between
Pennfylvania and Maryland, are ftill remembered by
the name of the Conejaghally war; fome of the he-
roes, who gained their military fame by their exertions in that war, have not been many years de-
ceafed.

The conteft between Pennfylvania and the Connecticut claimants has occafioned bloodfhed and numerous acts of outrageous violence, both before and
fince the revolution. And notwithftanding the decree of a court of Congrefs, determining the right
of territory to be in Pennfylvania, yet that ftate has,
fince the decree of fettlement, been obliged to fend
different military expeditions into that country. Though
confiderable feverity has marked the progrefs of fome
of thefe expeditions, yet they have not proved adequate to the object. Recourfe has been had to quieting laws; but thefe, though made on the moft gene-
rous principles, have been defeated by the claimants
in whofe favour they were made, and the commiffioners of peace obliged to fave their lives by flight, or
be taken prifoners. Even Mr. Pickering, the then
prothonotary of Luzerne county, but now the fecretary of ftate, when deciding on a beneficent law, which
he had done much to procure in their favour, was violently feized and detained many days a prifoner in
the woods, from whence he with difficulty efcaped.

Nor has this controverfy yet fubfided. A Pennfylvanian dare not even now fettle on his own land. One
who lately attempted it was fhot in his lodging,
and though, in the opinion of the court, the murder
was fully proved, a verdict could not be obtained a-
gainft the criminal. A combination has long exifted,
and ftill does exift, in that country, in declared oppofition to the laws, and too ftrong for the ordinary
powers of the civil magiftrate.

How different this from the conduct of the people
in the weftern counties. There, there was no neceffity to call to their aid the authority of Congrefs,
no armies had to be marched againft them, nor any
unconftitutional laws paffed impairing the rights of
contract in their favour. They fubmitted to the decifions
of the ordinary courts of the refpective ftates, if not
wholly without murmuring, yet without flagrant oppofition or perfonal violence.

C

_____

C H A P. II.

Of the State Excife Law.

UNDER the colonial government of Pennfylvania, in the year 1756, an excife had been levied on imported fpirits. The legiflatures of the colonies, having no power to levy impofts at the ports, took that method of difcouraging the confumption of foreign fpirits and raifing a revenue from it. The law was enacteft for a limited time, and the revenue arifing from it appropriated to the redemption of certain bills of credit. In March 1772,the former excife law was revived, and the tax was extended not only to wine, rum, and brandy, but to fpirits diftilled from the natural products of the province, excepting what was for the private ufe of the owner.

I never have underftood that the law as far as it refpected domeftic produce was executed. I knew nothing of it at the time, and though I was acquainted with many diftillers, I never heard of an excife-man vifiting them. I have made enquiry, fince that

time, of many who were born and refided in different
counties of the province, fome of whom had ftills,
and cannot difcover that they knew any thing about
the execution of that part of the law. Probably all
that was diftilled from domeftic produce was confidered
as for the ufe of the owner, and this was indeed, in
a great meafure, the cafe, for the citizens took their
rye and malt to the ftill, nearly on the fame principles as they took their grift to the mill, and paid for
the diftillation either in kind or an equivalent in money. At this time rum diftilled from molaffes became
an article of great confumption ; it was purchafed at
from two fhillings to two and fixpence per gallon by
the barrel ; and as it coft the farmers nothing to bring
it home in the waggons with which they hawled out
their flour, they found it to be more profitable than
their own whifkey.

In the time of the revolutionary war, when neither foreign rum nor molaffes could be imported, the
demand for domeftic diftilled fpirits for the army and
for general confumption became exceeding great, and
the manufacturing of it became fo profitable, that not
only the rye but a great quantity of wheat was confumed by diftillation. In many parts of the country you could fcarcely get out of fight of the fmoke of
a ftill-houfe. The citizens became alarmed, left the
army fhould fuffer for want of bread for the troops,
and forage for the horfes. The clergy from the pul-
pits, and in fome inftances by judicial warnings of
prefbyteries, inveighed againft this alarming deftruction of bread from the army and the poor, and againft
the ftill-houfes, as the general nurferies of intoxication

and licentioufnefs. There was no law then in force to prevent diftillers from felling in fmall quantities, confequently thofe who loved to get drunk at a fmall expence, reforted to the ftills. The manners of our youth were much endangered by the number of the ftills, and by affociating with fuch as ufually reforted to thefe recepticles of vice. The army foon felt the effects of this wafte of grain to an alarming degree.

In March 1779, the affembly enacted a law to prevent the diftillation of all kinds of grain or meal, but in October following it was repealed fo far as to permit the diftillation of rye and barley. The vaft number of hands employed in the militia and ftanding army had leffened the number of labouring hands; the low price of grain at the beginning of the war had difcouraged the farmers, and many through the ftate, who were difaffected to the revolution, or principled againft war, had raifed lefs grain than ufual, with a defign to prevent the army from being fupplied. Thefe circumftances, added to the confumption by diftillation, gave fuch a ferious alarm as rendered it neceffary not only to difcourage the diftilling of grain, but to lay an embargo on the exportation of grain and flour in the port of Philadelphia. Diftillation, by the abufes attending it, and exorbitant profits made by it, was become unpopular, and the neceffity of a revenue was become extremely urgent to preferve the exiftence of the government itfelf.

This was undoubtedly a fituation that juftified on every principle the levying an excife, and this con-

viction was fo general among the people, that a confiderable revenue was raifed from it during the continuance of the war.

In the year 1780, Congrefs refolved that an al-
lowance fhould be made to the army for the depreciation of its pay, and required the flates-refpectively to
liquidate and provide for the difcharge of it.   The
State of Pennfylvania iffued certificates for the liqui-
dated depreciation, and made it optional for the holders to receive paper bills emitted on the credit of the
State to the difcharge of the one third of the amount;
thefe bills being then much depreciated, though afterwards redeemed at par, many of the certificate holders
declined to accept of them. A large tract of land Weft
of the Allegany-river, and fome confifcated property,
were appropriated for the final difcharge of that debt;
but the confifcated property was but of fmall value,
and the mortgaged property could not then be rendered productive. When it was brought into the market
feveral years after peace was reftored, and fold by
auction, only a fmall portion of it could be fold at
any price, and what did fell went at a very low rate.
The rage for land fpeculation had not then commenced.

The legiflature always treated the depreciation
as a favoured claim, and the funds appropriated
for the difcharge of it not being productive,   on
the application of the officers of the Pennfylvania
line a law was paffed, by which the revenue arifing
from the excife was appropriated to the payment of
the intereft and the final difcharge of that debt,
though every other fource of revenue was then
brought into operation, even to an oppreffive extent,

yet the proceeds were appropriated to fatisfy the requifitions of Congrefs, and to other indifpenfible purpofes; confequently no provifion was made for the debt due for militia fervices, fupplies, &c. till the year 1785, when revenues were appropriated for paying the intereft of both the debt of the State, and of the United States, in the hands of citizens who were original holders. A fum was alfo given in aid of the excife, to difcharge the arrears of intereft due on the depreciation debt.

If the excife tax could have been collected, it would, in a fhort time, not only have paid the intereft, but difcharged the principal of the depreciation debt. In 1786, Mr. Robert Morris made a propofal to the committee of ways and means to take it on farm, and pay into the ftate treafury feventy thoufand pounds per annum; but farming of revenues having been practifed only under defpotic governments, and perhaps only practicable there, the propofal was rejected, but no doubt was entertained but that a neat fum to that amount might have been produced by it, if it could have been collected; but when it was beft collected it produced only fifteen thoufand pounds, and that only for two or three years; and this was chiefly raifed from imported fpirits and wines; but the neighbouring ftates not having excife laws, even the excife tax on foreign liquors was much evaded.

For fome time after the fettlement of the weftern Counties commenced, diftillation was not introduced, but the fpirits confumed there were brought from the eaft fide of the mountains, and during the war little progrefs could be made in promoting the manufacture of Spirits; consequently little attention was paid to the collection of excise in that country, though I find that the prothonotary of Westmoreland collected some in that County under his authority of collecting the tax on tavern licences. It might have been longer neglected, if the excise offices for those counties had not been urgently solicited by one Graham, who formerly kept the black-horse tavern in Market-street, and who obtained a commission for collecting the excise tax in all the western counties. A person of a more fair character and greater discretion would have been necessary for the successful discharge of that trust, but such did not apply.

Before this time, it was generally known that very little of the excise tax on domestic distilled spirits was then collected in the old settled counties; in most of them none at all. Mr. Bartholomew, the excise officer of Philadelphia, informed me that he had declined demanding it from the distillers of grain or fruit. The members of assembly from Chester county, some of whom were distillers, said that none was collected there. This was generally known to have been the case throughout the state at large, but more especially in those counties bordering on other states.

None of the neighbouring states having excise laws, rendered it the more impracticable and odious in Pennsylvania. The State of New Jersey, pressed with the debts contracted in the course of the war, and having neither commercial revenue, nor any lands to dispose of, consequently having no resources from imposts or land offices, as the neighbouring states of New-York and Pennsylvania had, attempted about this time to aid her revenue

by an excife, but never could bring it into operation :
It was wholly defeated in the firft attempt by a powerful combination of the citizens of that ftate.

Thefe circumftances were well known in the weftern counties, and occafioned them to be more reluctant in the payment of that tax. Thofe who had been
prejudiced againft the laws of Pennfylvania, and never experienced an excife tax, difcovered a ferious re-
pugnance to the execution of it. However the diftillers in Weftmoreland pretty generally fettled with the
collector of excife, and paid him confiderable fums of
money. He often converfed with me on the fubject,
and acknowledged that he fucceeded equal to his expectations.

The people however complained that the collector
acted contrary to law in feveral inftances, and he acknowledged he did to Col. Cook the Judge of the court,
and told him that the magiftrates ought to protect him
in doing fo in fome inftances, as it contributed to the
public fervices. He was informed that if he did not
confider himfelf to be bound by the laws in the difcharge
of his duty, he muft not be furprifed if the people
did not regulate their conduct towards him agreeably
to the laws.

However he met with no interruption, till fome
time after at the court of Weftmoreland, when in the
evening a man in difguife, fupported by feveral others,
called him to the door of his chamber, and attempted
to pull him out, telling him that he was Belzebub, and
would deliver him to a number of other devils who
waited for him without. But the collector being armed with piftols ftood on his defence, and with the affift-

ance of some in the room kept them out, nor would he suffer those in the room to go out during the night.

The collector commenced a prosecution against the person, who, he supposed, personated Belzebub, and some others, but satisfactory proof being given to the court, that the collector had mistaken the person, he was of course acquitted, and the collector's character was so freely treated by some of the gentlemen of the bar, that he left the court as soon as he perceived his mistake was discovered. An imputation of a mistake of that kind had been alleged against him formerly. To do him justice however, I suspect that he rather mistook the time than the person. Greater mistakes of the same nature have since been made by others.

Some time after this, however, he met with worse treatment in Washington county. He was there attacked by a mob, who, after shaving him, cutting off his hair, and dressing his horse's mane and tail in such a manner as to disfigure him, brought him into Westmoreland county and let him go. No doubt other attempts were made to intimidate and discourage him, but I have neither heard from himself nor any other person, of any subsequent outrages committed against him. I have never understood how much money he received. I believe in some instances he compounded for what he could get without trouble, and as there was no check on him, he probably detained the largest share of the money in his own hands. When the su-

D

preme judges came to hold a court of Oyer and Terminer in Wafhington, he commenced a profecution againft twelve perfons, who were convicted and fined, and compelled to pay high damages to the collector, which I am informed he received, and then refigned his commiffion.

Afterwards, a man of the name of Craig accepted of the office of excife for the weftern counties. His fon, who acted as his deputy, I was acquainted with; he behaved himfelf well, and appeared to be fuccefsful; but his father getting into fome quarrels, near the place of his refidence, complaints went againft him, and he was removed.

The reprefentatives from thefe counties were much importuned to have the law repealed, but this could not be done until fome other fund could be procured to appropriate as a fubftitute, and all the other funds were at this time overburthened. They were mortified however to fee the authority of the ftate degraded by the non-execution of the excife law. To remedy this evil feveral unfuccefsful endeavours were made to revife the law, and to procure more refpectable officers.

John Baird, Efq. then a member of the fupreme executive council of the ftate, and myfelf, applied to a refpectable perfon, well known in that country, and obtained his confent to ferve, but when the commiffion arrived he declined accepting it. Before the law was repealed, another perfon, well qualified for the appointment, accepted of it, and kept his office for fome time in Pittfburgh, but foon refigned it.

There were no riots but thofe I have mentioned a-
gainft Graham ; but as all thofe who held the office
received fome money, for which it was believed they
never accounted, (probably they did not receive
more than was a competent compenfation), thofe that
paid at firft, feeing others efcape with impunity, refufed to comply. They all knew, that in the old
counties it was generally paid only on foreign liquors.

Some may wifh to know how the people in fo remote a country knew fo well what was done in the
eaftern counties. It is neceffary they fhould be
informed, that a great proportion of the weftern farmers ufually go over the mountains, every year after
feeding time, to bring up their falt, when they generally vifit their friends, where they formerly refided, and are informed of the news of the country.
All the falt, and many other articles confumed in
the weftern counties, are purchafed from the ftore-
keepers on the eaft fide of the mountains, and carried
to the weftern counties on horfe-back, in cags, or
bags. In this way they have to carry it from above one
to two hundred miles.

It was long expected, that the thirteen ftates
would agree to veft Congrefs with the power of levying an impoft on goods imported. Under this impreffion the funding law of the ftate was enacted in
1785. The depreciation debt had been funded before, and one year's intereft had been paid on a great
part of the domeftic debt. This had been done with
a view to equalize the diftreffes of the citizens, and

give a check to the prevailing fpeculations on certificates, and raife the price in the market of thofe which
had not been alienated, till Congrefs could provide
otherwife for them, which was then daily expected
to be put in their power by the thirteenth ftate agreeing to the five per cent. impoft.

———

C H A P. III.

WHEN the federal government was organifed, and before provifion had been made for the public debt, the affembly of Pennfylvania repealed the law for levying a direct tax, and left the excife unrepealed. This meafure was much influenced by one of the members of Congrefs, who refided in the city, and had newly returned from congrefs at New-York; the fame who always introduced the meafures, originated by the fecretary of the treafury, in the form of refolves, in the Houfe of Reprefentatives; but it was oppofed by a numerous minority, of which the weftern members compofed a part. They wifhed to continue the direct tax a year longer, that the earlieft opportunity might be taken of repealing the excife law. So much embarraffed were the revenues of the ftate by the premature repeal of the direct tax, that in the next feffion the legiflature had to borrow fixty thoufand pounds from the Bank of North America on mortgage, and to negociate with the late proprietaries,

to get them to receive certificates inftead of cafh, for a
debt due them by the commonwealth.   How far dif-
appointing the public creditors of the ftate, by prematurely embarraffing its revenues, and continuing
the ftate excife when the direct tax was repealed, was
intended to promote the plan for affuming the ftate
debt, and levying a general excife, which tranfpired
foon after, the reader who has been attentive to thofe
meafures in their progrefs will be able to judge for
himfelf.

It is well known, that the plan reported by the
fecretary of the treafury to the fecond feffion of the firft
Congrefs was rejected at that time, and again brought
forward in the laft feffion of that Congrefs, and enacted
into a law, Congrefs then fitting in Philadelphia.

The legiflature of the ftate being then alfo in feffion, the members of the houfe of reprefentatives became exceedingly alarmed at the introduction of an
excife, and adopted refolutions expreffive of their fenfe
of the excife bill then before Congrefs.   The refolves
were defigned to have been fent to the Senate of the
United States, not as inftructions by which they were
to be bound, but as a declaration of the fenfe and wifhes of the ftate of Pennfylvania refpecting an excife
fyftem.

The fubftance of thefe refolutions were : Firft, A
declaration of a right in the ftate legiflature to give an
opinion on every thing of a public nature which has
a tendency to deftroy the rights of the people : Second, That the proceedings of Congrefs, tending to
the collection of a revenue by means of an excife,
ought to attract the attention of the houfe : Third, That

no public emergency then exifted to warrant the a-
doption of any fpecies of taxation, that would violate
the rights which were the bafis of the government, and
thereby exhibit the fingular fpectacle, of a nation oppofing the oppreffion of others, to enflave itfelf.

In the difcuffion of thefe refolutions there were
none who argued in favour of the excife. The objections were confined to the right of the houfe to interfere in federal meafures. I was a member at the time,
and voted in favour of the refolutions ; but had at firft
fome difficulty with refpect to the right of interference. Since that time we find, however, that other
ftate legiflatures have frequently interfered, by giving
their opinion on important federal meafures, without
being cenfured for it. The Yeas and Nays were taken on the refolutions, and the reafons given at large
on the journals. By the journals of that feffion of the
houfe of reprefentatives of the General Affembly, it
appears, that there were forty votes in favour of the refolutions, and fixteen againft them. Some, at leaft, of
the minority were as much oppofed to the excife as
thofe who voted in the majority, but thought the interference improper. The name of John Nevil, now
infpector of the weftern furvey, ftands with the majority. Confidering the difficulty of the queftion of interference, this was a very unanimous declaration of the
reprefentatives of Pennfylvania, and could not be
afcribed to the influence of a faction. The truth is,
the refolutions were moved and feconded, and zealoufly fupported by Col. Gurney and Mr. Richard
Wells, of the city of Philadelphia, well known to be
refpectable citizens and zealous federalifts. They

were alfo fupported by confultations with other inhabitants of the city, at the Coffee-houfe, where the principles of excifes were difcuffed freely, and at thefe confultations, and in the debates in the Houfe of Reprefentatives, the teftimony given by the old Congrefs againft excifes was much relied on. The weftern members did not affift at the confultations at the Coffee-houfe.

A great proportion of the people of Pennfylvania had expreffed their fenfe of the excife law, by the alarm they difcovered on receiving information of the fecretary's report in favour of an excife fyftem, and the joy they expreffed at hearing that it was rejected. This circumftance gave the members of affembly a good opportunity to know the fentiments of the people on the fubject, and this difpofition was not confined to any particular place. Only one member from the city of Philadelphia, and two from the county, voted againft the refolutions, and but one member from the weftern counties voted in their favour.

The firft ill treatment given to an excifeman under the federal law was in Chefter county, but the rioters were convicted, and punifhed feverely by the ftate courts. On that occafion, the foreman of the jury told the Attorney-general, that he was as much, or more, oppofed to the excife law, than the rioters, but would not fuffer violations of the laws to go unpunifhed. I expect fenfible jurors every where would act from the fame laudable principle. There were feveral other attacks made on excife officers in other parts on the eaft fide of the mountains, which it is not neceffary to be particular in ftating.

The people in the weſtern counties anticipated their experiencing peculiar hardſhips from the excife. Without money, or the means of procuring it, and confuming their whifkey only in their families or uſing it as an article of barter, which, though it in ſome refpects anſwered the place of money, yet would not be received in pay for the excife tax, they thought it hard to pay as much tax on what fold with them but at from two ſhillings, to two ſhillings and ſix pence, as they did where it brought double that price. Theſe, and ſuch like arguments, were not new. I found them in uſe againſt the ſtate excife when I went to reſide in that country. They aroſe from their ſituation, and the ſimpleſt perſon feeling their force, knew how to uſe them.

Some talked of laying aſide their ſtill altogether, till they would have time to obſerve the effects of the law on other places, and have time to reflect on the ſubject ; and this method was adviſed, in preference to a more violent mode of oppofition, by ſome who were apprehenſive of outrages being committed. But though ſeveral peaceable men laid aſide their ſtills or fold them, yet there never was any aſſociation or reſolutions among the inhabitants to that purpoſe. The contrary has been aſſerted by pretty high authority.

In the month of June 1791, the firſt year on which the ſtills were to have been entered there were no offices of infpection opened in the weſtern counties : And though the people were in great conſternation, no public or general conſultation was held on the ſubject, till the latter end of July following, when a meeting was advertiſed to be held at Red-ſtone old fort.

E

Individuals attended from different places, but not by delegation, and, being in harveft, few attended from a diftance. There were four or five from Weftmoreland, few from Allegany, or the diftant parts of Wafhington or Fayette. The hardfhips, naturally refulting from the execution of the excife law to that country, were explained, but at the fame time the conftitutional authority of Congrefs to enact it was afferted. It was refolved to petition Congrefs for relief, and no petition being prepared, a committee was appointed to meet at Pittfburgh to draught one. The committee was alfo authorifed to correfpond with the citizens in other places, who might be difpofed to petition Congrefs on the fubject, and it was recommended to the different counties to appoint committees to fuperintend the figning the petitions and forwarding them to Congrefs.

How this meeting could have been ranked by the fecretary of the treafury, in his report to the Prefident, preparatory to calling out the militia, among the caufes of the infurrection, and given as one of the inflances of unlawful combination, I know not. Surely fuch a meeting may be held, and fuch refolves paffed, in Great Britain, even after the fedition bills, which have thrown that nation into fuch a flame, are enacted into laws. I never knew that a meeting to petition government refpectfully, was efteemed criminal in any country that had the leaft pretenfions to freedom.

The truth is, as far as I was acquainted with the defign of that meeting, it was intended to promote fubmiffion, and not oppofition, to the law. There was no other alternative ; for to have argued that the law was juft and falutary, would have had no effect ; nor did I know of any perfon then in the country that approved of, or advocated it as a good law. Some, who wrote in favour of fubmiffion to the excife law, in the Pittfburgh Gazette, were prefent at the Red-ftone meeting.

Several of thofe who kept the largeft diftilleries, that I was acquainted with in thefe counties, defigned at that time to enter their ftills, if there was an opportunity. Some of thefe however afterwards changed their mind. Many of the uninformed people, being told by the warm advocates of the federal government, that after it was ratified we would have no more excifes, confidered the excife law therefore as unconftitutional. At the Red-ftone meeting this miftake was openly combated. It is not eafy to convince people that a law, in their opinion unjuft and oppreffive in its operation, is at the fame time conftitutional.

In Auguft a committee met at Wafhington, agreeably to the recommendation of the Red-ftone meeting, and in September a committee, compofed of perfons from the weftern counties, met at Pittfburgh. I prefume none of them were delegated, except perhaps from Wafhington county, for only in it had there been a county committee. From Weftmoreland there was but one perfon, and he was not delegated.

A petition was propofed by the general committee at Pittfburgh to be figned by the people, and feveral refolves were publifhed in the gazettee, fome of which were intemperately expreſſed, and refpeſted ſubjeſts but little conneſted with the excife law, ſuch as the ſalaries of office, the funding ſyſtem, &c.

About eleven months after, in Auguſt 1792, a number of perſons, from Waſhington, Fayette, and Allegany counties, formed the ſecond and laſt committee of that kind that was held at Pittſburgh. They prepared and publiſhed another petition to Congreſs, praying for the repeal of the excife law, to be ſigned by the people. The committee alſo publiſhed its ſentiments on the principles of taxation, and the ſuppoſed impropriety and injuſtice of an excife ſyſtem. Though it did not cenſure any other meaſures of government, it reſolved to take all legal methods of ob-ſtruſting the operation of the excife law, and to have no fellowſhip with ſuch as accepted offices under it, and to withdraw from them every aſſiſtance, to withhold the comforts of life, &c. They alſo recommended to the people to follow their example. A ſimilar reſolution had been publiſhed by the committee of Waſhington, about a year before.

I never knew that this example was followed by the people in any inſtance, or that the reſolution was obeyed by even all the members of the committee.

On the ground of diſcretion theſe reſolutions were cenſurable, and were in faſt diſapproved by many through the ſtate, who alſo heartily diſliked the excife law. That they were not, however, contrary to law, is acknowledged by the ſecretary himſelf, who informs us of his procuring teſtimony, in order to proſecute the perſons who compoſed the committee; but he adds, that the attorney general did not think it aſtionable. There

is no doubt but it is morally wrong in many cafes to
refufe our charity or affiftance to any of our fellow
men, when their neceffities require it; but thefe duties being of imperfect obligation, we are only refponfible to our own confcience and the opinion of the
world for the proper difcharge of them. There are
no doubt perfons in fociety whofe manners are fo difagreeable, or their character fo objectionable, as to
juftify us in refolving to have no fellowfhip with them;
and where the excife law is almoft univerfally believed
to be unjuft and oppreffive, men of this defcription
will be found pretty readily among the excife officers.
Indeed this obfervation need not be reftricted to places fo fituated; it correfponds with the fentiments of
people generally, where excifes have been long eftablifhed, and is the language of their laws.

The fe refolutions, however, were cenfurable on
the ground of policy. They difgufted thofe members
of Congrefs, that would otherwife have been difpofed to
have eafed, if not to have fully relieved, them from their
gounds of complaint, and offended the citizens at large,
who had fympathized with them; in fhort, they undoubtedly occafioned lefs refpect to be paid to their pe-
tions.

A defultory meeting was held, in confequence of an
advertifement, in Allegany county; it formed rules of
affociation, and publifhed fome intemperate refolutions,
but never had a fecond meeting. Col. Morton, the chairman, near whofe refidence the meeting was held, behaved always in an orderly manner, and difcovered great
firmnefs and difcretion through the whole of the infurrection. A meeting was advertifed to have been held

at Greenſburgh, in the ſame winter, James Guthry,
chairman ; but the ſuppoſed chairman contradicted
the advertiſement in the next week's gazette, denying
that there was any ſuch meeting, or that he was chairman, and we heard no more of it.   It may be remarked, that Guthry has uniformly ſupported the
character of a good citizen.   In ſhort, there was a diſpoſition prevailing with a few people to have the country organized into committees, but not excluſively to
popoſe the exciſe. The wages of the aſſembly-men had
been raiſed the year before, and people living at ſuch
a diſtance from market, having the neceſſaries of life
cheap, and not being ſenſible of the increaſed expence
of living in Philadelphia, were offended.   From this
circumſtance a greater number than uſual wiſhed to
bring themſelves forward as candidates, not to lower,
but to receive, the high wages ; to take a lead in committees ſeemed a probable means of ſucceſs. This circumſtance was ſuſpected to have promoted the progreſs of the diſturbances in ſome places, but the conduct of theſe characters came into diſrepute ſoon e-
nough to prevent their ſucceſs.

———

C H A P. IV.

I CANNOT diſcover that the meetings I have mentioned had any influence in promoting the inſurrection, or connection with it. They were not ſanctioned by the people, nor was there even the appearance of the people aſſembling to elect the perſons of which they were compoſed.

Though I have ſaid, that the reſolves publiſhed by theſe meetings were intemperate and impolitic, yet they are not without the patronage of reſpectable precedents, or rather examples, given by reſpectable and influential characters, even in our own country.

In the year 1777, the darkeſt period of the late war, when the ſtate of Pennſylvania was daily in danger of invaſion, and the government newly put into operation, a number of the moſt wealthy and reſpectable characters in the ſtate, chiefly in the city of Philadelphia, entered into reſolutions, with the declared intention of oppoſing, not a law, but the government

itſelf. They refuſed to hold offices under it, and, if
I remember well, to aſſociate with thoſe who did.   I
do not bring in this example as a juſtification of the
conduct of the other ; it had a very bad effect in weak-
ening the operations of the government at a time to
the laſt degree critical.   Yet, if I am not miſtaken, a
reſpectable judge of the ſupreme court of the United
States, and the late ſuperviſor of the diſtrict of Pennſylvania, were among the leading members of that aſſociation.   This inſtance ought to be improved as a
warning, and not as a precedent.   In Britain we obſerve the people, through the whole nation, conven-
ing either in aſſociations or occaſional meetings, in
vaſt multitudes, to cenſure the conduct of adminiſtra-
tion, and petition againſt the ſedition bills ; and we
ſee theſe aſſemblies publicly patroniſed by the firſt no-
bility and moſt influential commoners of the nation.
So far is this from being cenſured by the miniſtry,
that they are equally induſtrious in procuring popular
meetings to approve of their meaſures.   This is no
new thing in that nation.   The ſenſe of the nation,
given in that manner, has often not only prevented
bills being enacted, but has frequently procured the
repeal of obnoxious laws.   To prove this, many o-
ther inſtances might be mentioned.

It is true, it may be plead that popular meetings
are often conducted with indiſcretion, and have a tendency to promote licentiouſneſs.   This is admitted ;
but it does not therefore follow, that ſuch meetings
ſhould be prohibited by law or denounced by government.   Doing ſo, would be reducing the people to

mere machines, and fubverting the very exiflence of liberty. It is the duty of the legiflature not only to accommodate the laws to the people's interefts, but even, as far as poffible, to their preconceptions; for as a republican government refts on the people's confidence, whatever weakens that confidence faps the foundations of the government as effectually as treafon and rebellion, though not fo rapidly. There are few inflances of treafon and rebellion which may not be traced to indifcreet laws as their fource. It is generally one indifcretion exciting another.

It will not do to fay, that to hold meetings to remonflrate againft the paffing of a law is admiffible, but that to remonflrate againft an exifting law is improper. Such doctrine in this extenfive country is abfurd, for it muft always happen, that a great proportion of the people, who are to be governed by the laws, know nothing about them till they are enacted or in operation, confequently cannot petition againft their paffage.

It is equally abfurd to affert, that becaufe our laws are enacted by our own reprefentatives, therefore we ought to fubmit to them without remonftrance, till our reprefentatives, who know our circumflances, and partake of our interefts, think proper to repeal them. This doctrine is fupported by a prefumption, that a government of reprefentatives can never miftake the true interefts of their conftituents, nor be corrupted or fall into partial combinations, whereas the contrary is prefumable from the nature of man, and verified by immemorial experience.

F

If the people have a right to petition for the repeal of a law, or remonftrate againft its injuftice or inexpediency, furely they have a right to meet, publifh their fentiments, and correfpond through the whole extent of the country affected by the laws, without the imputation of combining againft the government. Their characters indeed are refponfible to public opinion for the indifcreet ufe of that right, and their perfons and property to the laws for the infractions committed on them.

Experience will not juftify the claim of implicit obedience to the laws even of a reprefentative legiflature. Even in fuch there may be combinations fo ftrong as to fubvert the conftitution itfelf; and as the difpofal of the public property and the adminiftration of the national force is neceffarily vefted in the government, temptations, too ftrong for the ordinary portion of virtue enjoyed by mankind, may prefent themfelves too fuccefsfully to the avarice or ambition of thofe vefted with the power of difpenfing the public will. Inftances of this are to be found in the hiftory of all nations, and proofs of it are not wanting even among ourfelves, though as a nation we are yet in our infancy.

In Georgia, we fee the legiflature the fellers, and the members of the legiflature and officers of the ftate, together with influential officers of the general government, the purchafers of land, to an amount unknown in the hiftory of contracts. In confequence of this enormous fpeculation we fee the people agitated to a degree of madnefs, and the fucceeding legiflature not only repealing the law, but erazing the memorials of it from their journals. How much better would it have been, how much more honourable to the ftate, to have liftened to the remonftrances of the people in time. The government of Georgia is a fair and full reprefentation of the people, and yet here we find a powerful leffon againft the claim of im-plicit confidence in the wifdom of reprefentative legiflatures.

But we need not look to the ftate of Georgia alone for inftances. The conduct there differs only in degree from what had previoufly taken place in other ftates. On examination it will be found, that generally where any of our governments had a fubject of fpeculation at their difpofal, much of it has found its way into the hands of fuch as had the difpofal of it, or their favourites. The land-offices of different ftates, even Pennfylvania itfelf, may be cited in proof of this doctrine.

Where a large territory is fubject to a reprefentative legiflature, it is fometimes very difficult to accommodate general laws to the various interefts and prepoffeffions of the different parts. In this cafe, it becomes the legiflature to prefer what is moft evidently juft and practicable to that which refined politicians may judge expedient. The greateft danger to republican governments arife from combinations and political fineffe. If the people have not fo much good fenfe as to fubmit to exactions, or fupport meafures that are reafonably juft and neceffary, they are not fit for a republican government. It is of importance that the neceffity of meafures which prefs hard on the people fhould be evident; and generally matters of urgent necessity are easily explained to the comprehensions of the people. When this is done they are generally found willing to submit to any burden.

This observation was verified in the course of the late war. When the Congress-money ceased to be a useful circulating medium, the people in those states, whose legislatures made exertions, submitted to pay an amount of taxes that will scarcely be credited in future time; and they did this without giving the governments any difficulty, until they became apprehensive that the fruits of their earnings went chiefly into the hands of speculators. Yet in one state only did this promote an insurrection. It is acknowledged that the oppression in Massachusetts was exorbitant before it produced opposition, and that the insurrection in that state was preceded by a long course of complaints and evident discontents. The legislature removed the causes of complaint after the opposition was subdued, and the insurgents were treated with lenity. The conduct of that state on this trying occasion reflects honour on republican government; still more happy, however, would it have been, if, by giving more early relief, the insurrection had been prevented. The citizens will bear amazing burdens in times of public emergency, or for the immediate discharge of debts contracted from evident necessity; but when once the impression of necessity is removed from their minds, and especially when the claims have become the objects of speculation, the people generally have not discernment enough to approve even of necessary arrangements for the support of public credit. Though they have pretty accurate ideas of justice or equity in the abstract, yet they cannot trace it through the refined mazes of a policy neceſſary for funding ſyſtems. Indeed, to carry theſe ſyſtems to any great extent, the government ſhould poſſeſs not only all the internal reſources of revenue without competition, but alſo all other internal governmental powers and patronage to the utmoſt extent.

It is a doctrine now avowed in the Britiſh parliament, that when laws are enacted dangerous to the liberty and intereſts of the people, ſubmiſſion to them is not a queſtion of morality but of prudence. Perhaps government ſhould always act under impreſſions of the truth of this poſition, but the citizens ſhould examine it with the utmoſt caution before they reduce it to practice.

We are certainly under a moral obligation to preſerve our own life and the life of our neighbours. Every inſtance of actual oppoſition to government, obliges it to have recourſe to force and coercion for its own preſervation, for the authority of government cannot be diſtinguiſhed from the government itſelf. Though forcible oppoſition has often been made to particular laws, without the remoteſt intention in thoſe who oppoſed the law to overturn the government, yet it is not to be ſuppoſed, that thoſe who adminiſter the government will be moved to change their meaſures by a defiance of their power to ſupport them. Nor indeed can this be done in a republican government, without ſuch an imputation of weakneſs as will invite to forcible oppoſition from every diſcontented party. Therefore citizens who conceive themſelves oppreſſed by partial laws, ſhould conſider, that a de-

fiance of the power of government, by forcible oppofition to the authority of the laws, eventually leads to
hoftility and bloodfhed, and that there is no telling
the end of thofe meafures from their beginning.
Every thing that has a tendency to agitate the public
mind to an unufual degree, ought to be avoided, becaufe when the mind is highly agitated with refpect
to public meafures it is too much difturbed to judge
deliberately, and is predifpofed to act without difcretion. The public mind may be agitated by thofe who
cannot direct or controul its exertions. We are under a moral obligation to refpect government, not only as a divine ordinance, but alfo as a moral compact,
binding the people to one another for its fupport.

It is certain, however, that the government and
laws of fome countries are not worth preferving, and
even where a government is good in itfelf it may be
perverted in the adminiftration. As it is for the promoting of mutual happinefs and fecurity only that
government is valuable, therefore the power of alter-
ing or amending governments is exprefsly declared to
be in the people, who are the judges of their own
happinefs, by fome conftitutions. It is, however, ra-
dically in them, whether expreffed in a written inftrument or not.

When the change of a government, a revolt from
it, or a temporary oppofition to its laws, fuch as the
oppofition of the colonies to the ftamp and tea acts was,
is believed to be morally right, it is yet a matter of
the greateft delicacy, to calculate with accuracy with
refpect to the prudence or policy of commencing the
oppofition contemplated. When the mind is highly

agitated, it is very unfit to examine the resources to support opposition, or to calculate with precision the probable consequences of it. That this was the case in the late insurrection will appear evident in the sequel.

But if those who administer the government attempt to issue denunciations against the liberty of expressing opinions of their measures and objects, or to prescribe rules by which men must be regulated in expressing their opinions, the very attempt will increase the evil it is intended to correct. When those in trust attempt to exercise authority over the discretion of the citizens, otherwise than in the unequivocal language of the laws, as the attempt cannot be supported by coercion it will only bring the measures of government into contempt, and operate as a stimulus to indiscreet censure. Instances might be given in proof of this observation if it were necessary. Candid investigations of the measures of government have their uses even though they may be mistaken, and scurrilous writings, though they are pernicious in themselves, can do little harm; they rather attach people of discernment more closely to the government. Those who conduct the measures, and dispense the favours of government, have generally the advantage in newspaper writings; not only men of discretion, who approve of the measures, will write in their favour, but panegyrists, sycophants, and even the greatest masters in the arts of scurrility, will generally be found on the side of government in every country, whether its measures be good or bad. And though sometimes indeed a Junius may start up on the other side;

this is rare; and the writers in favour of government often treat refpectable citizens and the mafs of the people with great freedom, and generally efcape the denunciations of thofe entrufled with the public ad-miniftration. It is never a good omen when the mea-fures of government are in danger of fettering by in-veftigation.

The meetings which have been enumerated I confider as lawful and harmlefs in themfelves; but fome of their refolutions, as I have before obferved, were cenfurable in point of difcretion. It is my own opinion, that if they had been more generally attended by men of difcretion, they might have been advantageous. They were not permanent affocia-tions.

There was, however, an affociation of a more per-manent nature commenced in the winter previous to the infurrection. A great proportion of the Mingo creek regiment of militia became members of it. It is faid, that during its exiftence it was frequently at-tended by three hundred perfons. The rules of this inftitution, and various powers which it is reported to have exercifed, imitated the language, and affumed the forms of regularly conftituted authority. This affo-ciation never was announced in the newfpapers, and its exiftence was known to but few.

Though the whole country difapproved of the excife, yet the people in the fettlement where this af-fociation was formed, feem to have been more zea-lous in their difapprobation of it than many others. It is true, their rules did not apply particularly againft the excife, nor contain any thing unlawful, yet the circumftance of being affociated made them formidable in what they undertook, and encouraged them to undertake what they otherwise would not have done as individuals.

It is in this that the difference between occafional focieties and permanent affociations confift. In Maffachufetts, where the people of every town is incorporated into a permanent affociation, when they undertake any thing, either good or bad, they act with greater vigour. By this means it was that they made fuch glorious exertions at the commencement of the revolution, and by the fame means alfo the infurrection in that ftate became fo formidable, and was conducted with fo much fyftem.

It has been generally faid, that one object of their affociation was to prevent people from committing outrages on excifemen. This might have been the object of a number of the affociates, and it might have produced this effect for fome time. Perhaps it was owing to this that general Nevil was not attacked at his own houfe fooner, for undoubtedly there was greater refentment againft him than any of his deputies, for reafons that I fhall mention in the fequel; and it does appear that defigns were entertained againft him by fome of the affociates previous to the attack on his houfe. This affociation was the more dangerous that it was fecret. And though, as has been obferved, it was not actively concerned in many of the outrages preceding the infurrection, yet various concurring circumftances render it more than probable, that that unfortunate event was principally to be afcribed to its inftrumentality.

G

CHAP. V.

THE firſt actual outrage was committed in September 1791, on a Robert Johnſon, collector of exciſe for Waſhington and Allegany counties, by a party of armed men diſguiſed. The attack was made on him near Pigeon creek. After cutting his hair, they tarred and feathered him, and in this ſituation compelled him to walk ſome diſtance.

The next act of violence was committed on a man of the name of Wilſon, who was in ſome meaſure diſordered in his intellects, and affected to be, perhaps thought he was, an exciſe-man, and was making enquiry for diſtillers. He was purſued by a party, taken out of his bed, and carried ſeveral miles to a ſmith's ſhop; there they ſtriped off his cloaths and burnt them, and burning him in ſeveral places with a hot iron, they tarred and feathered, and in that ſituation diſmiſſed, him.

Not long after this, one Roſsberry ſuffered the puniſhment of tarring and feathering for advocating the excife law. An armed banditti feized and carried off two perfons who were witneffes in the cafe of Wilfon, who had been abufed by the rioters. A formidable attempt was made to feize the infpector himfelf in Wafhington town, where he was expected, by a numerous party difguifed. He had been apprifed of their coming, and did not attend at the office. In Auguft 1792, capt. Faulkner, who had let his houfe to the infpector to hold his office in, was attacked on the road by a perfon with a drawn knife, and threatened that his houfe fhould be burned for permitting an office of infpection to be held in it. He efcaped, on giving a promife to prevent the further ufe of his houfe for an office, and accordingly gave public notice in the newfpapers, that the office fhould be no longer kept in his houfe.

In April 1793, an armed party attacked the houfe of Wells, whofe refidence is in Fayette county, but did not find him at home. They broke open the houfe and threatened the family. On the 22d of November following, the houfe of Wells was attacked again, in the night. They then obliged him to furrender his commiffion and books, and required him to publifh a refignation of his office, within two weeks, in the newfpapers, on pain of having his houfe burned.

James Kiddoe and William Coughran, who had entered their ftills, were firft threatened, and afterwards attacked. Some pieces of the grift-mill of the former were carried away, and the ftill of the latter was deftroyed, his faw-mill rendered ufelefs, and his grift-mill materially injured; and he was ordered to publifh what he had fuffered in the Pittfburgh Gazette.

An armed party in difguife, attacked and broke into the houfe of John Lynn, where the office was kept, and after prevailing on him to come down ftairs, they tied and threatened to hang him ; then took him to the woods, cut off his hair, tarred and feathered him, and fwore him never to difclofe their names, or permit an excife office to be held in his houfe; and binding him to a tree, left him in that fituation till morning, when he extricated himfelf. Thefe outrages all happened fouth of the Monongahela.

In June 1794, Wells, the collector for Weftmoreland and Fayette counties, opened his office, at the houfe of a certain Philip Regan in Weftmoreland county. The houfe was at different times attacked by armed men in the night, who frequently fired on it; but they were always repulfed by P. Regan and Wells the younger.

I have taken this enumeration from the fecretary's report. However, I have paffed one inftance mentioned by him, viz. that Wells the collector was injurioufly treated at Greenfburgh, in Weftmoreland, in 1792. I paffed it, becaufe I was convinced it was without foundation. On the moft minute enquiry, I have not found the fmalleft trace of any injury or infult that he received there; nay, he got affurances that none in the town would injure him. He was told indeed, in friendly converfation, that they could not undertake for other parts of the county, and that fince no perfon in the county would accept of the office, he might conclude that his holding it there would not be acceptable. Though the man's perfon was little known in that county, yet few were flrangers to his perfonal character previous to his obtaining the office.

The account of his being ill treated at Greenf-burgh, is connected by the fecretary with a fimilar af-fertion refpecting the treatment he received at Union Town, in Fayette county. This, however, alfo ap-pears to have but little foundation. On the firft day appointed for entering the ftills, a number of diftil-lers attended ; but the collector did not appear. On the fecond day, for he was to have attended one day in the week, a greater number of diftillers appeared ; but the collector was not to be found, though called and diligent enquiry made for him. He was known to be a timid man, and very probably was afraid of their numbers, and this might have been the reafon why a greater number attended the fecond day ; but they were neither armed with weapons nor threats. When he undertook the office he ought to have dif-covered more boldnefs and lefs apprehenfion. This conduct invited to further infults. I am perfuaded, that at this time no plan for attacking or mal-treating excife-men had been concerted or matured by the diftillers.

When either public or private trufts are under-taken by men who diflike the bufinefs themfelves, they cannot be expected to difcharge it with energy. To obtain the compenfation will be their principal aim, and all their efforts will be directed to that object. It will be the fame with fuch as poffefs neither prin-ciple nor fenfe of honour, and fuch may be expected

to obtain offices where the field for felection is very
much narrowed.   How far this obfervation will apply to the cafe of the excife officers in the weftern
counties, will be feen in its proper place.

In two inftances, the barns of perfons who had
given information againft offenders, &c. in Allegany
county, were burnt, probably by the offenders themfelves, though this could not be proved.   Some o-
ther injuries were committed, and threats were publifhed in the newfpapers, under the fignature of Tom
the Tinker.   Thefe threats, contained in letters figned by Tom the Tinker, were directed to certain perfons, with exprefs orders to have them publifhed;
and the editor of the Pittfburgh Gazette did not think
it prudent to refufe to admit them.   I cannot give
a better account of the famous fignature of Tom Tinker, which figured fo highly about this time, than by
adopting the words of Mr. Brackenridge on that fubject.

" A term had come into popular ufe before this
" time, to defignate the oppofition to the excife law ;
" it was that of Tom the Tinker.   It was not given,
" as the appellation of whig originally was, as a term
" of reproach for adverfaries; but affumed by the peo-
" ple who were active in fome of the mafked riots,
" which took place at an early period. A certain John
" Holcroft was thought to have made the firft applica-
" tion of it.   It was at the time of the mafked at-
" tack on a certain William Coughran, who rendered
" himfelf obnoxious by the entry of his ftills; and the
" menders, of courfe, muft be tinkers, and the name,
" collectively, became Tom the Tinker.   Advertife-

" ments were put up on the trees, and in the high
" ways, or in other confpicuous places, under the fig-
" nature of Tom the Tinker, threatening individu-
" als, or admonifhing them in meafures with regard
" to the excife law." *Incidents, page* 79.

It afterwards appeared that they did not originate
with Holcroft, though the inventor of them has never
been difcovered; thefe letters were only made ufe of in
the fettlements adjacent to the Monongahela, till after
the infurrection broke out. Then, however, they were
fent to diftant places.

In the latter end of 1793 and the beginning of
1794, there appeared to be a very general wifh among
the diftillers, and other people of reflection, that the
ftills fhould be entered, and a general fubmiffion to the
law enforced. They were convinced, that the defultory, outrageous, and incendiary oppofition that was
given to the execution of the law, was likely to introduce a very bad ftate of fociety. That it was putting
it in the power of bad men, emboldened by the ha-
bit of commifting daring outrages, to difturb the peace
of fociety, and to render the enjoyment of life and
property infecure. They knew that though the prefent outrages were only directed againft the execution
of the excife law, if thefe efcaped with impunity, the
execution of every other law might fhare the fame
fate in its turn. The demand for whifkey for the
fupply of the army put it in the power of the diftillers
to procure cafh for the payment of the excife tax, and
the contractor confining his purchafes to fpirits on
which the excife had been paid, gave a powerful inducement to a compliance with the law.

With a view to promote this compliance, a number of the moſt influential perſons including a number of the moſt reſpeaable diſtillers, agreed to promote ſubmiſſion to the exciſe laws, on condition that a total change was made in the officers, and ſuch men put into office as the people could confide in ; they alſo expreſſed their willingneſs to recommend ſuch charaaers and render themſelves reſponſible for their fidelity. This agreement was entered into at the court of Fayette county, in the winter or ſpring previous to the inſurrection. I had the firſt information of it from James Roſs, Eſq. ſenator of the United States, who had been preſent and contributed to this agreement, before he came to the ſenate in April 1794. I aſked him how far the change of the officers was intended to go, and if they were confident they could precure good men to accept of the offices. He told me the change was intended to go to all the officers of the ſurvey, and that they were confident of being able to procure ſuch as would faithfully diſcharge the duties of the reſpeaive offices, and enjoy the confidence of the people, and he aſked me if I could recommend ſuch for Weſtmoreland county. I told him that having been long from home, and having no opportunity of conſulting, I could not recommend : That if I did recommend a good man without knowing whether he would ſerve or not, and he declined it, it would render it more difficult to get another to accept of it. I had experienced this inconveniency under the ſtate exciſe.

This diſpoſition coming to the knowledge of thoſe who were obſtinate and undiſcerning, and who had already committed exceſſes, they became more outrigerous, proceeded to frelh acts of violence, and expreffed as great a degree of refentment againft thofe who complied with the law as they did againft the officers who acted under it. The exertions of thofe who oppofed the law being the refult of an infatuated ftate of mind and a miftaken zeal were vigorous, and being conducted in a clandeftine manner, there could be no defence againft their effects; this encreafed the difpofition of difcreet men to fubmit, but it deterred them from actually entering their ftills. They were furprized that no coercive exertions were made by the federal judiciary in fupport of the law, and thofe who complied with the duties it required. About that time I received letters from different diftillers near Loyalhanna in Weftmoreland county, requefting my opinion both as to their beft mode of proceeding, and whether government was likely to make any exertion to put the law in execution, and protect thofe who were willing to fubmit; for though there had been no riots in that part of the country, neither had there been any office of infpection, nor entries of ftills; but they had heard of the treatment thofe had met with who entered them in cther counties, and did not know but they might be treated in the fame manner. I informed them that it was their duty to enter their ftills whether they ufed them or not, that there was no ground to expect that the law would be either repealed, or altered in that refpect, during that feffion of Congrefs, but referred to themfelves to judge of the fafety of their perfons or property. I had fufpected no danger of that kind in that part of the country when I left home. With refpect to the opportunity of entering, that laying with the infpector, I

H

could tell nothing about it. Some of thofe in the mean time, compounding privately for the excife in Pittfburgh, fold their liquor to the contractors. They would have much rather entered their ftills; but even felling their liquors to the contractors raifed fufpicions againft them, and occafioned threats from a diftance and refentment from fome of their neighbours, and rendered it neceffary for them to temporize, during the troubles that followed, more than they otherwife would have done. The new alterations in the ex- cife law were not enacted till fome time in the month of June, and could not be known at that diftance till after that month was expired.

From the relation already given, it is evident, that an oppofition to, or non-compliance with, the execution of the excife law, had exifted in the weftern counties of Pennfylvania, for the fpace of three years; or, to ufe the expreffions of the fecretary of the treafury, " The op- " pofition to thofe laws in the four weftern counties " of Pennfylvania, was as early as they were known " to have paffed. It has continued, with different · " degrees of violence in the different counties, and " at different periods.—But Wafhington has uni- " formly diftinguifhed its refiftance, by a more excef- " five fpirit than has appeared in the other counties, " and feems to have been chiefly inftrumental in kin- " dling, and keeping alive the flame."

There might be fome difference of opinion be- tween the fecretary and others, about the inftances that are entitled to the term oppofition. Perhaps, circulation of opinion, or declaration of fentiments, and every lawful means of promoting remonftrances

againſt it, or petitions for its repeal, or even reſolv-
ing to ceaſe from diſtilling, if that had been done,
might be better expreſſed by the term diſapprobation.
But not to contend about this, it will be admitted,
that the attack on Robert Johnſon, on the 6th of September 1791, and all the ſubſequent acts of violence,
were acts of oppoſition to that law, and were ſo many
defiances to the power of the judicial authority of the
United States. Various and flagrant inſtances of oppoſition I have already recited, till I have brought
the narrative to the avenue of that criſis, when the
oppoſition burſt forth with an exploſion, that, as has
been ſaid by reſpectable authority, electrified the
whole United States. It remains to be enquired, what
means the reſponſible head of the executive department exerted, to coerce this oppoſition, and to prevent
its more general ſpread.

———

CHAP. VI.

THE firſt inſtance that we find of co-ercion having been attempted, was the ſending Joſeph Fox, deputy marſhal, to ſerve proceſſes iſſued by the diſtrict court againſt the perſons concerned in the riot on Johnſon. He went to the inſpector, and on his advice returned home again without going to the proper place, or attempting to ſerve the writs; but with the inſpector's advice alſo, he ſent the proceſſes under cover as private letters, by a poor ſimple man, who had been uſually employed in driving cat-tle, &c. If the inſpector could have contrived a ſurer method to degrade the government in the eſteem of the rioters, and invite inſults, it is beyond my comprehenſion; and unhappily the poor man, who was ignorant of what he was doing, was the vic-tim of this injudicious plan.

What better could the inſpector expect. If the people were well diſpoſed where the proceſs was to be ſerved, why diſcourage the deputy marſhal from go-

ing forward? If they were not well difpofed, why
fend a poor creature who, not knowing what he delivered, could not give teftimony of his having ferved
the proceffes? Would not this contemptible method of
ferving proceffes irritate even a well difpofed man on
whom it was ferved? The authority of a commiffion from
government, and the refpeftability attached thereby to
the perfon that bears it, generally procures a degree of
reverence to an officer of juftice. The fheriff or con-
ftable will be refpefted when the officious bum will probably be well flogged, but in this inftance the poor
man was taken for a bum and treated accordingly,
without knowing the nature of the fervice he was employed about. He was feized, whipped, tarred and
feathered, and it is faid that his money was taken from
him, and finally, being blindfolded, he was tied in the
woods, and remained in that fituation for five hours.

No farther exertion was made on the part of government till the fall of the year 1792, that the fupervifor of the revenue was fent "to afcertain the real ftate
of the furvey, to obtain evidence of the perfons who
were concerned in Faulkner's cafe, and of thofe who
compofed the meeting at Pittfburgh, to uphold the
confidence and encourage the perfeverance of the officers acting under the law, and to induce if poffible
the inhabitants of that part of the furvey, which appeared leaft difinclined, to come voluntarily into the meafure, by arguments addreffed to their fenfe of duty,
and exhibiting the eventual dangers and mifchiefs of
refiftance."

I wifh for the fake of the perfonal refpeft I have
long entertained for the fupervifor of the revenue,
and his family, that he had not introduced his journey

to Pittſburgh, and put me to the diſagreeable neceſſity of animadverting on it.   Were I indeed to relate it in the manner I have heard it deſcribed, the reader would be induced to think it a romance rather than a real narative.   It is ſufficient for my purpoſe to ſtate that he went to Pittſburgh in the moſt clandeſtine manner poſſible, confined himſelf within a very narrow circle of the citizens while he remained there, refuſed to go to Waſhington town, though he was warmly ſolicited to go there and aſſured of ſafety, and though it was in that county that the offence was committed, to prepare for the proſecution of which was the principal objeĉt of his miſſion, and where only evidence was to be procured.   Staying but a few days at Pittſburgh, he returned to Philadelphia with the rapidity of a poſt rider, accompanied by a military guard through the moſt peaceable part of the country, where there were many reſpeĉtable citizens with whom he was well acquainted, and others who would have been glad to have ſeen him, and would have thought it a pleaſure to do him any reaſonable ſervice.

Not contented with diſcovering this total want of confidence in the moſt diſcreet people of that country, when he returned to Philadelphia he made an unprovoked attack in the news-papers on the magiſtrates, clergy, and all the other inhabitants of the whole weſtern counties ; I ſay unprovoked ; for though a ludicrous account of his journey had been publiſhed in the Pittſburgh gazette and republiſhed in Philadelphia, yet if it was a crime it could not be aſcribed to the people whoſe charaĉter he traduced, for few of them knew he had been up till they heard of his being gone again.

Though I reside within two miles of the great road, by which he returned, the first information I had of his having been up was from that very publication in the gazette. If I had known he had been there I would undoubtedly have waited on him, and invited him to my house ; there were others who would have done so as well as me.

There had been no insult offered or injury done to any excise officer, nor actual opposition given to the execution of the law in all the country through which he passed and repassed, and at that time the distillers there generally would have been easily induced to have complied with the law ; but the supervisor's conduct went far to suppress the growing disposition towards compliance, which even the secretary himself acknowledges to have existed at that time. He indeed procured evidence against two men for being concerned in the riot at Faulkner's, but the evidence was false. The two men were not only innocent but meritorious, and the proofs of their innocence were so decisive as not to leave the least doubt remaining ; therefore though a bill had been found at the district court, in consequence of the perjury, the prosecution was discontinued.

The witness was a recruit, and at that time an hostler of Capt. Faulkner's. I know nothing of his character ; but I have sufficient reason to presume that Capt. Faulkner's own testimony would condemn no person before a court of justice where his character was known. I never knew who it was that suborned the witness to swear against Mess. Kerr and Beer, but I am persuaded the supervisor's moral principles were too good to permit him to be knowingly concerned in it. All the information the fecretary is pleafed to communicate on this, is, that there was a miftake in the perfons; fortunately the miftake operated againft perfons whofe character and fituation protected them from falling victims to the moft grofs and flagrant depravity. It might have been otherwife with perfons equally innocent.

We are further informed that teftimony was procured by him of the perfons who compofed the Pittfburgh Committee, and in a letter of the fecretary to the governor, he fays that Mr. Gallatin was one of them ; this is alfo a miftake, for Gallatin and myfelf were both attending the General Affembly of the ftate in Philadelphia at the time of the Pittfburgh Committee.

Thefe proceedings encouraged thofe who were difpofed to oppofe the execution of the excife law, to exult in the weaknefs of the adminiftration of the revenue, and confirmed their belief, that a law which could not be executed would be repealed. When the head officer of the Diftrict was afhamed to appear in defence of it, people who knew there was no danger did not afcribe his behaviour to fear, even thofe who were convinced of the neceffity of fubmifion and would otherwife have contributed to promote it, thought it prudent to be filent.

From this time the number and boldnefs of thofe, who violently oppofed the law, and maltreated the officers who executed it and the citizens who complied with it, vifibly encreafed. It was not till after this that perfons were put in jeopardy for entering their fills ; and the fecretary acknowledges that the laws

appeared during 1793 to be gaining ground, that feveral principal diftillers who formerly held out had complied, and that others difcovered a difpofition to comply,
which was only reftrained by the fear of violence. I
will add that as far as I was acquainted with the diftillers, the compliance would have been general, if adequate protection had been afforded by government.

It was not however an expenfive protection that
was defired or neceffary. The prefence and authority
of a court of juftice would have anfwered every neceffary purpofe, and lefs would not do. The neceffity of a federal court going into that country, or of competent powers being vefted in the ftate courts, had been
fuggefted to the Prefident, and urged on the fecretary of
the treafury, who at that time was not only the refponfible head of the revenue department, but who alfo
at that time originated the revenue laws, as well as
directed the arrangements for the execution of them.

On a full conviction of the propriety of this meafure, Congrefs in March 1793 enacted a law to enable
the federal judiciary to hold fpecial feffions nearer the
place where crimes were committed, than thofe to
which the feffions of the circuit court had been fixed by
law. Thofe who anxioufly wifhed to fee the dignity
and authority of the laws fupported, expected that a
fpecial feffion would have been held in the weftern
counties with all convenient fpeed. If this had
been done, I am certain there would have been no
Infurrection.

But far from applying this cheap, rational and
efficacious remedy, the diforders were permitted to go
on and encreafe till July 1794. Previous to this how-

I

ever, on the fifth of June, authority was vefted in the
ftate courts to try caufes arifing under the revenue
laws.   Though this important improvement in the
laws was too long delayed, yet if it had been fairly
exercifed, even at this late period, extraordinary exertions would have been unneceffary, but thefe ordinary and falutary methods of preventing the evil appear
never to have been ferioufly defigned.

, Previous to the neceffary powers being vefted in
the ftate courts, proceffes had privately iffued out of the
diftrict court at Philadelphia, but the execution of
them was delayed till July following, when the marfhal was fent to the weftern countics to ferve the proceffes in the midft of the hurry of harveft, when men's
minds are agitated with unufual care and their bodies
with vigorous exertions, and when to the heat of the
feafon and the competition of labour is generally added
the ftimulus of ardent fpirits. At this unfortunate
period the marfhal arrived and ferved the proceffes,
which required the diftillers to appear at the diftrict
court in Philadelphia. I do not mean that people drink
more ardent fpirits in harveft in this coutry, than in
other places, where there is no other fubftitute. It is
drunk on thefe occafions in as great quantities on the
eaft fide of the mountains as it is on the weft.

He ferved all the proceffes that were directed to the
diftillers of Fayette County, thirty four in number,
without interruption, and had been equally fuccefsful
in ferving all thofe in Wafhington County, till the
very laft writ, when he unfortunately went into Pittfburgh.

Before I proceed further it is proper to remark, that during the firſt two years the number who committed infractions on the laws were comparatively ſmall and confined to but a few places, that in the laſt year as the diſpoſition among the diſtillers to comply with the law became more evident, the oppoſition to it became more violent, and was carried on in other and more alarming methods, that during this period the treaſury department either wholly neglected it or tampered with it, in ſuch a manner as was only calculated to encourage the oppoſition and diſcourage every exertion of well diſpoſed citizens to ſupport the law. It is an undoubted fact that the manner in which the execution of the law was conducted, while it invited oppoſition gave alarming apprehenſions to men of diſcernment ; for, they could not otherwiſe account for it than by ſuppoſing, that the diſorders were deſignedly foſtered until they would produce a more ſerious iſſue. Many of them knew that he who ſtood at the helm of the revenue department had no averſion to being employed as a pilot in a ſtorm. When the whole method of conducting the coercion of the laws, both as to time and manner, is compared with the criſis produced by it, and the ſubſequent proceedings relative to that criſis, are taken into conſideration and judiciouſly examined, the candid reader will be the better qualified to judge of the reaſonableneſs of theſe apprehenſions.

It is true the ſecretary aſſigns ſome reaſons in his report for this negligence, but they are not found, they are indeed ſcarcely plauſible. Did the laws give him any more power to diſpenſe with the application of their coercive powers, than it did to the people in

their non-compliance. The conftitution has indeed vefted the humane and falutary power of pardoning in
the Prefident, but has not vefted the power of granting impunity in the commiffion of crimes, nor of difpenfing with the execution of the laws in the fecretary.
That impunity, which evidently contributes to promote oppofition to the laws, and increafe the number
and the crimes of offenders, is undeferving of the name
of lenity. It is a refinement in cruelty.

C H A P. VII.

WHEN the infpector came to Pittf-
burgh, he expreffed his furprife and fatisfaction that
he had fucceeded in ferving the proceffes without
meeting with either injury or infult: what a pity it
was that he delayed to ferve the laft one? Some who
were prefent when he expieffed furprife at his fuccefs,
were equally furprifed that he fhould have expected
any oppofition. However, a too fuccefsful method
was foon found to promote oppofition and excite outrage, I do not fay with defign.

The next day, in company with the infpector, he
went to ferve the laft writ on a diftiller named Miller,
near Peter's creek. On leaving the place, a number
of men were obferved as if in purfuit of them and
one gun was difcharged ; not, however, it is believed,
with a defign to do execution. It is well known that,
if the defign had been to fhoot one, or either of them,
they could not have efcaped from fo many men, few

of whom I fuppofe would have miffed their aim at a pigeon or the head of a fquirrel. Appearing, however, to be in bad humour, the marfhal and infpector rode off.

It is ufual in that, and perhaps in every other, country, where day labourers are fcarce, for the neighbours mutually to affift each other as their grain becomes ripe, and this being the throng time of harveft will eafily account for fo many people being together as has been reprefented; the number has been differently ftated, fome accounts making it only ten, while others have extended it as high as thirty.

The marfhal behaved well, and would have been finally fuccefsful, if he had finifhed ferving the writ before he called on the infpector. I have never heard a reafon affigned for his ftopping fhort, and going to Pittfburgh, before he completed the bufinefs; or, for his bringing the infpector with him. The infpector knew there were defigns againft himfelf, and he had procured arms, and otherwife prepared his houfe for an expected attack. He ought not to have involved the marfhal in the fame rifk with himfelf, and the marfhal ought to have confidered that, however unreafonable the diftinction is, the people in Europe as well as here, have always made a great difference between an officer of excife and the officer of a court of juftice. The laft feems, as if he fhared in the folemn refpectability of the judiciary, and the firft, as if he partook of the odium of the tax, the collecting of which he fuperintends.

The people of Wafhington and Allegany counties, have been charged with a capricious inconfiftency of character. They have complained of perfons of bad character being appointed for collectors of the excife tax, and were offended at general Nevil accepting of the office of infpector, whofe popularity of character was acknowledged by themfelves. This paradox, however, may be explained.

During the continuance of the ftate excife general Nevil was one of the greateft declaimers againft it, and of the moft open encouragers of oppofition to it. When Graham, the ftate excife-man was fhaved, had his hair cut, and expelled from the county, if he did not patronize that outrage he openly approved of it, and faid they did not ufe the rafcal half as bad as he deferved. In the affembly of the ftate, which preceded that which fat when the excife law was enacted by Congrefs, he voted againft the repeal of the ftate direct tax in order to make way for repealing the ftate excife. In the fubfequent affembly he voted for the refolutions againft the paffage of the excife law then before Congrefs. He and I fat and voted together for them, and we had always agreed in our principles refpecting excifes, though I never agreed with him in opinion that the excife officers ought to be ill-treated.

It was but a few days after he voted for the refolutions cenfuring the law, that he himfelf accepted of the office of infpector of that very furvey, in which he had diftinguifhed himfelf for his oppofition to the collecting of the ftate excife. The people were the more irritated againft him, on being informed that when he was told that he would forfeit the good opinion of his neighbours, from whofe good will he had held any office which he chofe, and which they had in their

power to beſtow, anſwered he did not regard their
good will, he had got an independent ſalary of 6oo
a year ; I ſuppoſe he meant Dollars, but it paſſed
among the people for pounds. I for ſome time
thought the whole ſtory fabricated in order to excite
more effectually the popular odium againſt him, but
I was afterwards informed of it by authority, too ſub-
ſtantial to leave room for doubt, and too well diſpoſed
to admit a ſuſpicion of deſign.

The authority of the law, and the dictates of cool
philoſophy will not admit of the people connecting
their ſubmiſſion to the law with their reſpect for the
man. But we muſt in our dealings with men, take human nature as it is, and admit that prejudice and paſ-
ſion will have their ſway in directing the conduct of
the great maſs of mankind. All are not lawyers, all
are not philoſophers, nor do lawyers and philoſophers
always regulate their conduct by their own precepts.

. They looked on the inſpector as giving up his
principles for a bribe, and bartering the confidence
they had in him for money, and were the more irritated at his ſpeaking ſo contemptuouſly of their good opinion, which he had been formerly ſo ſolicitous to obtain. There is alſo a great averſion among the maſs of
the people to ſalary officers. This has even diſcovered itſelf againſt the county judges, though their ſalaries are but moderate.

The inſpector was certainly early ſenſible of his
loſs of popularity. I obſerved it when he came to
Philadelphia, the firſt winter after he had accepted of
the office. When I called to ſee him at his lodgings, he
told me with joy that he had lodged in Greenſburgh

all night and been well treated. I expreſſed my ſurpriſe that he ſhould have any other expectations. He
anſwered that he had heſitated greatly about venturing
into it, but not finding any convenient road to paſs
it he had finally determined to go in. I have not
found that any threats had been made againſt him
there, or any other place at that time. Certainly if we
are in the way of our duty we ought to diſcover confidence. Cauſeleſs fears invite inſult.

The ſecretary aſſerts that Waſhington County
has uniformly diſtinguiſhed its reſiſtance by a more
exceſſive ſpirit, than has appeared in the other counties, and ſeems to have been chiefly inſtrumental in
kindling and keeping alive the flame. This character is admitted to be well founded. That part of it which
lays adjacent to the Monongahela and contiguous to general Nevil's reſidence has been called the center of oppoſition, and was undoubtedly the cradle of the
inſurrection. As their character is equally good with
thoſe of other parts of the weſtern counties, the only
reaſon I have heard aſſigned for their diſtinguiſhing
themſelves in this manner was their reſentment
of general Nevil's conduct. It was with theſe very
people he had formerly enjoyed that popularity,
which brought him into the ſupreme executive council,
the Convention, and frequently into the Aſſembly
of the ſtate for Waſhington County, before that part of
it where he reſides was included in Allegany county,
and it was to that part of Allegany, which was taken
from Waſhington, to which the violences committed in
it were confined.

K

The committee of conferees who met with the President's commiffioners at Pittfburgh, of whom we fhall hear further prefently, ftated this prejudice againft the officer, as a caufe of the oppofition, and the declaration that Miller made of his own feelings is a proof that refentment prevailed over every other confideration. It is afferted that he faid that he felt himfelf mad with paffion, that he thought having to pay 250 Dollars and attend the court of Philadelphia would ruin him : That he felt his blood boil at feeing general Nevil along to pilot the officer to his very door: That he had been as much againft the excife law as any body, when old Graham, the excife man was feized, had his hair cut, &c. he had heard general Nevil fay they ought to have cut the ears of the old rafcal, and when the diftillers were fined he talked as much againft it as any body, and thofe feelings were not peculiar to him alone, they were general in that part of the country.

I would willingly have avoided this digreffion if I could have done juftice to the caufe without it, but as I undertake to develope the caufes which promoted, and the circumftances which charaterifed, the firft popular tumults which alarmed and threatened to convulfe the moft extenfive federal republic on which the fun ha e er fhone, and which ocafioned the equipment and marching of the firft formidable militia army raifed under the federal goverment, and the firft inftance of brother being called to fight with brother, or of or an army of 15,000 men being marched from two to four hundred miles, in order to affift the marfhal of the diftrict to feize and tranfport a few perfons

to a prifon, in order to ftand a trial above three hundred miles from their place of refidence ; every ftep
taken in this important crifis will be of importance to
pofterity, and improved by them either as precedents
to be imitated or miftakes to be avoided. / The firft
caufes which have led to, or impelled, the moft alarming events in fociety, have too generally been over-
looked in hiftory. Thefe, however, are of the greateft importance to be known, becaufe by an early attention to them great mifchiefs might be prevented at
a fmall expence.

C H A P. VIII.

THE marſhal returned from Miller's to Pittſburgh, and the inſpector went to his own houſe ſome miles diſtant from Miller's. On the ſame day the Mingo creek regiment rendezvouſed in order to form a ſelect corps of militia, as their quota of the 80,000 men required by Congreſs. In the evening before they parted, they received information of the inſpector having been with the marſhal at Miller's ſerving writs, and of his having been chaſed away from there. Early next morning John Holcroft, the reputed author of Tom Tinker's letters, and about thirty-ſix others, moſt of whom had been at the militia rendezvous, with arms in their hands, appeared at the houſe of the inſpector; on being aſked by him what their buſineſs was, and anſwering in a ſuſpicious manner, they were, without further provocation, fired on from the houſe, and after returning the fire, they were fired on by the negroes from the adjoining buildings. Being thus unexpectedly attacked in flank they retired, having ſix wounded, one of them mortally; the infpector's family received no injury; he had been apprifed, fometime before the arrival of the marfhal, of an attack being meditated againft him by fome members of the Mingo creek affociation, and prepared to repel it by fetting thick plank againft the windows, and by procuring a fufficient number of arms to put the negroes in a ftate of defence. This was not known to the affailants.

Some of the circumftances relating to this tranfaction, have been differently ftated, by the late fecretary and others. The number of the rioters has been called about one hundred, and they are charged with having commenced the attack. They did not, however, exceed thirty-fix and it has been proved on oath before the circuit court, that the infpector began the attack before any outrage had been attempted by Holcroft's party. No doubt he had reafon to fufpect that their defign was to compel him to furrender his papers and refign his commiffion. He had been warned of fuch a defign, and it was probably only accelerated by his affifting at ferving the writs, and perhaps conducted by other hands. Unfortunately, however, it did not end here. That refentment which formerly difcovered itfelf by cafual exceffes in which comparatively few were engaged, and thofe few generally perfons of violent paffions and little difcretion, now affumed the tone of unreflecting madnefs, and drew into its vortex many perfons of good morals, and who ufually difcovered a refpectable meafure of difcretion in all their dealings as men and citizens.

By the mortification of the defeat, and by the flame
of refentment kindled by one of Holcroft's party being
killed, and fo many wounded, all regard for confequences was fwallowed up by the paffions of the moment, and uncommon exertions were made that night to
prepare for accomplifhing their object next day. The
vicinity of the Mingo creek affociation which included a
large proportion of that regiment, contributed greatly
to their fuccefs ; by means of that affociation they
were prepared like a difciplined phalanx to act
with vigour agreeably to whatever direction they took,
and were as a centre for others to rally round. It is
generally agreed that next morning not lefs than 500
men moftly armed, rendezvoufed at Couche's fort,
a few miles from the infpector's houfe. Many attended folely becaufe they had not firmnefs fufficient
to refufe.

While they were deliberating what was beft to be
done, the reverend Mr. Clark, a venerable and very
old clergyman, expoftulated with them on the impropriety of their enterprife, and ufed his utmoft endeavours to diffuade them from it ; but they confidered his
fentiments to proceed from the cold caution and timi-
dity naturally attendant on extreme age ; and looking on
him, perhaps, to be in his dotage, and unfit to advife in
affairs not fuited to his time of life, they unfortunately defpifed his counfel, and fuffered themfelves to
be carried on by the hurricane of their irritated and
blind paffions.

From Couche's fort they marched to the infpector's
houfe. They elected a committee of three to fuperintend the enterprife ; the committee appointed ma-

jor M' Farlane to command the party, fubject however to its direction. The orders were to demand and obtain the infpector's commiffion and papers, and to offer no violence to his perfon, family or property, farther than would be abfolutely neceffary for accomplifhing this object. The horfes were left under a guard in the woods, and the committee took their feat on an eminence at fome diftance from the infpector's houfe.

Major Kirkpatrick, with a detachment of eleven men from the garrifon at Pittfburgh, had arrived that morning to affift the Infpector, who when informed of the force that was coming againft him thought it prudent to withdraw to a place of concealment, and not having a profpect of defending the houfe left it in charge of his kinfman Kirkpatrick, with directions to make a capitulation in favour of the property if practicable, if not to defend it as long as poffible.

When Major M' Farlane with the affailants approached the houfe, a flag was fent from the Committee to demand of the infpector to deliver up his papers. On anfwer being returned that the infpector had left the houfe, a fecond flag was fent, and demand made that fix perfons fhould be admitted into the houfe to fearch for his papers, and take them. This demand however was abfolutely refufed. Notice was then given by a third flag, for the miftrefs of the family and fuch other females as were in the houfe to withdraw, which being done the firing commenced. About fifteen minutes after a call was heard from the houfe, and thofe within ceafed firing; upon which major M' Farlane ftepping from behind a tree, and commanding

his party to defift from firing, received a deadly
fhot from the houfe and inflantly expired. The affailants believing that the ceffation of firing in the houfe
and the call from it, was a feint to put them off their
guard, and that M' Farlane was killed by a fhot aimed at
him in time of parley, concluded that he was murde-
red, and becoming exceedingly enraged, renewed the
firing with great vigour. While a meffage was fent
to the Committee to enquire whether the houfe fhould
be ftormed, a man without any orders fet fire to fome
ftraw in the barn, which cummunicated the flame to
the whole building, and foon extended itfelf to the adjacent buildings. The intenfe heat and danger of the
flame immediately communicating to the dwelling houfe,
obliged Major Kirkpatrick and his party to furrender,
and they were received and difmiffed without injury.

When it is confidered that the affailants believed
that their leader was fhot with defign by Major Kirkpatrick himfelf, and that they difmiffed him and his
party without injury, it muft be admitted that notwithftanding they were enraged to a degree of madnefs,
they difcovered no inclination for wantonly fhedding
blood. Kirkpatrick and M' Farlane had been both
officers through the whole courfe of the late war with
Great Britain. What a pity, that thofe who had
fought together in fo good a caufe fhould have had the
misfortune, the one to fhed the other's blood in a caufe
fo ill judged and fo indifcreetly conducted. I never
faw M' Farlane fo as to know him, but I had long
heard him fpoken of as a well-behaved refpectable citizen, who had made an independent fortune by honeft

industry, and I cannot find that he was ever concerned in any other outrage before this day which to him was fatal.

Many incidents relative to this unhappy affair have been very differently reprefented. However they are not very important: but it will readily be obferved that in one particular of fome importance, I have contradicted the report of the late fecretary. When the affailants demanded the Infpector's papers, he afferts that they were anfwered, that they might fend perfons to fearch the houfe, and to take away whatever papers they could find appertaining to his office. But not fatisfied with this they infifted unconditionally, that the armed men, who were in the houfe for its defence, fhould march out and ground their arms, which Major Kirkpatrick peremptorily refufed, confidering it, and reprefenting it to them, as a proof of a defign to deftroy the property. This refufal put an end to the parly. However what I have ftated is the truth, confirmed by folemn teftimony taken before the circuit court, and the truth or falfehood of this fact was what in a great meafure diftinguifhed the character and marked the aggravation of the crime. As ftated by the fecretary, it was their object to treat the detachment of the Federal troops as enemies in a ftate of war, and to treat the houfe as a garrifon which they had a right to plunder or not, as they faw caufe. If this was true, it was a rebellion in form, and conftituted unequivocally the crime of treafon. If his ftatement was not true, it was only a riot of the fame nature of thofe attacks formerly made on Wells and others, only differing in force. Though his account of it is certainly fallacious, yet it was on the fuppofed validity of it

L

that the affociate judge gave the certificate preparatory
to calling out an army, and occafioned the offence to
be tried on a charge of treafon.

The houfe of the infpector was burned, and befides
his furniture, which was valuable, a number of certificates and other papers of importance to a large
amount, were alfo confumed. The certificates, however, being loaned and regiftered, were not loft. It
was a pity, that as he was warned of the danger and had
early prepared for defence, he did not think of removing his own private papers. Major Kirkpatrick
had been a brave and experienced officer, but furely a
defperate defence, without even a chance of fuccefs,
and with the certain deftruction of much valuable property, can be intitled to no other epithet than rafhnefs.
True bravery is always connected with prudence.
The marfhal, and colonel Prefsly Nevil, fon of the
infpector, came up juft after the houfe was burned.
There is reafon to prefume that if colonel Nevile had
arrived in time, he would have faved the property, by
agreeing to the terms of the affailants, agreeably to
the inftructions of his father, which major Kirkpatrick difregarded. The marfhal muft have been convinced that he was in jeopardy before, by being in
company with the infpector; his putting himfelf in
evident jeopardy again, when he had no writs to ferve
nor means of fuppreffing the riot, may fpeak in favour
of his courage and the goodnefs of his heart, but not
of his prudence; he and colonel Nevil were difmiffed without injury, but not without difficulty and rifk.

It is to be regretted, that citizens of good moral
character and difcretion fhould have engaged in fuch

a criminal enterprife ; yet fome good arofe out of this circumftance. If it had not been for fuch characters being embarked with thofe of another defcription, undoubtedly much more blood would have been fhed. There were feveral, who expreffed an intention of killing major Kirkpatrick, and who threatened colonel Nevil and the marfhal ; but there was on this and all other occafions through the infurrection fo many men of difcretion as prevented any perfon from being killed or maimed by the infurgents, except the few that were wounded at the attack on Nevil's houfe.

Before they parted, probably at the funeral of major M'Farlane, they appointed a meeting to be held at Mingo creek. This meeting was compofed of a number of thofe who had been at the infpector's houfe, fome others in the vicinity, who had refufed to join in that meafure, and a few individuals from Pittfburgh and thofe parts of Fayette county which lay moft contiguous. At this meeting Meffrs. Bradford, Marfhal, Cook, and Brackenridge, whofe names became fo confpicuous afterwards, appeared publicly, for the firft time, on the ftage. It appears that Bradford and Marfhal were confulted at the town of Wafhington, previous to the fecond attack on Nevil's houfe, and it is faid that at firft they declined having any thing to do with it ; but having once confented they were afterwards confidered as leaders. At this meeting Bradford, in a violent and lengthy harangue, openly advocated what had been done, urged the propriety and neceffity of unanimity in making it a common caufe, &c.

Marfhal endeavoured to change the ftate of the queftion into an enquiry, what was beft to be done, in preference to deciding on the merits of what had been done.

Brackenridge, in a speech of considerable length, drew their attention by amusing them and seeming to countenance their conduct ; but before he concluded he ventured to suggest, that though what they had done might be morally right, yet it was legally wrong, and suggested the propriety of their consulting their fellow citizens in the other parts of the survey, and in the mean time of their sending commissioners to the President. He endeavoured to convince them of the bad policy of having those that had not been engaged in the attack on the inspector involved, because in that case they could not act as mediators for those who were obnoxious The meeting was divided in opinion about the sentiments he expressed ; some thought he was warm in the cause, but the more violent were offended : It was pleasing, however, to those who, like himself, were not yet involved. He had been sent for by some of the leaders, but declined coming till he was advised to it by colonel Nevil, who assisted in procuring others to accompany him, to be witnesses of his conduct. He retired before the meeting resolved on any measures.

The only measure agreed on before the meeting broke up was, to call a meeting of the four counties, which they published in the following words. " By " a respectable number of citizens, who met on Wed- " nesday the 23d instant, (July,) at the meeting-house " on Mingo creek, it is recommended to the town- " ships of the four western counties of Pennsylvania, " and the neighbouring counties of Virginia, to meet,

" and choofe, not more than five, nor lefs than two,
" reprefentatives, to meet at Parkifon's ferry, on the
" Monongahela, on Thurfday the 14th day of Auguft
" next, to take into confideration the fituation of the
" weftern country."

Though this was moved for by the well difpofed,
and cautioufly worded by the chairman and fecretary,
and defigned by them as a means of flopping the diforder, and procuring an amnefty for the guilty, yet that
it was defigned to be ufed by Bradford and fome others,
to draw the whole weftern counties of Pennfylvania
and Virginia into the vortex of infurrection, is evident
from their fubfequent conduct.

Though no other plan was propofed at the meeting,
it was but a few days until Bradford, who now affumed
the direction of the bufinefs, planned and procured
the execution of another enterprife, which, though not
fo formidable as that already atchieved, was equally an
outrage on the laws and alarming to government. It
was the robbing of the weftern mail. This plan was
executed three days after the meeting, on the poft-road,
about ten miles from Greenfburgh, and twenty two
from Pittfburgh, by a namefake and near relation of
Bradford's and a man named Mitchel, both from Wafhington county. It is not certain that any but himfelf
were concerned in laying the plan, but it was only two
days after the mail was robbed that Bradford and others
went to Canonfburgh, feven miles from Wafhington,
with the Wafhington and Pittfburgh mail in their fad-
dle bags. When they opened the mails, that from
Wafhington contained no letters on the meafures that
had been purfued; but the Pittfburgh mail contained

letters from general Gibfon, colonel Nevil, Mr. Bryfon, and Mr. Day which gave great offence. They contained a ftatement of the attack on Nevil's houfe, and the fentiments expreffed by Bradford at the Mingo meeting. Thefe were taken out, and the reft put up carefully, to be returned to Pittfburgh.

Though thefe letters contained little elfe than a ftate of the facts as they really happened, they were made the engine of bringing about the Braddock's field meeting.

At Cannonfburgh the following circular letter was agreed upon, and directed to the militia officers in the fame manner as an order would have iffued from the proper authority, and was in feveral regiments as promptly obeyed. By fuch officers as wifhed to promote the meafure the people were called on as for a ufual tour of militia duty, without being informed of the contents of the circular letter which is as follows :

" Sir.

" Having had fufpicions that the Pittfburgh poft would carry with him the fentiments of fome of the people in the country, refpecting our prefent alarming fituation ; and the letters by the poft being now in our poffeffion, by which certain fecrets are difcovered, hoftile to our intereft, it is therefore now come to that crifis, that every citizen muft exprefs his fentiments not by his words but his actions. You are then called on, as a citizen of the weftern country, to render your perfonal fervice, with as many volunteers as you can raife, to rendezvous at your ufual place of meeting, on Wednefday next ; and from thence you will march to the ufual place of rendezvous at Braddock's field, on the Monongahela, on Friday the firft day of

Auguſt next, to be there at two o'clock in the after-
noon, with arms and accoutrements in good order. If
any volunteers ſhould want arms and ammunition, bring
them forward, and they ſhall be ſupplied as well as
poſſible. Here, ſir, is an expedition propoſed, in which
you will have an opportunity of diſplaying your military talents, and of rendering ſervice to your country;
four days proviſion will be wanted, let the men be
thus ſupplied."

This general order was ſigned *I. Canon, B. Parkiſon
D. Bradford, A. Fulton, T. Speers, I. Lochry,
J. Marſhal.*

Colonel Marſhal had been an early ſettler in the
weſtern counties, and a uſeful citizen, during the
courſe of the late war with Britain, and the territorial
controverſy with Virginia. He was ſucceſſively, Regiſter, High Sheriff, member of the ratifying convention,
of the legiſlature, county lieutenant, and again regiſter
in Waſhington County; and was reſpectable for the
diſcretion he diſcovered in the diſcharge of the duties
of the reſpective offices he filled. In the ratifying convention, he voted in favour of amendments previous
to ratification, but refuſed to ſign the reaſons of the
minority. Moderation was thought to have been a leading trait in his character. He is an induſtrious man,
and poſſeſſes property to a large amount. From theſe
circumſtances, the part he took in the inſurrection was
truly ſurpriſing. He had come from the north of
Ireland in his youth.

Bradford had been deputy of the attorney general
of the ſtate, from the time that Waſhington had been
erected into a ſeparate county. He was originally from
Maryland, where he ſtudied law, and had been a member

of the Virginia Affembly, before the fettlement of the boundary line of the ftate, and ftill practifed law in fome of the courts of that ftate. He had favoured the plan of forming a new ftate. At the time of the adoption of the federal government, he was one of its moft zealous advocates in that country.

Parkifon, a Pennfylvanian by birth, has always refided in that ftate. He alfo was a federalift, and had fupported general Nevil's intereft formerly, was reputed a good citizen, a man of influence in his neighbourhood, had been a juftice of the peace before the revifion of the conftitution of the ftate, was prefident of the Mingo creek affociation, and one of the committee who fuperintended the operations in the attack on Nevil's houfe.

Canon was from Chefter county in Pennfylvania, had long been a refpectable citizen fouth of the Mohongahela, lived in the town called by his name, had attached himfelf to the government of Virginia, and favoured the idea of a new ftate. He was afterwards a member of the legiflature, and was an early advocate for the federal conftitution, and a fupporter of general Nevil's intereft in that country.

Fulton was from Maryland ; he was not only a federalift, but an open advocate of the excife law, indeed the moft openly fo, of any I have met with in the weftern counties, and an avowed friend of the Infpector. He kept a large diftillery, and expected by the operation of the excife law to have a confiderable advantage over the fmall diftillers. He had alfo erected a brewery. I have never been able to account for the inconfiftency of his conduct.

I know little of Speers or Lochry. The laſt was lately from Cheſter county and attended Col. Marſhal's mill. He perhaps ſigned without reflecting what he was doing. The other had lived ſeveral years at Canonſburgh and kept ſtore ; he might have been active at this time , but I preſume he was not very influential.

There were but three days from the date of the orders to circulate the information and prepare for the rendezvous. Great exertions were made however in communicating the circular letters, and though many who probably wiſhed to ſupprefs them durſt not, there were ſome who did keep them ſecret, and ſome clergymen and others in the ſouth of Waſhington county were active and ſucceſsful with their neighbours in diſſuading them from going. What had already taken place was aggravated and miſrepreſented, more were ſaid to have been killed and wounded than really were, men's minds were in a ſtate of conſternation and ſuſpenſe, and the ambiguous manner in which the circular orders were written excited men whoſe minds were already agitated to expect that ſome wonderful diſcovery had been made, and that ſome great event was about to take place.

In this interval three men from the town of Waſhington undertook to carry the mail back to Pittſburgh. Under cover of this errand they correſponded with a committee of the town, informed it of the meaſures that were purſuing, and particularly of the deſigns of Bradford and his friends againſt the perſons in Pittſburgh, who had written to Philadelphia a ſtatement of the preſent ſituation of the country, and of the danger the town might be expoſed to on their ac-
M

count. They also assured the committee that a number of well disposed men would mix with the others to attend the rendezvous at Braddock's field, in order to have the better opportunity of preventing excesses. Three of the persons, who had written the letters, and who had it in their power to retire for some time without much inconveniency, and who of their own accord were disposed to do so, agreed to submit to the form of an expulsion by the committee.

On the day of rendezvous it was supposed, that a mixed multitude, not much short of seven thousand, appeared on the ground. But from examining the population of the country from which they were collected, it is not probable that their number was near so great. Many of those who did attend were without arms. Several field officers in the vicinity of Braddock's field attended, with as many of their friends as they could collect, to be prepared to prevent excesses, and save Pittsburgh if it should be in danger, and some of the field officers of the most formidable and warlike corps who attended are known to have been well disposed to peace and order.

The greatest number was from Washington county, but though those from the Regiment about the town of Washington came in force, with the general of the county and their colonel at their head, yet it is notorious that general Taylor and colonel Stokely were uniformly opposed to the whole system of outrage and resistance. Colonel Hamilton of the Mingo creek Battalion was also opposed to it, and when he heard of the orders of march coming to his Regiment, though he had not seen them himself, he rode with all possible speed to the county town to countermand them, but too late to have effect. Every thing was conducted with a rapidity characteristic of the ind scretion that governed the conductors of the measures. General Wilkin with a great many others of his Allegany county Brigade were well disposed. This was particularly the case with colonel Patterson, and colonel M⸱ Nair and their friends, and also with the principal part of the citizens from Pittsburgh. There was but one Major and a company of about 60 men from Wellmoreland county, who appeared in a state of preparation according to the orders. The Major is said to have discovered a warlike disposition. Many however from the two adjacent townships in West more and county went to be spectators of what was carrying on and encreased the croud. Some of these might have gone with a bad disposition, and some might have caught the infection when they were there. I have not however heard of any remark made on the conduct of any of them, except the Major to whom I have alluded. I am certain the colonel and majors of the nearest Wellmoreland Battalion were well disposed. There were not more than twelve men from Fayette county at Braddock's field. The orders had been sent to colonel Cock, who concealed them from his most intimate neighbours, and went alone to endeavour by his advice to prevent excesses. The few others from that county had been informed of the meeting by rumor.

Colonel Cock residing in the nearest part of Fayette to Mingo creek had attended that meeting with the same view. He was chairman there and at a number of the subsequent meetings. He had been Member of the

firft convention of Pennfylvania, and was judge of
the court of Weflmoreland, and lieutenant of that
county till Fayette county was erected, of which he is
now an affociate judge. Being an elderly, and efteemed
a difcreet man he is generally made chairman in all
meetings of which he is a member. He has rarely
been known to pafs the bounds of difcretion if we except
in the ardour of his zeal for the adoption of the Federal
government, he was proportionably mortified at the
excife law and fome meafures that led to it being enacted by that government, but had no hand in the oppofition made to the excife, and put himfelf into fufpected
fituations in order to reftore order. He being generally
known through Pennfylvania was much fpoken againft.
He went to Philadelphia and entered into recognizance,
but there was no caufe of action found againft him. His
having been chairman in all meetings and committees
connected with the infurrection, is the reafon ef this
digreffion.

Bradford reviewed the troops on the ground, and
is fai l to have affumed the powers and to have received
the honours of Major-general. There is no doubt but
that he received every honour that could be conferred.
The infatuated diforganizers idolifed him, and thofe
who held him in contempt, and looked on the meafures
with horror, were many of them the moft obfequious in
their attentions to him. They believed that at that
moment expulfion or even more fevere punifhment
depended on his will. His denunciation of cowards
and traitors, and holding up Roberfpiere's fyftem of
terror for imitation at the Mingo creek meeting, was
well known to th m, and fpread a temporary panic.

A committee was apointed at the rendezvous, who refolved that general Gibfon and colonel Nevil fhould be expelled, and authorifed the Pittfburgh committee to put this refolution into execution. It was refolved that the army, as it was called, fhould march to Pittf-burgh. On this occafion the people of Pittfburgh went forward to prepare for giving them the moft hof-pitable reception in their power, that they might pafs through it with good humour. Bradford alfo fent to the commandant of the garrifon to inform him that no harm was intended, and to requeft being permitted to pafs peaceably. They marched in, however, by the Monongahela road which did not lead to the garrifon, and being furnifhed with refrefhments in Pittfburgh by the towns-people, they croffed the Monongahela without giving any difturbance.

After croffing the river many returned to their homes, and thefe were no doubt the moft orderly. A great number of the well difpofed people had previoufly gone to their homes from Braddock's field. A num-ber, however, ftayed over night near Pittfburgh, and in the night burned a fmall barn, the property of ma-jor Kirkpatrick, with the grain it contained, which was then the property of a tenant. They attempted alfo to burn the dwelling houfe, but were prevented by the interpofition of colonel Hamilton, &c. who with difficulty faved it. About the fame time, a party who had parted from the main body and remained in Pittfburgh, at-tempted to burn Kirkpatrick's dwelling houfe in the town, but were prevented by the interpofition of colonel Cook, and a brother of major M'Farlane, who

had been killed, aſſiſted by the addreſs of Mr. Brackenridge.

It will naturally be enquired what was the objeƈt of
this mighty rendezvous of men. Nothing appears to
have been done or attempted by thoſe who direƈted it,
but ordering two more of the citizens of Pittſburgh to
be expelled.   This might have been as well accom-
pliſhed by ſending a deputation to Pittſburgh to deſire
that it ſhould be done.   However hard it might have
appeared to require it, the men would have been wiſe
enough to have gone out of the way themſelves till
times had altered.   To underſtand this we muſt go
back to the private meeting at Canonſburgh.   It had
been there agreed upon to attack the garriſon at Pittſburgh, and ſeize the arms and ammunition for their own
defence.   They conſidered the conduƈt of Congreſs
in ſeizing the Britiſh poſts, arms, &c. while they remained colonies, petitioning the throne, acknowledging their dependance on it, and endeavouring to have
their juſt grounds of complaint removed, to be a precedent perfeƈtly applicable to their caſe.   It was in
conſequence of this determination that the rendezvous
was ordered, but the objeƈt was kept ſecret ; there
were ſome preſent who diſſented.

Thus an enterpriſe of a moſt daring nature was
determined on during an hour or two ſpent in a tavern,
by men unauthoriſed even by thoſe who had already
rendered themſelves obnoxious; for thoſe men were
not delegated, and not more than two of them had
been perſonally engaged in the attack on the inſpeƈtor's
houſe. Not only to determine on ſuch a daring and dangerous enterpriſe, but to endeavour to draw the whole

people of the weftern counties into the execution of it, blindfolded, was fuch an inconfiderate meafure as I am at a lofs for words to exprefs my fentiments of ; but I have no doubt that long before this time their own re- flections have painted the impropriety of their con- duct on their own minds, in colours more glowing than can be reprefented by language.

' It was not thus that the revolutionary conteft was commenced. There was not only the flow delibera- tion of the wifeft men felected from every colony, but of the moft difcreet men in every county and townfhip, and the magnitude of the object was fet be- fore the people in the moft remote fituations, before they were drawn into the arduous conteft. May the con- duct of the Canonfburgh committee be an example to deter from fuch rafh and impetuous proceedings !

When colonel Hamilton, and fome others, had dif- covered the defign of attacking the garrifon, and per- fuaded Bradford and Marfhal to countermand the or- ders, he told them that the arms were for an expedi- tion againft the Indians under general Scott.   Brad- ford, without even confulting Marfhal or anfwering a word to Hamilton, wrote the countermand, and hand- ing it to Hamilton afked him if that would do.   He inferted in a poftfcript what he had been told of Scott's expedition as a reafon of the countermand ; this firft brought the defign of the rendezvous to light ; but it feems it was now given up ; but the rendezvous being carried on, fome who attended ftill believed that to have been the object of it, till they were convinced of its being laid afide by the event.   Marfhal wifhed to

have countermanded the orders foon after they were
iffued.

Bradford promifed Hamilton and others to advife
the militia, who met at Wafhington, not to march to
Braddock's field.   They were convened in the court-
houfe, and Meff. Rofs and Stokely addreffed them with
the moft powerful reafons, to diffuade them from proceeding further.   Bradford notwithftanding his agreement
to the contrary, addreffed them with vehement declamation in favour of proceeding.   They had liftened
attentively to the firft fpeakers, but appeared to be fo
influenced by Bradford's fpeech, that when Marfhal rofe
after him to offer fome reafons againft proceeding, he
could not be heard, and that night his houfe was tarred
and feathered   This expreffion of refentment feems
to have been the reafon of his proceeding farther in
that courfe, from which he feemed defirous of retreat-
ing ; from this and fome other inftances it appears he
was not fo much a leader, as he was led by Bradford,
and pufhed forward by his dread of thofe, whofe meafures he had at firft inconfiderately countenanced.

This was the only open attempt that was made to
addrefs the people who were collected by the circular
letter, and if it had not been for Bradford the attempt
would have been fuccefsful.   It was with great difficulty they were got to parade for the march after leaving
the court houfe ; few but young men and boys appeared
willing ; but it was not thought proper they fhould go
alone, and if any marched it had been agreed among
the moderate people that they would go in company.
Colonel Stokely, though he had openly oppofed the

meafure, put himfelf at the head of h's regiment, Mr. Rofs the fenator, general Taylor and others who were equally oppofed to the meafures went alfo.

I have been the more particular in re sting the rendezvous at Braddock's field, as it had the moft formidable afpect, and approached neareft to the defcription of a combination againft the governm nt, of any inftance that happened during the diforders; vet when examined, it does not prove to be a combination of the people of any county, but of fix men in a tavern, who wifhed, probably, to inflame the people into a combination, which, however, did not take place, for there appears to have been no plan laid, nor combination entered into, at the rendezvous. Ordering the expulfion of the two men and directing the march to Pittfburgh, was conducted by a committee compofed in part of very orderly well difpofed men, who thought it imprudent to object to any meafure dictated by Bradford, whofe terror was aided by the occafional interference of fome defperate men who were not of the committee. The march to Pittfburgh, and the expulfion; though very difagreeable to the committee members from Pittfburgh, was agreed to even by them. No man ever commanded an army, fo great a proportion of which were traitors to the caufe. nor had fuch a deference paid to him with fo little fincerity, as Bradford, on this occafion.

Though this formidable parade made an aftonifhing noife and appearance, it vanifhed in fmoke like a rocket, and left no trace of its tranfactions behind, except the march to Pittfburgh, for the purpofe of parade; yet its effects were undoubtedly more pernici-

N

ous than thofe which were produced by any preceding
excefs.   Till now the flame had been confined to a
fmall fpace ; but from this it fpread to a diftance. The
countenance given to the rendezvous and the acquiefcence in Bradford's meafures, apparent in the conduct
of judges, attornies, the fenator of Congrefs, and other
refpectable citizens, including the whole of the magiftrates, other officers, and merchants, of Pittfburgh, the
motives for which were not underftood, gave the appearance of unanimity in the caufe, and inconfiderate
people in other places became afhamed that they had
done nothing.   It had been reported from the Mingo
meeting, that Bradford and Brackenridge had pledged
their lives and fortunes for the lawfulnefs and fuccefs
of the meafures ; their legal abilities were extolled by
infatuated people at the time, and it was believed that
under their direction the plans muft be well laid, and
judicioufly conducted, and the countenance given at
Braddock's field by fo many men of found judgment
and refpectable character was efteemed an infallible
teft of the goodnefs of the caufe.   However neceffary
this temporizing conduct was on the occafion, it had a
very bad effect on the country at large.   It was believed, however, by thofe who practifed it, that this was the
moft certain method of faving Pittfburgh, and preventing
the effufion of human blood.   Bradford's movements
were too rapid to allow time for defenfive arrangements,
or to find out in whom they could have confidence.
The time had been when Marfhal would have been
one of the firft applied to on fuch occafions ; the manner in which he and fome others now acted, made every
perfon be fufpected till his fentiments could be une-

quivocally known, and the impreſſions of terror made prudent perſons cautious in divulging their ſentiments.

It was but a few days after this that a party went to the reſidence of Wells in Fayette county, burned his houſe, and compelled him to reſign his commiſſion, and ſwear not to hold the office in future. He was collector for Weſtmoreland and Fayette counties. This party appears to have gone from the parts of Weſtmoreland adjoining, and to have been joined by a few from Fayette. There appears to have been a ſmaller proportion of men of common diſcretion engaged in this than in the attack on Nevil's houſe. The houſe of Wells was burnt without reſiſtance or oppoſition, and againſt the remonſtrance of the moſt prudent; ſeveral were forced by this party to go along with them contrary to their inclination.

Threatening letters were ſent into the center and ſouthern parts of Weſtmoreland to excite them to go againſt Webſter, collector of Bedford, and many poor people in thoſe parts had cauſe of complaint againſt him, which did not exiſt againſt other exciſe officers. He had made a practice of ſeizing liquors on the road from poor people, who were carrying it to procure their ſalt, or other neceſſaries; ſome inſtances of this might be mentioned that were very inhumane: ſometimes he was contented with receiving the exciſe tax and letting the liquors paſs, but generally he kept all, and ſometimes detained the horſes for a time, reſtoring them again as a matter of favour. This hardſhip fell generally on the poor, for he let others paſs, even though they called and drank at his tavern, with their loads. It was believed he did not account with the public for the proceeds.

That his conduct was not agreeable to law was afferted
by the infpector, when he was applied to, but no redrefs
was given, nor was the practice relinquifhed. The
law authorifing feizure was not made till June immediately preceding the infurrection.

The party who went againft Webfter were comparatively fmall, fome of them were from Bedford
county, but much the greateft number were from the
parts of Wellmoreland adjoining, many of whom had
had their liquors unlawfully feized by him. They
thought it robbery, nor do I know if they thought
amifs. The law fubjected diftilleries to the officers,
but did not at that time fubject people travelling on
the road who had nothing to do with the entry of ftills,
more than a man taking his grift to the mill, had to do
with the tax having been paid on the mill by its
owner.

Webfter made no refiftance, but brought out his
papers, and tore and trod on them. The party differ-
ed among themfelves. Some were for tarring, feathering, &c. Fire was fet to his hay ftacks and ftables,
but the more moderate party were the majority. They
extinguifhed the fire and protected the man from any
other injury than infulting language. Not agreeing
how he fhould be treated they took him along with
them fome miles, and apprehenfions being entertained
by himfelf and fome others, of the outrageous party
falling back and treating him ill when the others were
gone, he was taken into Wellmoreland and there being lodged in fafety that night, he was permitted to
return home the next day without further injury. He
had expected the vifit, probably before it was thought

of by thofe who made it, and had taken refuge in the town of Bedford; but finding himfelf unfafe there he returned to his own houfe and prepared for the event.

Immediately after the meeting at Mingo creek, Bradford wrote to the principal perfons in the neighbouring counties of Virginia, preffing them in the moft urgent manner to fend Delegates to the meeting, which was appointed to be held at Parkifon's Ferry. His fending this letter, and the ftyle in which it was wrote, indubitably proves the improvement he defigned to make of the Parkifon meeting. His robbing the mail, and directing the rendezvous at Braddock's field, were calculated to inflame the minds of the people previoufly to that meeting, and encreafe the number of thofe who would be rendered defperate by their crimes. In this he was but too fuccefsfull. The threatening letters to excite the people to attack Wells and Webfter, though they have not been traced to Bradford, were no doubt a part of the plan, and by their means and the Braddock's field rendezvous, the infatuation was vaftly extended and the number of offences was encreafed, between the meeting at Mingo creek and that at Parkifon's Ferry. Even in Virginia an Excife officer had fled, and a riot was committed at the place of his refidence.

———

CHAP. IX.

AFTER the writs had been ferved on
the diftillers of Fayette county, they held a meeting
to confult what was beft to be done, at which other
difcreet perfons befides the diftillers attended. They
felt exceedingly hurt at being obliged to attend the
Diftrict court in Philadelphia, after competent powers
had been vefted in the ftate courts. Yet although the
news of the riots and their fatal effects reached them ;
and although it was known that parties of armed men
were then affembled, in fome of the neighbouring
counties, in order to intercept the infpector of the revenue and the marfhal; an idea of combining with the
rioters was not even fuggefted at the meeting ; but on
the contrary it was unanimoufly agreed, that in future
the diftillers fhould either abandon their occupation,
or enter their ftills, and that thofe who had been
fummoned fhould immediately evince their fubmiffion,
by entering an appearance to the refpective fuits. In

purfuance of that agreement an exprefs was actually fent
to Philadelphia, council was retained, and inftructions
for legal and confciencious defence were given ; but
it feems that the writs were made returnable at a
time when no court was fitting ; and this error in point
of law was deemed fufficient to vitiate the procefs ;
and to fuperfede the neceflity of entering the appearance of the feveral defendants.   During this meeting at Union town, a letter was received, with the propofition for the meeting of the four Weftern counties by their delegates at Parkifon's Ferry. But fo predo-
minant was the apprehenfion, that fuch an affemblage
would encreafe the degree of inflammation, and extend
the influence to greater numbers, and fo eager was
the hope that the riots might be confined to the place
where they originated, and might fubfide or be quel-
led, without any extraordinary interference, that this
propofition was reluctantly read, and never taken into
confideration. *See Gallatin's fpeech, pages* 9 *and* 10.

In the county of Weftmoreland no writs had been
ferved nor riots committed, confequently they had no
meeting of diftillers nor received any letters ; but on
feeing the appointment of the Parkifon's Ferry meeting
in the gazette, the influential people determined to
pay no attention to it, being apprehenfive that the inflammation might be fpread by it rather than fuppreffed,
and that it might be conftrued as giving countenance to
the riots which led to that appointment. This advertifement made fimilar impreffions on the people of Pittfburgh
alfo at the firft ; but on obferving the rapid progrefs
of the inflammation, and the fucceffion of exceffes
which had been promoted, efpecially the rendezvous

at Braddock's field ; the choofing of difcreet delegates
to attend the Parkifon meeting, appeared to be the only
feafible means of ftemming the current of diforder, until the people, who were fo highly inflamed, would
cool down, and until the cautious and timid would
fhake off the panic, or lay afide that exceffive caution,
by which they were governed, and ftand forward in defence of the laws, and of that liberty, whofe name was
proftituted to blazon the moft tyrannical meafures.

Thefe alarming circumftances made the fame impreffion on all the four counties, without any opportunity of confultation ; confequently the townfhips they
contained were generally reprefented at that meeting ;
but from the fhort time there was to give warning of
this fecond determination, no means could be adopted
to regulate the elections or to imprefs the cautious part
of the citizens with a fenfe of the neceffity of their
attending.   The general ftate of thefe elections cannot be better defcribed than it is done by Mr. Gallatin,
in his fpeech page 13 :

" The meeting was partly a true reprefentation of
the people, but it was partly not fo ; for as there is not
in this ftate any regular townfhip meetings ; a few individuals collected in any one townfhip might appoint
deputies, and the truth is that in almoft every cafe, a
minority of the Inhabitants of the refpective townfhips
did make the appointments, in every townfhip like-
wife where there were any violent characters, fuch
characters would undoubtedly attend the election,
while on the other hand moderate men and friends to
order were cautious either in attending the elections,
or in fuffering themfelves to be elected.

The meeting at Parkison's Ferry was a pretty full though not a true or equal reprefentation. There were upwards of 200 delegates, three of thofe were from Ohio county in Virginia and two from Bedford county in Pennfylvania, befides thofe from the four counties. The place of meeting was unfavourable, being in the neighbourhood in which the refiflance had originated, and within a mile of the dwelling houfe of M' Farlane, who had been killed, and there were probably a greater number of fpectators than of delegates.

The delegates convened on an eminence under the fhade of trees; colonel Cook was appointed chairman, and Albert Gallatin, fecretary. It was foon difcovered that there were a number of inflammatory perfons among the delegates, few of them however had talents. Bradford opened the meeting, with a flatement of the events that had taken place, and concluded with reading the letters that had been taken from the intercepted mail, with fome inflammatory comments on them.

At this time the arrival of Commiffioners from the Prefident, with powers for reftoring order in the Weftern Country, if a correfponding difpofition was met with among the people, was announced to the Meeting. After a fhort paufe colonel Marfhal rofe and expreffed fome fatisfaction at the information of the arrival of Commiffioners; but faid that they fhould not on that account neglect the bufinefs of the meeting, and read fome refolutions that had been agreed on between Bradford and himfelf. The firft refolution, being againft taking the citizens out of the vicinity

O

for trial occasioned no contest ; the second and most
important resolution, runs in the following words :

" Resolved that a standing committee be appointed,
to consist of—members from each county, to be denominated a committee of public safety ; whose duty it shall
be to call forth the resources of the western country,
to repel any hostile attempts that may be made against
the citizens, or the body of the people."

This, compared with the subsequent resolution,
was prefacing the proceedings of the meeting by a direct question, whether the western counties would
raise the standard of rebellion or not. This was certainly a bold attempt to form a combination hostile
to the government both of this state and the United
States. If such a resolution had been offered, before
such a number of persons had become desperate by
being involved in the preceding riots, it would not have
been heard with patience ; but now it required both
great address and fortitude to parry it. Fortunately there
was among the delegates a man well qualified for this
purpose. His fortitude was no doubt the greater, as
he knew he was in no danger at home for what he might
say here. I mean Mr. Gallatin, the secretary. He rose,
and began by criticising on the word hostility ; asked
what it meant, or from whence the hostilities were
to come. He alleged if it was the exertions of government that were designed to be opposed, the term was
improper ; the exertions of government on the citizens
in support of the laws being coercion and not hostility. He encouraged them to expect no other means
of coercion from government but through the judiciary, and after a number of sensible observations moved to

refer the refolution to a felect Committee. But fo great was the prevailing panic, that notwithftanding the number of well-difpofed members that were in the meeting, he was not feconded ; after fome delay, however, Marfhal himfelf offered to withdraw the refolu - tion on condition, that a Committee of fixty fhould be appointed, with power to call a new meeting of the people or their deputies. This was inftantly agreed to, and a new refolution was fludioufly modified, fo as to enfure its adoption, and was agreed to by the meeting. In it a determination was exprefled to fupport the ftate laws, and afford protection to the citizens ; this was an important ftep towards the reftoration of order ; for at that time no man thought himfelf fafe in many places in telling his real fentiments ; Threats were not only circulated in anonymous letters, but were contained in the mottos on liberty poles ; one was erected on the morning of the meeting and within view of it; it was erected under the direction of one of thofe who figned the Braddock's field orders. The motto of it was ; *Liberty and no excife, and no afylum for cowards or traitors.* Every man was efteem- ed a coward or traitor, by thofe diforganizers, who difapproved of their meafures.

Mr. Gallatin had the fortitude to object to the ex- ception againft the excife, originally contained in the refolution for fupport of the municipal laws, and pro- cured it to be ftruck out ; but durft not offer an affir- mative refolution in favour of fubmitting to it. Indeed the doing fo at this time would have been imprudent, nor would fuccefs, in fuch a refolution, have been

of ufe, till fubmiffion to the municipal laws had been
reftored.

In fhort the refolutions, being five in number,
were difcuffed, and referred to a committee confifting
of Bradford, Brackenridge, Gallatin, and Herman
Hufbands of Bedford. who new modelled them before
the next day's meeting, at which they paffed without
much difficulty. The committee of fixty or of one
from each townfhip, was appointed to meet at Redftone old fort, on the 2d of September, and a committee confifting of twelve members, three from each
of the four counties, was appointed to confer with the
commiffioners from the Prefident. Thefe, with one
exception, were well chofen.

The commiffioners came to a houfe near the meeting before it adjourned. This rendered the fituation
of the friends to order more delicate. It was urged
by fome that the meeting fhould not be diffolved till
they would know and decide on the terms propofed by
the commiffioners. With great addrefs, however, they
were prevailed on to adjourn without day. Men of
difcernment knew that nothing would bring the people to a proper fenfe of their duty, without time for reflection, and for the prefent agitated ftate of mind to
fubfide. They knew alfo that if time could be procured to diffeminate knowledge among the people every
thing, that was neceffary, would be gained. Therefore
to reftore quietnefs and gain time was the great object
with Gallatin, and thofe who thought as he did.

Brackenridge probably was actuated by the fame motives as Gallatin ; but fupported the meafures in a different manner. He often kept up the appearances,

and fometimes ufed the boafting language, which were
acceptable to Bradford's party, and oppofed Gallatin.
Yet he always contributed to bring the proceedings to
the fame iffue.

James Edgar, one of the affociate judges of Wafhington county, gave confiderable affiftance in prevailing on this meeting to adopt reafonable preliminary
meafures ; for fuch meafures as would lay a foundation
for the complete reftoratin of order were all that was
expected or aimed at this meeting, and this was obtained. There were ferious objections againft keeping
the people long together, and againft holding the conference with the Commiffioners at this place ; nor was Redftone old fort, appointed for the meeting of the committee of fixty, well chofen, nor were the members, of which
it was to be compofed, well felected. They were chofen out of the Parkifon meeting delegates, by their
colleagues, before they left that place. Thofe who were
moft fit in fome inftances excufed themfelves from
attending, and their places were fupplied by rafh and
inflammatory perfons who were willing to go. To this
circumftance I was attentive at the time, and obferved it with fenfible regret.

On the 20th of Auguft, the conferees waited on the
commiffioners at Pittfburgh, according to a previous
appointment. Thomas M'Kean, Chief Juftice, and
general William Irwin, commiffioners in behalf of the
ftate of Pennfylvania, had alfo arrived at Pittfburgh. All
the conferees, except Bradford, were ferioufly difpofed to fubmit to the laws and the reftoration of order.
It was evident at the Parkifon Ferry meeting, and on
fome other occafions, that Marfhal wifhed only for a

safe opportunity of abandoning the caufe; and this opportunity was now offered. On the firft confultation held
by the conferees, they all, except Bradford, agreed that the
intereft of the country, and their duty as citizens, rendered
fubmiffion neceffary and proper. Some perfons, who
they expected had influence on Bradford, were employed to converfe with him on the fubject, and
againft the next day he feemed perfectly reconciled
to fubmiffion.

The Commiffioners propofed an amnefty for all
offences committed before that date, and certain be-
neficial arrangements, for adjufting delinquencies and
profecutions for penalties now depending, to be made,
and communicated by the officers appointed to carry
the faid acts into execution. Thefe arrangements were
underftood in converfation to apply to all arrears
due for excife, and penalties for not entering their
ftills. The conferees were alfo invited to recommend
fuch officers as they would have confidence in for the
execution of the excife law.

The conditions, on which thefe privileges were
offered, were, that the general committee, to meet
at Redftone old fort, fhould explicitly declare their
determination to fubmit to the laws of the United
States, and that they would not directly nor indirectly
oppofe the execution of the acts for raifing a revenue
on diftilled fpirits or ftills, and that they would explicitly recommend a perfect and entire acquiefcence under the execution of faid acts. That they alfo would
recommend that no violence, injuries or threats, fhould
be offered to the perfons or property of officers, or
complying citizens.

The conferees, for themfelves, promifed an entire aquiefcence, and to recommend the fame to the committee at Redflone; which they agreed to call four days fooner than had been appointed.

The Commiffioners on behalf of the State, propofed an amnefly for all indictable offences againft the laws of the State, on condition of their keeping the peace and complying with the terms propofed by the United States. Thefe Commiffioners, as well as the Commiffioners of the United States, laboured much according to the opportunities afforded them, to bring the people to a proper fenfe of their duty and intereft, and to remove their difficulties, and correct their miftakes.

While the Commiffioners were at Pittfburgh, a very feditious libel was pafted up on the Market-houfe, and afterwards publifhed in the gazette. It was wrote in the form of a dialogue, and infulted the Commiffioners, the militia of the lower counties, and particularly the militia of New-Jerfey, in a very irritating manner, and contained a number of the ftrongeft popular arguments againft the execution of the Excife law, and boafts of the intrepidity of thofe who were oppofed to it. It was wrote in a ftyle and manner well fuited to encourage and embolden the ignorant and obftinate part of the people, which was the clafs that now gave moft trouble. It might well pafs for a production of Tom the Tinker, and indeed it was believed to have flowed from that fource; though on enquiry it turned out to be the production of one who had been always a friend to the Excife and the government, though he had not been active in endeavouring to reftore order; in this refpect he was neutral.

Though the conferees had done every thing in their power to obtain the moft favourable terms, and though the commiffioners of the United States, and of the commonwealth, had granted every thing that was in the power of the federal and ftate executive to grant, with very few exceptions even in the opinion of Bradford himfelf, yet many of thofe who ftood moft in need of the offered amnefty became inflamed againft the conferees, and circulated a report, that they had received bribes; this incredible ftory gained ground particularly among the Germans, who, with a number of the moft ignorant every where, but particularly adjacent to the Monongahela, thought that the conferees fhould have agreed to nothing lefs than an unconditional repeal of the excife law. They did not comprehend the difference between the executive and legiflative authority; nor was there time to inftruct them.

The conferees, knowing the importance of time in the prefent ftate of the country, were importunate with the commiffioners to obtain it, but their own authority being limited to a fhort day, it was not in their power to grant this requeft, which was however of the laft importance in giving effect to all they had granted.

C H A P. X.

ON the 28th of Auguſt, the committeé of ſixty met at Redſtone old fort (Brownſville). While they were collecting, an armed party arrived from the upper parts of Waſhington county, who paraded the ſtreet with a drum beating. This party conſiſted of about ſixty or ſeventy infantry, well armed with rifles, and a few light horſemen mounted in uniform. This, and the reports of extreme inflammation among Tom Tinker's men, together with a letter under that ſignature, which it ſeems the editor of the gazette thought it even now imprudent to refuſe to publiſh; and in which the conferees are charged with being traitors, encouraging Tom's friends to perſevere, and containing ſevere denunciations againſt cowards and traitors; and the ſeditious and inſulting dialogue, which I have before mentioned, coming out about the ſame time, and then ſuppoſed to be from the ſame quarter, and the meeting being in the vicinity of an inflamed neigh-

P

bourhood, I fay all thefe circumftances confpired to intimidate the delegates to a degree inconfiftent with that calmnefs and reflection neceffary for deliberation. This was fo evident that fome of thofe, who had the quieting of the country much at heart, hefitated about the propriety of attempting to fupport the report. Gallatin, however, was difpofed to try it, and others agreed with him in making the attempt.

It foon appeared that the declared object of the armed party was, to chaftife Samuel Jackfon, a wealthy miller in the neighbourhood, for having called the committee *a fcrub Congrefs*. He had ufed this expreffion in jeft at Pittfburgh, in company with the conferees, where it was confidered as inoffenfive; but being carried abroad, and artfully mifreprefented, occafioned the march of the party in arms, who being highly agitated and heated with drink might have given another example of fcandalous outrage, had not the committee interpofed; by its influence a vifit to Jackfon's dwelling by the party, was prevented, and they were prevailed on to accept of an acknowledgement and a treat from him as a complete atonement for his offence. Thus this matter ended, but the party continued at Brownfville till night, and by their prefence and threats overawed the meeting.

When the committee proceeded to bufinefs, Bradford urged to take the vote immediately, expreffing his furprife that any man fhould hefitate or be unprepared to decide; from his manner, it was evident that, notwithftanding his agreement to the terms of fubmiffion at Pittfburgh, and his promifes to the commiffioners and his colleagues, he was now determined on a fummary rejection of the report ; and it was then generally believed that the armed party was brought there for the purpose of supporting him, and averawing the meeting. This indeed was afterwards found to be a miflake, and that this party knew nothing of the meeting at Brownf-ville, until they were far advanced on their way to it ; they lived in a part of the country where little infor-mation circulated, and though they were, perhaps as much inflamed againft the excife law, and the officers as any others, yet they were not engaged in the attack on Nevil's houfe, nor any of the fubfequent riots, but were excited to this undertaking by fome of Jackfon's neighbours, who had a private difference with him. However their prefence and behaviour made the fame impreffion on the committee, as if they had come with the exprefs defign to overaw them, and anfwered the fame purpofe to Bradford.

It required great addrefs in the committee to pro-cure an adjournment of the queftion till the next day. On this occafion James Edgar, in an addrefs containing ironical compliments on Bradford's ftrength of mind, which he probably took to be real, and arguments in favour of time for weak men like himfelf to make up their mind, delivered in a ftyle well adapted to the hearers, and which could not give offence, con-tributed greatly to procure the adjournment.

Means were ufed to prevail on the armed party to retire that night, and the next day the gallery of fpec-tators was much thinned, but reports were circulated that Bradford who lodged on the Wafhington fide of the river that night, had bound himfelf faintly with a number of others to fupport the oppofition by force of arms, until government would be brought to agree un-equivocally to their own terms; it appeared by what followed that the idea of a complete revolution was now taken up by Bradford, and it was certain that several of the most obstinate of those who originated the present violent measures were among the spectators, and perhaps some of them members of the committee; but Marshal and others of the most respectable men among them had totally withdrawn from their interest.

The committee was opened next morning by a long, sensible and eloquent speech by Mr. Gallatin; he alone would venture to open the business in this direct manner. In this speech, no motive to submission was left unexplained, nor any objection left unanswered; he was supported by Mr. Brakenridge, who having no new ground of argument left unexplained, enforced and enlarged on the arguments already offered and ad-dressed their consciences and their fears. His argument was of the more importance that it was decisive; formerly he had temporized in such a manner as to induce the rioters to believe he was a friend to their cause.

But like the spirit which at unlucky occasions actuated the Israelitish king, the frenzy which actuated Bradford during the whole of this period, at this unlucky moment impelled him to rise and address the committee in a most extravagant harangue, in the course of which he urged the propriety of erecting an independent government, and alleged that the Fede-ral government had only tempered with Spain and Britain about the Mississippi and the western posts, and trifled with the Indians. Let us be independent, faid he, and we will accomplifh thefe objects in a few months. For a fource of fupplies he propofed killing the firft army that came againft us, and fupplying ourfelves with arms and ammunition as the French had done. This harangue did not contain fufficient good fenfe to be relifhed, even by many of his admirers, though it excited their inflammation, and ftill more intimidated the Committee, who from the fuppofed combination formed over night were, many of them, afraid that this inflamatory difcourfe was the fignal of actual violence. They were however miftaken. If this was the moft abfurd and inconfiftent exertion Mr. Bradford made, it was his laft in that way. He left the meeting when he faw the vote went againft him, and afterwards figned the terms of fubmiffion, and advifed others to fign them ; but reflecting that it would not cover the offence he had committed at this meeting, he left the country before the army came up.

The arguments were concluded by Mr. Edgar ; fome part of his fpeech ftruck my attention fo much, and I recollect it fo well, that I will trouble the reader with a fhort extract of it.

He ftated, that he had been a member of the convention which ratified the federal conftitution, and had in it objected to the unqualified power of levying excifes, but that they had fubmitted to it, many of them had advocated it in all its parts : Their officers, legiflative, executive and judicial had fworn to fupport it, and they had all voted for members of Congrefs and applied to the government for protection under it, which was a folemn acknowledgement of their allegiance to it, with all the powers with which it was

vefted. That what they might think a premature and
inexpedient exercife of the power of levying excifes,
could never juftify them in renouncing allegiance to
the government, and would equally juftify a refiftance
to every law, becaufe every general law occafioned
complaint from fome on whom it preffed hard.

He gave an affecting defcription of the diftreffing
fituation into which they had inconfiderately brought
themfelves, and ftated the fympathy with which they
had been treated by their friends, who when they had
nothing to fear on their own account had yet put themfelves in fufpicious fituations, and made in fome refpects a common caufe with them, with no other view
than the more effectually to difpofe government to
grant an oblivion for their paft offences, on condition
of their future fubmiffion to the laws, and which could
not be granted on any other condition ; that now that
object being as liberally offered as they had any reafon
to expect, if it was obftinately refufed, they would not
only have themfelves to blame for the hardfhips they
would bring on themfelves, their families and country,
but for ingratitude to their friends, who had laboured
with fo much zeal to extricate them from their difficulties. With fuch expoftulations, and a number of
cogent reafons and advices, he concluded a pretty long
fpeech. The refpectability of his character for true
piety, good morals, and eafy manners, as well as the
good practical fenfe expreffed in his difcourfe in a fimple
and affectionate manner, drew the attention of all def-
criptions of the audience. His gray hairs which gave
him the appearance of being older than he really was
had alfo fome effect.

I had never heard speeches that I more ardently
defired to fee in print than thofe delivered on this occafion. They would not only be valuable on account
of the oratory and information difplayed in all the
three, and efpecially in Gallatin's, who opened the way,
but they would alfo have been the beft hiftory of the
fpirit, and the miftakes, which then actuated men's
minds. But copies of them could not be procured.
They were del'vered without any previous preparation
other than a complete knowledge of the actual ftate of
things, and of human nature when in fimilar circumftances. This knowledge, and the importance of the
occafion on which it was exhibited, produced fuch inge-
nuity of reafoning and energy of expreffion, as never perhaps, had been exhibited by the fame orators before. But
after all that could be done by reafoning. it was a matter
of great difficulty to get a vote taken. When the vote
was taken, the meeting were not unanimous, there
were 34 Yeas and 23 Nays ; fix men it is afferted faid
afterwards that they had given in the Nay ticket inftead
of the Yea, by miftake ; the certainty of this cannot
be known, though if it had not happened they need
not have told it, for no one knew how another voted.
The vote was on the following refolution. *That in
the opinion of this committee, it is the intereft of the
people of this country to accede to the propofals made by
the commffioners of the United States:* The majority
through fear refufed to put the queftion on the laft
propofition, though it was on agreeing to it that the
eventual fuccefs of the meeting depended. Their
fears were certainly greater than their danger, for
though feveral members fpoke decifively in favour of

submiſſion, no inſult was offered to them. Their panic was not only inſpired by the place and circumſtances, but many of them were afraid of miſchief at home. The Tom Tinker's letter recently publiſhed had concluded with ſevere threats, againſt thoſe who would comply. Indeed threats of burning houſes, tarring and feathering &c. were now made by a deſcription of people, whoſe voice is not heard in ſociety in ſettled times. I have ſaid before that ſeveral of the committee-men were not well ſelected, ſome of them I knew to be of the moſt inflammatory characters.

C H A P. XI.

IT was plainly perceived that longer time was neceſſary ; a new committee of 12 conferees was appointed to procure it, if poſſible. The conferees who had been with the commiſſioners before, though they knew that time alone was neceſſary to bring the people to a ſenſe of their intereſt and duty, before the terms were finally ſubmitted to them, believed it could not be obtained, and as there had been imputations againſt them, they declined the appointment, and 12 new conferees were appointed, of whom only 8 waited on the commiſſioners at Pittſburgh, who had it not in their power to grant longer time as their own authority was to expire in a few days.

On the terms propoſed by the commiſſioners not being decided on by the committee of 60, they withdrew them, and ſubſtituted new ones to be ſubſcribed by the people individually in their town meetings, or election diſtricts ; this mode of taking

Q

the fenfe of the people had been recommended by the committee of 60, and fome of the new conferees appointed the method of taking the fenfe of the people in diftricts, and others in townfhips for their refpective counties.

The teft to be fubfcribed was in the following words : " I do folemnly promife henceforth to fubmit to the laws of the United States ; and that I will not directly or indirectly oppofe the execution of the act for raifing a revenue on diftilled fpirits and ftills, and that I will fupport as far as the law requires the civil authority in affording the protection due to all officers and other citizens."

Thefe terms were agreed to on the 2d September, but it was the 4th before they were got printed ready for the conferees to leave Pittfburgh ; confequently there was but fix days to fpread the neceffary information through a country, containing 70,000 inhabitants, (exclufive of the extenfive county of Bedford, for which the teft was alfo intended,) fpread over a territory not much lefs extenfive than the ftate of Connecticut, which fends feven members to Congrefs, and interfperfed with mountains and large bodies of unfeated lands. Four of the conferees not attending left fome large diftricts wholly without the means of information, but though exertions were made to circulate the neceffary information, yet there was no opportunity of impreffing on the cautious citizens, who had from an excefs of prudence declined attending all the former meetings, the neceffity of attending this one, and the people generally had no opportunity of perufing the teft they were required to fubfcribe, until the hour they met on the ground to fign their names ; not then had they had time, or opportunity for deliberately making up their minds.

The word *folemnly* was confidered as an oath, and from henceforth, as an acknowledgement of having offended heretofore, which with much the greater number of the inhabitants in general, and many diftricts with refpect to the whole inhabitants, was not true. The commiffioners indeed agreed that thofe objectionable words fhould be ftricken out, and publifhed it in the gazette ; but the gazette did not, nor could not arrive in moft places till after the day of figning. In fome places However the people fuppreffed thefe words themfelves. The word indirectly was underftood by many as calculated to bind them from even petitioning againft the excife law for the future, and the fhort fpace of an hour or two at a confufed meeting did not afford leifure nor compofure for thofe who were capable, and fo difpofed, to inform and advife the people. It is well known that a legiflative body compofed of the wifeft citizens will not pafs a law for the leaft important purpofe, without various readings on feveral different days ; it could not be expected that an uninformed mafs of people could make up their mind to fubfcribe what amounted to a new teft of allegiance, with fo little time or compofure for deliberation. The difficulty was much encreafed by the number and fmallnefs of the diftricts in which they were covened ; this gave an opportunity, for fuch as feldom attended elections, and whofe voice was never heard on other public occafions, who had not horfes to ride nor cloaths to put on, to attend the meetings, overaw them, and infult the very perfons, by whofe fympathy their families had been preferved from famine. This took place in fome townfhips and fmall diftricts, where no exceffes had formerly been committed. By this def- cription I do not mean to implicate the induftrious poor. There were no people behaved better than moft of thofe. I have obferved ftriking inftances of the virtue and ufefulnefs of this clafs of men ; their advice was often attended to, when men who were on ordinary occafions influential, would not be heard. It is known, that to all new fettlements there is a conftant ingrefs of the moft indolent people, who are not only flothful, but ignorant and obftinate, and who having nothing to lofe and little expectation of bettering their condition by induftry, delight in promoting confufion. This defcription of people was become bold and dan- gerous at this period, and the non-attendance of a great proportion of thofe who having given no offence were determined to *fign* no teft, gave the greater oppor- tunity in fome places for diforderly perfons to domi- neer ; they did fo in fome places to fuch a degree as to prevent in a great meafure the defign of the meeting from being obtained. Though they did not exceed a fourth or a fifth of the number prefent, yet defperation and threats of burning fupplied the place of numbers, and it was not thought prudent on that day to put the law in execution, as the country diftricts did not know the fituation the county towns were in, or whether taking perfons to prifon might not lead to further riots.

In the refult, however, out of above forty different places of meeting for the purpofe of fubfcribing the affurances, at only two of them were the papers torn by

a defperate banditti. One of thefe was at the place
where the people who needed an amnefty were numerous, the other was that in which I refide, where very
few had been guilty of any exceffes. At one place in
Allegany county the figning was prevented by violence
or terror, where it was the intereft of many to have
fubfcribed ; at a few other fuch places, the fubfcribing
was done with difficulty. Neverthelefs thofe who had
been deeply engaged in the exceffes generally figned,
except a few of the moft ignorant and obftinate ; there
were fome indeed who had dared to engage in the greateft outrages, who had not courage to fubfcribe for their
own fafety, left they would be confidered as defert-
ers.

      In fome of the townfhips next to the frontiers, even
the people who attended the meetings abfolutely refufed to fign, becaufe there were none among them who
had given offence, or at any time oppofed the execution
of the excife law.   They took it amifs that they were
called upon ;   and fome diftricts in the upper parts of
Wafhington were not warned. Indeed the people generally, who had been much diftreffed all round the extenfive
frontier, had no hand in originating, or carrying on the
difturbances, nor did they appear at all in it, till they were
folicited to fend delegates to Parkifon's ferry to promote
the reftoration of order, and as far as I could obferve
or be informed, they uniformly contributed to that defirable object in every inftance, till the fubfcribing
was called for, and then they faid, *let them fign in the
places where they are involved.* Some, however, were
perfuaded to do it from policy.   They had not only
behaved well themfelves, but from fome places offered

their fervices, particularly to general Wilkin to quell the infurgents.

The whole county of Fayette acted on the fame principle. They had fubmtted to the authority of the marfhal, and regularly entered for their appearance to the action, and knew that there were few if any criminals among them ; they therefore refufed to fign to the terms of the commiffioners ; but in order to fatisfy government with refpect to their intention, they formed refolutions of their own, and at a meeting of delegates from the feveral townfhips, unanimoufly agreed to fubmit to the laws of the United States and of this ftate, and not to oppofe directly or indirectly the acts for raifing a revenue on diftilled fpirits, ftills, &c. agreeably to the terms propofed by the commiffioners to the committee of fixty. They alfo called on the people to meet in election diftricts, to declare their fubmiffion to the laws. Comparatively few attended, efpecially in the places furthermoft removed from the difturbances, and where leaft heat or agitation had prevailed ; of thofe who did attend, 580 voted for fubmiffion, and 280 againft it. Yet notwithftanding the refufal to fign the terms prefcribed by the whole county of Fayette, and by feveral townfhips in the north of Weftmoreland, there was only one prifoner brought from Fayette, and none from the other, when the judge and the army went into the country ; the perfon brought from Fayette was found to be innocent ; he had been in Kentucky when the riots were committed in the weftern country.

The commiffioners returned to Philadelphia before the day of figning, except Mr. Rofs, who ftayed to receive the lifts of fubfcribers, and to obferve the temper that would be difcovered on that occafion. He alfo was obliged to go to Philadelphia before all the returns were come to hand. The tumults that took place on the day of figning, and the heat and agitation which difcovered itfelf in a few places, particularly among the uninformed part of the Germans, for a few days after it, induced feveral of the judges and other perfons of information to agree in opinion with Mr. Rofs, that it would be neceffary to have an army fent into the country ; but this opinion was alfo made up without time for information, and confequently was foon changed.   It was but a few days, in fome places the very next day, after figning, that many of thofe who had been moft riotous on the day of figning, came, fome of them in tears, begging permiffion to fign ; in fome places their figning was received, with certification, that it would not be admitted as a claim for amnefty, in other places they were refufed the privilege altogether.   When they reflected, they faw that they were deferted by thofe on whom they had depended, and who, perhaps, had advifed them, or by their example encouraged them to mifchief.

From a view of the fubject it is evident, that if but one week had been allowed for the people to deliberate on the affurances they were required to fign, the fubmiffion to the laws would have been complete, at leaft there would have been fo few exceptions, that they would have given no alarm ; there were none within my knowledge but what would have figned in half that time. Signing affociations, binding the citizens to affift one another in fupport of the laws, had been promoted at Pittsburgh by general Wilkin and others, and generally signed ; this example was generally and successfully imitated ; such an association was entered into in the township in which I reside, the third day after the signing, and in many other places equally soon.

The commissioners, however, are not to blame for not giving longer time ; their own powers expired with the time given to the people ; they were nearly expired before it was determined to submit it to the people, in that manner, and it was the influence of terror on the committee of 60 at Brownsville, occasioned by the wickedness of a few, perhaps, of one man, which rendered submitting it to the people necessary. The reasons, that determined the President to limit the authority of the commissioners to so short a period, will be given in their proper place.

Though it may be admitted that there was a latent predisposition to violence among a few individuals, who had been formerly attached to the inspector, and encouraged by him to oppose excise officers, under the state, and though this was known to himself, and he was prepared for defence, yet no such thing was generally known in the country, and its breaking out at the time was owing to accident, and circumstances of a local nature. Inconsiderate and useless resistance by shedding blood too abundantly, which the inspector was the more successful in doing, by being prepared in a manner of which the assailants were not aware, excited a more formidable attack, and drew many into the vortex of riot, who would have been far from engaging in it, if they had had time to deliberate on the consequences. Numbers thus inconfiderately involved in crimes became defperate, and endeavoured by drawing others into the fame fituation to make it a common caufe, and being unfortunately aided in thefe miftaken views by Bradford, Marfhal, and others, who attempted to give a more violent complexion and greater magnitude to the mifchief, by drawing the whole weftern country into a combination againft the excife law, and for this purpofe contriving the rendezvous at Braddock's field, and ufing every means to inflame the minds of the citizens, and to overawe with terror thofe who might oppofe their defigns, and for this purpofe magnifying the numbers at Braddock's field, and advertifing that thoufands had been on their march to join them, from places where there was not a perfon who knew of the rendezvous. I fay, by thefe mad exertions, the infurrection progreffed for a few days like the paroxifm of an inflammatory fever, fpent its force in frequent irregular convulfions, and finally fubfided almoft as fuddenly, and to many as unexpectedly as it commenced; the moft alarming fymptoms were difcovered at Braddock's field, and the laft ftruggle was a feeble attempt to raife a party a few miles fouth of Greenfburgh.

The courts had not been interrupted in their progrefs, on the Monday previous to the day appointed for figning the affurances to government, the court at Greenfburgh was opened by a fenfible fpeech, well adapted to the occafion, by prefident Addifon, and he was not infulted nor the bufinefs of the court interrupted, and he went through the circuit without meeting with any embarraffment.   As the ocean which is agitated for fome time after the ftorm has fpent its force,

R

fo was the agitation that appeared among the people after the day of figning; but they afterwards became calm as formerly, except as to the anxiety that arofe from apprehenfions of what was to follow, and reflections on the paft.

The agitation having fo perfectly fubfided, an advertifement was put in the gazette, calling on the Parkifon's ferry delegates to hold another meeting on the 2d of October. The meeting was advertifed by fome of the fame perfons who had but about a week before given their opinion that an army would be neceffary; but fo fudden and perfect was the prefent calm, that they were convinced that fuch affurances of fubmiffion could now be procured, as would render the march of the army totally unneceffary.

The delegates met, and agreed to the following refolutions: "Refolved unanimoufly that it is the opinion of this meeting that if the fignature of the fubmiffion be not univerfal it is not fo much owing to any exifting difpofition to oppofe the laws, as to a want of time and information to operate a correfpondent fentiment; and with refpect to the greateft number, a prevailing confcioufnefs of their having had no concern in any outrage, and an idea that their fignature would imply a fenfe of guilt."

By another refolve they gave affurances of fubmiffion in the very words prefcribed by the commiffieners; and by a third they refolved to fend David Redick and myfelf, with thefe affurances, to the Prefident of the United States, with authority in behalf of the meeting, to explain to him the more circumftantially the ftate of the country, in order to enable him to judge whether an armed force would now be neceffary to fupport the civil authority in thofe counties.

I had not attended this meeting, but the refolves were tranfmitted to me, and a letter from prefident Addifon, affuring me that he had converfed with diftillers and others, refiding in the parts of the county where the oppofition originated, and that they had given the ftrongeft affurances of their fubmiffion. I had otherwife fufficient proofs that the laws could be fupported in every other part of the weftern counties.

———

C H A P. XII.

ON the road to Carlifle we heard alarming
accounts of the army, rendezvoused at that place, being very ungovernable and exceedingly inflamed againft
the people of the weftern country indifcriminately.
We ftill flattered ourfelves that thefe reports were not
well founded, till we met with fome officers of the
weftern army on their way to Pittfburgh with recruits,
who confirmed the reports we had heard from others.
We lodged at a tavern three miles from Carlifle, and
pufted for travellers going to Philadelphia, which we intended doing if we fhould not meet the Prefident at Carlifle; but when the people of the houfe difcovered that we
were from the weftern counties, they were much alarmed, and preffed us exceedingly to abandon the thought
of going through Carlifle, offering at the fame time
to conduct us by another rout. They defcribed the
rage of the army againft all the people from the weftern counties, in terms which they thought fufficient to

deter us from approaching it ; and in giving a relation of the licentioufnefs and ferocity of the troops, told us of their having already killed two men in cold blood.

We had no fooner difmounted at the tavern in Carlifle, than I was afked to walk afide by a gentleman who was waiting to fee me. The Carlifle paper had mentioned our coming ; confequently we were expected. He informed me of the inflammation prevailing in the army being apparently too ftrong to be reftrained, and of their threats againft us, and advifed that we fhould be cautious how we expofed ourfelves ; that the refentment againft us was particularly exafperated from an apprehenfion that it was our errand, to give fuch affurances to the Prefident, as were intended to prevent their march to the Monongahela. He affured me that his object was purely to prevent injury to us, and difhonour to the army. and requefted me to pay attention to his advice. He had been a refpectable officer during the late war, but not attached to the prefent army, nor a dweller in or near that place. I have not had an opportunity fince that time of acknowledging his well timed and humane caution. Though I did not credit the extent of his impreffions at the time, I was foon convinced they were not exaggerated. We obferved the proofs of it in the behaviour of feveral individuals, and were confirmed by the information of others, in and out of the army.

Having early in the morning waited on the Prefident to deliver the papers, and obtained on appointment for an interview, we withdrew in a fhort time. This was to have been expected ; it was about feven o'clock ; but before ten the report was current through both the town and the army, that the Prefident had dri-

ven us out in fix minutes, and was not to fee us again ;
and notwithftanding the Prefident's eftablifhed character for difcretion and politenefs, and the frequent interviews to which we were admitted, this ridiculous
ftory was believed by many in the army during the
whole expedition, and has been reported fince, through
diftant parts of the United States. Long after the
return of the army, I was told it by one of the geneials
who commanded in the expedition, and who was furprifed to hear that it was not true.

Though we were cautious of mixing with the
army at large, we took every opportunity of converfing
with the officers from different places, in order to have
an opportunity of removing the miftaken impreffions,
and correcting the falfe information, they had received,
and to know more perfectly the general character
of the army.   In one inftance obferving a regiment
newly arrived from Philadelphia ; as foon as the men
were difmiffed from parade, we mixed with fuch
of the officers as we were acquainted with, and dined
in company with the Colonel.

When we informed him of the fuccefsful exertions
that had been made to reftore fubmiffion to the laws ;
and mentioned one individual, who had diftinguifhed
himfelf with induftry and addrefs, he anfwered us that
that very man, if he was met with, would be fkewered, fhot,
or hanged on the firft tree.   I had before been informed of two lifts put into the hands of fome in the army, containing the names of certain perfons, who were
to be fo treated when met with, and that the very perfon alluded to by the Colonel was in both of them.
I underftood I had the honour to fill a place in one
myfelf.   The colonel treated us decently, but his ex-

preffions confirmed my belief of a fact, the truth of which I had till now willingly doubted.

But the defigns of affaffination were not againft us exclufively. Thofe among themfelves who had reafoned in favour of the fubjection of the military to the civil law, or fuggefted that thofe who killed a citizen in cool blood fhould anfwer to the proper courts, and that the army were only employed to aid the Judiciary in the exercife of its proper functions, and not to ufurp or exercife thofe functions themfelves, were in as much danger, and equally the objects of threats, as the whifky men, and in fact were called fo.

Two men had been killed, one on the great road near Lebanon, and the other at a houfe in the neighbourhood of Carlifle. The one on the road was killed by the Jerfey troops. He provoked an officer by foolifh and infulting language, and on laying hold on one of the bayonets of the guard, who were ordered to arreft him, he was run through the body. He was evidently drunk or deranged. Surely fo many men in arms could eafily have fecured one unarmed fool, without killing him. The other was killed by a light horfeman from Philadelphia, who went into the country to feize fome perfons who had afifted at erecting liberty poles in Carlifle. The young man, who was killed, was not only innocent, but very unwell. The party left him under guard of one of their number, until they would fearch the barn for others. The fick boy declaring his innocence, and that he was not able to ftand, attempted to go into the houfe without leave ; the light horfeman ordered him to ftop, on the peril of being fhot, and if he could not ftand to fit or lay down, and in the mean time cocked his pistol. When the boy was in the posture of laying himself down, and the light horseman about to uncock his pistol, it went off and shot the boy mortally. I state this case, as I had it from the best authority, and as taken from an examination of the light horseman.

But admitting, as I believe we ought, that those acts of man-killing were not murder, yet they ought not to have been done, because they might easily have been prevented ; after the President had commenced the army, by his discourses, of the propriety, and enforced by his authority the necessity of the subordination of the military to the civil power, and after he had given an unequivocal testimony of his sincerity by obliging those who killed the two men, to enter recognizance with bail, for standing their trial at court, no more accidents of the kind happened.

The authority and influence of the President had lowered the tone, though not changed the temper of the outrageous part of the army, while we were at Carlisle. The proper attention he paid to us, on account of the errand we came on, and the restraint his orders imposed on their designs, gave great mortification to that part of them that continued longest in Carlisle ; the last interview to which we were admitted was on the evening previous to the President's fitting out for Patowmack. While the conversation continued, a general officer, with others, walked before the window, and railed against the President for conversing with us ; saying, that he never would recover the popularity that he lost by countenancing insurgents. Owing however to that salutary restraint, thus imposed on them

by the Prefident, all the fire was fpent in threatening
what they would do ; laying their hands on their
fwords, which many of them had not been accuftomed
to wear, they would fwear there was no need of judges
and juries, let them only fee the men and they would
fkewer them.

I was the lefs furprifed at this difplay of the
inflammatory agitation of the human mind, that I
had fo recently been acquainted with its ebullitions,
in a variety of efforts in the courfe of its fermentation
and fettling on its lees in the weftern country. I had
heard the word of terror pronounced in fuch loud accents, as that like a magic fpell it chilled the blood and
petrified the fpirits, almoft as far as the report of it vibrated with the air that wafted the alarming found. I had obferved in the rapid reign of indifcretion, plans executed
almoft as foon as an infatuated imagination conceived
them and fome thoufands of thoughtlefs, of outrageous,
and of well difpofed citizens rendezvoufed together in one
hetrogeneous mafs, and tens of thoufands put on paper as on their way to rendezvous, (who by the by had
not heard of the plan) and all for no vifible object,
nor to anfwer any purpofe, but expofe the madnefs of
thofe who conducted the career of folly. I had feen
the effervefcence in human fociety operate fo powerfully as to throw the fcum to the furface, and caufe the
purer parts to fuccumb for a moment, fo far as to fix
a general character of impurity. While things were
in this flate, I have heard men talk as if they were all
Samfons, who each could kill his thoufands with the
jaw bone of an afs. I had known myfelf and many
others threatened with having our property burned,
ourfelves tarred, feathered, &c. but faw none of thefe

S

dreadful threats executed. After the poor excisemen were overset, there was no person otherwise hurt, than by the effects of temporary terror on the mind. I knew of a black lift too, containing a certain number of the beft citizens to be hanged or fhot, who are all yet living. I clearly faw that the very fame fpirit was operating in the army, that had thus convulfed the weftern country, and hoped that it would alfo evaporate in air, efpecially as it would be held under reftraint by the authority and influence of difcreet and experienced officers. I had no doubt but that there was a majority of well difpofed people in the army, who wifhed to fupport the laws, as well as there had been in the weftern country, though by the bluftering noife and high handed meafures of the rioters, people at a diftance were induced to believe that all the inhabitants were infurgents. By mixing with the people myfelf, I found this was not the cafe, even where the outrages originated. In like manner, by taking every prudent opportunity of mixing with the army, I was convinced that many were difpofed to fubmit to difcipline and fupport the laws; but thefe were not the men who made the noife. The caufe however was very different; the caufe of the army was laudable, and their turning out meritorious; the caufe of the infurgents on the other hand was criminal. However when I reflected on the vaft mafs of undifciplined men, who were collected and fo well equipped, affuming the height of military airs, without the habits of military difcipline, having no apprehenfions of danger to prefs them together, no enemy to encounter, nor in fact any object to afford them an opportunity of difplaying

their prowefs; I fay, when I reflected on thefe circumftances, together with the inflammatory fymptoms which
were fo prevalent, and might foon pervade the whole
mafs ; it gave me unpleafant fenfations. I was not
without apprehenfions that fuch convulfions might
be the refult, as would not only be ruinous to the weftern counties, but proftrate the very government and
laws, which they were called forth to fupport. I knew
they had fhed blood, in a manner that difcovered that
they were not very folicitous to avoid it. I knew
that fome of no mean rank were mortified that thofe who
had fhed blood were obliged to enter recognifance, and
give bail. It is well known that at Carlifle the army was
once in that fituation, that one part of it was ordered to
charge the others, and if a difcretion, which by ftrict
rules might have been efteemed criminal, had not
been exercifed by the fficer who was ordered to make
the charge, brothers blood might have been fhed in
abundance. It is well remembered that the ftreets
and avenues of Califle were occupied by the army,
during the night, and that an apprehenfion of the town
being burnt excited a general panic. To what height
thefe alarming heats might have gone. if the Prefident
had not arrived fo feafonably, it is impoffible to tell.
Though there were officers poffeffed of virtue and experience there before he arrived, yet their authority
was not fufficient to preferve order. Indeed while the
army continued at Carlifle, drinking was carried to greater excefs, than I had heard of it being done among the
infurgents, and wine will inflame the paffions as much
or more than even whifky.

However it is a queſtion that never will be decided, whether the authority and influence of a Preſident would have been effectual if that Preſident had not been general Waſhington. The man, that had commanded our armies ſucceſsfully through the late war, and whoſe military character was ſo reſpectable, had an influence over military men, that few others could expect to poſſeſs.

There was not ſo much of the inflammatory ſpirit obſervable in the left wing of the army as in the center, nor was there any perſons killed by them, by accident or otherwiſe. In one or two inſtances, where there was danger of ſome fooliſh men who mixed with that wing being ſkewered, general Morgan, by pretending to reſerve them for ignominious puniſhment, ſaved them, till they could be ſafely difmiſſed, or kept his men from killing them by threatening to kill them himſelf. He kept his diviſion on the parade while on their march, until he called on the people reſiding near the encampment, and paid them immediately a reaſonable price for what the army had taken or deſtroyed ; conſequently there were few complaints made by the citizens of marauding or deſtruction committed by that wing. General Smith, who commanded the Maryland brigade, complied ſtrictly with the Preſident's orders in diſcharging ſuch of the men as were diſorderly. At fort Cumberland he called on the Captains to make report of characters of that deſcription, of which he diſcharged about 50 in one day ; this not only purged the army, but was a caution to thoſe that remained ; the conſequence was that the route on which he marched cannot be traced by the ſufferings and complaints of the citizens; nor was there fo high a degree of inflammation among the Maryland troops as appeared in the reft of the army; even among the troops from Virginia the tone was not fo high, nor the fpirit fo ungovernable, as in the right wing; however, more frequent examples of punifhment were made among them.

Notwithftanding the inflammatory and ungovernable fpirit that prevailed in the army, it was reftrained from actual outrage; but doing this required great addrefs. If a fevere example had not been made of two men in the camp at Carnaghan's in Weftmoreland, for difobedience and mutiny, it is the opinion of the moft experienced officers who were there, that the country would have been ruined; and there were fuch ferious apprehenfions of their punifhment occafioning a general mutiny, that it was a matter of great hefitation with the commander in chief of that wing, and other officers, whether the fentence could be executed without a general mutiny. Through the decifion, however, of general Irwin, to whofe perfonal intrepidity it was owing that the culprits were brought to trial, and through the confidence that was entertained in general Chambers's brigade, the fentence was executed without difturbance. By way of precaution, general Chambers had his brigade paraded in fuch a manner as to be ready to charge the regiment to whom the culprits belonged, and in front of which the fentence was executed, if a mutiny had been attempted. This inftance of difcipline is believed to have had an excellent effect in preventing a total fubverfion of difcipline, and reftraining the difpofition of marauding, which at that time threatened to involve the country in great diftrefs. It

will appear hereafter that an apprehenſion of a mutin-
ous diſpoſition prevailing in the army, had a diſagreeable effect on the proceedings of the judiciary.

General Chambers had made ſome examples of diſcipline, before his brigade left the ſettlements, where it
was raiſed. This was no doubt one reaſon why it ſet
ſuch an example of good behaviour and ſuſtained the
character of being the moſt orderly brigade in the right
wing of the army. To this I heard the commander in
chief of that wing, ſecretary Hamilton, and many other
officers bear ample teſtimony; but there was another
reaſon of greater weight, which influenced that character.

The ſeſſion of aſſembly, which was convened during
the inſurrection, obſerving a reluctance in the militia to
turn out in their claſſes, and conſidering that there was a
great number of citizens in the lower counties who had
religious ſcruples againſt bearing arms, gave a bounty
to encourage the enliſtment of volunteers, and many
of the citizens whoſe duty it was to go procured ſub-
ſtitutes. The militia corps from Philadelphia, and the
counties near it, were chiefly compoſed of ſuch of this
deſcription; there was a ſmaller proportion in general
Chambers's brigade than in the others, and of conſequence a greater proportion of ſuch citizens as turned
out in their proper claſſes; and it is among thoſe that
we may always expect to find the greateſt reſpect paid
to the laws. With orderly citizens, moral principles
and a ſenſe of honour will go far in ſupplying the want
of diſcipline.

There was another deſcription of volunteers, both
from New-Jerſey and Pennſylvania, who neither came

from the inducement of a bounty nor the expectation of plunder, but purely with a view to support the government and law. Many of these were men of large property, and extensively engaged in business. They came at much expence and made great sacrifices, many of them being unused to personal hardships stood the unavoidable fatigue of such a journey beyond expectation and without murmuring. Indeed I was agreeably surprised to see them arrive at Bonnet's camp in such good health and spirits, after so much fatigue. It had rained on them almost every day, from the time they left Bedford till they arrived at that place, and though they were every way the best equipped and supplied of any troops that ever had marched in the service of the United States, yet the excessive rains and exceeding badness of the roads rendered the march very fatiguing and uncomfortable, especially as a proportion of the road was on mountains naturally swampy. I do not say that none of them murmured, for some of them filled the news-papers with complaints and sarcasms on the whisky-men. By reading some of those letters, that were published, it would have been thought the county of Bedford was full of the most daring criminals, and the army harassed to death, pursuing them over roads, that endangered the life of man to pass, &c. whereas there were only four prisoners taken or sought after in that county, two of whom resided within a few miles of Bedford town, the other two were from the Glades, 30 miles distant from Bedford, and no resistance was attempted by them. In some of these letters, the difficulties they encountered are magnified to a very high degree. " In short no expedition during the last

war, nor even that of Hannibal over the Alps, could
equal the infuperable hardfhips which we fuffered,'
is the language of one of them.   But thefe foolifh ex-
aggerations ought no more to fix the character of thefe
corps, than the conduct of a few defperate infurgents
ought to fix the character of all the inhabitants of the
four weftern counties.

It muft be expected, that a proportion of thofe who
went out as volunteers, in what were called the gentleman corps, were men of the moft ardent fpirits, who
perhaps miftook the warmth of their paffions for patriotifm ; for, it is not uncommon in either religion or po-
litics to find mankind miftake the agitation and biafs
of their own paffions for zeal or patriotifm, and in the
cafe before us there might have been incidental prejudices arifing from other caufes ; but notwithflanding
the inflammatory materials of which thefe corps were
in part compofed, I have authority for faying, that
they not only fubmitted to fatigue with the perfeverance of veterans, but moft of them acted with a becoming fubordination to orders ; among thefe, however,
more than any other corps, did the bluftering threats
prevail, which fpread fuch a general alarm.

C H A P. XIII.

ONE evil of a peculiar nature arofe from this ftate of things. The militia corps being in fo great a proportion compofed of fubftitutes, or perfons induced to enlift by bounty, &c. and the militia generally not being dreffed in uniform, they were defpifed by thofe who compofed the gentleman corps, who always fpoke of them in the language of contempt, and to this day, in relating the incidents of the campaign, every thing bad or mean, that was done, they fay was done by the militia. Perhaps this had too much foundation in truth, owing to the materials of which the militia was in part compofed; but it is exceedingly impolitic to render the militia contemptible. The character of the militia ought to be had in the higheft honour, and the laws fhould be fo calculated as to render them the moft refpectable. They are as much the reprefentatives of the citizens, when they are called to fupport the laws of their country, as th

T

members of Congrefs are their Reprefentatives to make thofe laws.

To render the militia refpectable, no fubftitute fhould be admitted, unlefs in extreme cafes, and even in thofe cafes the perfon admitted fhould be of equal character, and have as much at ftake in the refult, as the citizen whofe place he fupplies. In fhort he ought to have an equal ftake, at rifk, in the common-wealth, and no exoneration fhould be admitted on account of religious fcruples. Thofe citizens, who have no fcruples againft being legiflators, magiftrates, or jurors, ought not be admitted to benefit by fuch fcru-ples, when they are neceffarily called on, to fupport the laws of their country, which are the common inheritance of all the citizens. The man, who enjoys affluence or the honour of holding public offices, ought not on that account to be exempted from the rifk and fatigue of militia fervice, in fupport of the govern-ment, in which he has more at ftake than his lefs for-tunate neighbours. In the diftribution of natural evils, the abodes of honour and affluence are not more free from difeafes and pains, than the abodes of thofe, who enjoy a more fcanty portion, neither ought they to be more indulged when political difeafes fhake the commonwealth. In fuch cafes they ought to fubmit to common rifk with thofe, whofe lot it is to be in equal ftations in the fervice in which they are employed. To have the militia diftinguifhed into gentlemen privates, and plebean privates, is wholly anti-republican. A ftanding army is preferable to a militia thus diftinguifh-ed. In the late expedition, the name *militia* was under-ftood to have the fame idea affixed to it, as *plebean* or *lower order of citizens.* An army, arranged in this manner, never can have confidence within itself, nor embrace the confidence of their fellow citizens.

When it becomes absolutely necessary to call out the militia to suppress insurrections, or to aid the civil magistrate against combinations too powerful for the ordinary administration of the laws ; if the militia were composed of the citizens drawn in their proper classes, no one corps could be held in contempt by the other, and every corps would have within itself a sufficient number of orderly citizens, whose respect to their own character and to the laws would be sufficient security against marauding and other outrages. A militia, called out on these principles, in this country where the principles of government are so generally understood, and where mildness of temper is a leading feature in our character, would certainly be the least dangerous, and also the most successful ; for the insurgents in this case would be less desperate, as they would have less to dread. They would consider the army, as their fellow citizens, discharging their duty in obedience to the laws, on the same principles with a court, jury or sheriff, and not as officious knight-errants, who were stimulated, perhaps, by the resentments of political party spirit, or the antipathies sometimes arising from local situation. Nor would they view them as an undisciplined band of substitutes, induced to undertake the service by the receipt of bounty and the expectation of plunder, without any regard to the love of the government or the detestation of crimes. This description of men are just so much worse than a standing ar-

my, as they are lefs in the habits of military fubordination.

Being informed from the beft authority at Carlifle, that in the city of Philade'phia, every perfon, except the volunteers, whofe duty it was to go on the weftern expedition, and who had the means of doing it, procured fubftitutes, it is equally certain that this was alfo
the cafe in thofe counties, where people entertained religious fcruples, and to a certain degree through all the
ftates, on which the requifitions were made. From thefe
circumftances, and finding that the word militia was a
term of reproach attached to the clafs regiments by the
volunteer corps, I was the lefs furprized at the licentious and inflammatory fpirit, which at that period formed to confp'cuous a trait in the character of the army,
and which it coft the Prefident fo much labour and
attention to fubdue. Indeed it gave me very fenfible
pleafure to difcover fuch corps, as contained a confiderable proportion of citizens who turned out in obedience to the laws, and not from any finifter inducement;
as thefe were the men who had the greateft common
intereft in fupporting the government, and reftoring
obedience to the laws, where their authority had been
infringed. I had confequently the moft confident
expectations, that in their own conduct they would give
a falutary example of obedience to that authority they
were employed to fupport, and fhew a refpect to that
order, which it was the object of the expedition to reftore. And I felicitate myfelf and my country, that I
was not difappointed in my expectation. The people
of the weftern country generally had the fame impreffions; for I have been well informed that they difcover-

ed much greater confidence in thofe citizens, who turned out in their claffes, in obedience to the laws, and treated them with more refpect, where they could diftinguifh them, than they did others.

The volunteer corps were more generally men of liberal education, and therefore as gentlemen had a fenfe of honour, and would not floop to the bafenefs of plundering or committing wanton deftruction, and the moft refpectable among them were fenfible of the importance of fetting an example of obedience to the laws in their own conduct; and even fuch of them as had but little refpect to the laws, or who thought they were not obligatory on them in dealing with thofe, whofe difobedience they were called to fupprefs, (and fome of them confidered every man who drank whifkey to be of that defcription) yet paid a reluctant refpect to the exprefs orders of the Prefident; I fay reluctant, for they murmured at them, and with difficulty fubmitted.

The oftentatious vaunts, and ferocious threats, loudly exprefled by the bluftering blades in thefe corps, which were perhaps exaggerated by fame, and the peculiar circumftance of their being compofed in part of fuch characters, as never were feen in arms in the defence of their country, when the fuccefs and barbarity of a powerful invading enemy required the utmoft exertions of all the virtue and energy the country could afford for its defence, at a time when the citizens of the moft remote frontier fettlements marched in the moft inclement feafons to the diftant fhores in fupport of the then vibrating caufe of virtue and mankind; I fay, thefe circumftances made an impreflion unfavourable to the character of thefe corps in the minds of the faber citizens generally through the state, but especially those in the western counties, who were the objects of their threats, without respect to innocence or guilt. These circumstances gave an apprehension that hatred to the western people generally, rather than patriotism, was the motive of their being volunteers in the cause ; and as hatred always begets hatred and distrust, so it happened in this case, at least so far as to mar that confidence which well disposed people would otherwise have entertained; however, the discreet and humane behaviour, which some of these corps discovered on some trying occasions, went far to remove this prejudice; and it is certain that the licentiousness of a few contributed more than any other cause to fix these unfavourable impressions ; but even that circumstance arose naturally out of the principles of their selections.

As that extreme degree of inflammation which discovered itself in the army, has been the occasion of serious reflection, and given ground to doubt, whether a militia army is the best calculated for the internal support of government, and their suitableness for that purpose is supposed to be rendered the more questionable by having recourse to historical facts, which relate to a war of brothers, from that of the ten tribes of Israel against Benjamin at Gibeah, down to modern times ; it is proper therefore to examine further into the incidental, or extraneous causes of the inflammatory spirit in the army, besides what arose from its structure, and the other circumstances I have related ; for if in the result of the enquiry, it should be decided against a militia, it will afford a strong, if not a conclusive, argument in favour of standing armies in time of peace, and if

this is once admitted, eftablifhing an hereditary monar-
chy becomes abfolutely neceffary, as a thing of courfe,
or at leaft, an ariftocracy as firmly eftablifhed, as that
of Venice, with all its multifarious perplexity of checks
and tyrannical guards, calculated for the eternal exclu-
fion of equal liberty. But this mortifying refult ought
not to be admitted, without the ftricteft fcrutiny and the
fulleft conviction.

That the citizens would have been confiderably in-
cenfed at being called out from their farms and their
merchandize, to go fuch a diftance to fupport the execution of the laws, even though they themfelves difapproved of the law that was oppofed, would not have
been furprifing. But if there had been no extraneous
excitements, fympathy would have been mingled with
their refentments, and their object would have been to
reclaim rather than kill, and to reconcile rather than
infult. They would have been careful to diftinguifh
the innocent from the guilty, and the ignorant and
miftaken from the intentionally wicked, and have paid
a facred refpect to the authority of the laws in their
own deportment, while they were contributing to bring
their fellow citizens to punifhment for their difobedience. 1 fpeak of the temper difcovered at Carlifle,
rather than their after conduct ; in the refult, however,
it will appear, that that temper was not quite extinguifhed. Among the extraneous excitements may be reck-
oned the great pains that had been taken to fet the conduct of the weftern country people indifcriminately in
the moft obnoxious point of view ; even thofe, who had
exerted themfelves with the greateft induftry, were
characterifed as the chief promoters of the infur-

rection, and the outrages were greatly aggravated both with respect to their object and extent. Indeed the leading rioters themselves contributed to this last circumstance; they exceedingly magnified their own numbers, boasted of their prowess, and by blustering threats intimidated those who were opposed to them, and produced a scene of temporizing, for a time, in some places, which was well calculated to deceive the people in the eastern country; but it was at no time true that judges, magistrates, clergy, members of Congress and Assembly, were opposed to the execution of the law, nor that any of them even temporised, except in particular situations, and for a short time. These slanders were the reports of excisemen, and spies, and were not well founded.

The evident reluctance of the militia to turn out rendered it necessary to address them with recruiting orations, calculated to rouse their passions. For this purpose, trifling incidents were magnified into crimes, and the most orderly citizens were characterized as offenders. Indeed many were induced to expect, that the whole country would be given up to military execution and plunder.

When the commissioners were in Greensburgh on their return to Philadelphia, a few drunken worthless persons, one of whom had a complaint against a servant belonging to the chief-justice, came in the night to the tavern, where the commissioners lodged, and demanded entrance; but on being refused admittance, and threatened by the landlord to be fired on if they persisted, they retired for some time, but returning again they made another attempt, and threw some stones at the house, with which they broke one pane of glass in a window

in the fecond ftory. General Irwin upon this, putting
his head out of the window, threatened to fhoot
fome of them if they did not difperfe; they immediately fled, and did not return again. The difturbance was not fo great as even to awaken fuch of the
commiffioners as were afleep, but from what they
were heard to fay, there is no doubt but they defigned to ufe the commiffioners ill. They threatened to
give the commiffioners a hafty paffage to Philadelphia,
but they were few in number and of the meaneft of the
rabble; there was nothing ferious to be apprehended
from the attack. They have fince been punifhed feverely by the ftate courts, and if the governor has not
remitted their fine, are yet in prifon, for none of them
had wherewith to pay it. This outrage was of fo little
importance that the commiffioners did not even give
it a place in the catalogue of riots contained in the
report which they made to the Prefident, as proofs that
order was not fufficiently reftored when they left the
country. Yet this attempt, triffing and unimportant as it
was, was in the recruiting harangues and popular orations,
magnified to an alarming atrocity, and the whole country charged with being worfe than favages, they having
maltreated ambaffadors of peace. I have myfelf feen
members of the legiflature mobbed and dragged out
of their lodgings in the open day. I have feen the
legiflature itfelf kept in durefs by a mob, obliged to
do the moft important bufinefs, for which they were
not competent at the time. My own lodging and
that of other members of the legiflature have been attacked and a whole window broke in the dead of the
night. I have known the houfes of judges of the fupreme court, and other refpectable citizens, mobbed in

U

the fame manner, and all this was done even in the city of Philadelphia, and by citizens, feveral of whom occupy high official ftations and eat the bread of the government at this day, and though thofe combinations were too ftrong for the ordinary power of the civil magiftrate at the time, yet no extraordinary methods were taken to fupprefs them. The temporary inflammation was fuffered to fubfide, and the whole city was never charged with being guilty of it. No refpectable citizen was engaged in breaking the pane of glafs at Greenfburgh, yet this circumftance, blazoned as it was, had an amazing effect in exciting the militia to turn out, and to inflame them againft the whole people of the weftern counties. In going to war with favages, we often hear advocates for extending mercy to them, but the people of the weftern country were, by thofe who then gave the tone to public opinion, confidered as wild beafts only fit for extermination, and to fkewer the Whifky-men, not to reclaim them, or to aid the judicary, was the declared object both in New-Jerfey and Pennfylvania. I have the charity to believe, however, becaufe I wifh to believe it, that in moments of cool reflection many of them recollected that numbers of thofe very men whom they exterminated in imagination, croffed the mountains in the depths of the winter fnows, and traverfed the frozen roads of the lower country, when their path might have been traced by their blood, to fave the city of Philadelphia from the Britifh, and to protect their brethren at the moft diftant fhores of New Jerfey.

One regiment of troops, for three years, and another of militia, marched from Weftmoreland in the winter of 1776, when our caufe was at the lowest ebb. The exertions and fervice of this regular regiment was perhaps equal to that of any other on the then eſtabliſhment, and the militia diſtinguiſhed themfelves in a ſkirmiſh with the Britiſh near Woodbridge, as well as in the difcharge of other dangerous and fatiguing fervices.

The publication I have already mentioned, publiſhed by one who was a friend of government, and who wrote in the character and manner of an infurgent, on purpoſe to excite the militia in New-Jerfey and the lower counties of Pennſylvania, had an incredible effect in exciting and inflaming the citizens of that ſtate and others ; particularly the following words contained in it: " Brothers, yqu muſt not think to frighten us with fine arranged lifts of infantry, cavalry and artillery, compoſed of your water-melon armies taken from the Jerfey ſhores ; they would cut a much better figure in warring with the crabs and oyſters about the capes of Delaware. It is a common thing for Indians to fight your beſt armies at the proportion of one to five ; therefore we would not hefitate a moment to attack this army at the rate of one to ten &c." This, together with the ridicuie contained in it againſt the commiſſioners, paſted up on the market houfe, and publiſhed in the gazette, at the very crifis when the neceſſity of arming the citizens depended on the decifions of the moment, connected with a mifreprefentation of the infult offered to the commiſſioners of peace at Greenſburgh, excited indignation and rage in almoſt every breaſt. This dialogue, having been afcribed to Brackenridge, on account of a faint imitation of his ſtile, which the author attempted, together with a letter from him to Mr. Tench Coxe of Philadelphia, wrote at a time when there was danger of letters being intercepted, and which it feems was mifunderflood, occafioned a very high degree of refentment againft him, and the whole weftern country.

A report made by the fecretary of the treafury to the Prefident, containing a narrative of the inflances of the oppofition made to the execution of the excife law in the weftern counties, was alfo calculated to inflame the army in a high degree.

The object of this report, however, was not folely to influence and inflame the militia againft the weftern country, but perhaps to convince the affociate judge of the propriety of giving the important certificate, neceffary to enable the Prefident to call forth the militia, and the Prefident of the propriety of exercifing that power.

The narrative begins with denouncing thofe people for holding and circulating opinions, which if they were criminal, had been entertained and circulated by the moft refpectable authority in the United States long before, and it goes on to enumerate the acts of oppofition with the higheft colouring they would poffibly bear, and intermixes real facts with mifreprefentations, or even worfe, and concludes in fuch a manner as to leave an impreffion that there was not a good citizen in that country but the excife officers. This coming from fo refpectable a quarter, not only made a deep impreffion on the militia, but excited thofe who were the fecretary's admirers to a high degree of inflammation ; and to make the greateft exertions to inflame others

againſt thoſe who were citizens of the weſtern country ;
by theſe no difference was made, between thoſe who
were guilty of breaking, and thoſe who were active in
ſupporting, the laws, nor between thoſe who reſided
near where the riots prevailed, and thoſe who lived a
day's journey diſtant. Further obſervations will be
made on this report in another place.

 "I have already mentioned that the inſpector and
Marſhal left Pittſburgh in a canoe, and going down the
Ohio till they were paſt the Pennſylvania line, came
through Virginia till they got over the mountains. I
have alſo mentioned that three or four others were very
tyrannically and fooliſhly expelled from Pittſburgh,
during the aſcendant of Bradford, when his terror
gave efficacy to his demands, when the citizens of
Pittſburgh were under apprehenſions that that place
was doomed to deſtruction, and when many others
would have wiſhed themſelves and their property well
away from it. Pittſburgh is ſituated on the verge of
the ſettled part of the country, and when the rendezvous was at Braddock's field, the communication between it and the country was in a great meaſure cut
off.

 Several of thoſe who were thus expelled felt themſelves exceedingly hurt, and expoſed the character of
the people indiſcriminately, in a manner, that while it
procured ſympathy to themſelves, at the ſame time
excited indignation againſt the citizens of the weſtern
country. The inſpector and marſhal might have come
very ſafely through the weſtern counties by going a few
miles up the Allegany river. The roads north of
Greenſburgh were not ambuſcaded, nor am I convinced

that the apprehenfion of the roads having been way-laid at any time was well founded, except when the mail was robbed ; but this outrage gave reafonable ground to fufpect that they were near the Monongahela. The others that were expelled were accompanied by two members of the Pittfburgh committee as far as Greenfburgh, and faw no appearance of any interruption on the road. Colonel Nevil halted in the eaftern parts of Weftmoreland till after the Parkifon ferry meeting, and was not difturbed.

A democratic fociety had been erected at Wafhington town, a few months preceding the infurrection, and it publifhed fome intemperate refolutions refpecting the conduct of government relative to the navigation of the Miffiffippi, the appointment of a chief juftice and a fenator as ambaffadors to Europe, &c. But I do not remember that they faid any thing againft the excife law. Their refolutions were written in imitation of refolutions that had been publifhed in Kentucky. Though there is no proof that thefe publications had any influence in promoting the infurrection, yet the damned democratic focieties, as they were called, were confidered as the caufe of it by many in the army, from the generals down to the privates. I found too, that it was generally thought that the country was full of thofe focieties, though in fact there was but one, and that one had been of fhort duration and compofed of but few members, feveral of whom I find were of the beft difpofed citizens; fome of them, however, took a prominent ftation in the infurrection, of which number Mr. Bradford was one.

The journals of Congrefs and the debates publifhed

In the news-papers in the winter following, will give a standing testimony of the irritation that prevailed at that time against democratic societies, not only in the army, but in the councils of the United States. This attempt in government to suppress popular societies had a tendency to revive them when they were on the decline. I have ever thought it impolitic in government to denounce, where it cannot punish. Societies cannot be suppressed in a free government, nor should it be attempted. They will do good or ill according to the good sense and discretion of those who compose them, therefore in order to reform societies we must begin with making men wiser and better; when they blazon the measures of administration or panegyrize the persons who conduct them, they are not denounced, therefore when they do otherwise they must be tolerated.

After making competent alowances for those extraneous causes of irritation, and for the materials of which many of the militia corps were composed, &c. a decision in favour of employing the militia, when an armed force is absolutely necessary to be employed in supporting the execution of civil or criminal process, is conclusive. I say when an armed force is absolutely necessary, for surely a sherili's *posse*, taken from the mass of the freeholders, is the most proper force for that purpose. It has the example of past ages, and the testimony of experience in its favour; and if this force had been employed in due season, another force would not have been necessary in the western counties.

It is beyond my purpose to enquire or develope what effects would have resulted from employing a stand-

ing army in the execution of civil or criminal procefs ;
but when the revengeful temper, and nefarious endeavours to gratify that temper, through influence obtained in the army and with the judiciary, that was exhibited in the weftern expedition, and which will be related
in the fequel, is conlidered, it will readily be admitted,
that if a mercenary army had been employed on that
occafion in preference to a militia, inftead of the puny
attempts that were made, there would have been fuccefsful exertions, to facrifice innocent victims to party
fpleen and perfonal rancour.

___

CHAP. XIV.

ABOUT seven o'clock in the morning
of the day on which we arrived at Carlifle, we waited on
the Prefident, and delivered to him the refolutions of
affurance agreed on at the fecond meeting at Parkifon's
Ferry. We found him alone, and were received and
treated with politenefs and attention. After a fhort
converfation he informed us that he was juft going out
about fome bufinefs relating to the army when he faw
us approaching, and that after breakfaft he was going
to fee a divifion of the army march, that therefore he
could not examine the papers at prefent, but would
converfe with us on the fubject at ten o'clock that
morning.

When we waited on him at ten o'clock, we found him
in company with governor Howell, to whom he introduced us. Col. Hamilton then fecretary of the treafury
was prefent all the time, but governor Howell

X

withdrew before the converſation ended. The Preſident opened the converſation with a diſcourſe on the ſubjeċt of the reſolutions. In which he expatiated at conſiderable length on the evils occaſioned by the inſurrection, and the injury reſulting from it to the cauſe of liberty and the general intereſts of republican government in the world. He ſaid that the outrages, committed againſt the government, and the peace of the citizens in the weſtern counties, had agitated the United States from one end to the other, like an electrical ſhock, and diſpoſed them very generally to turn out in ſupport of the violated laws ; he ſpoke of the reſpectability of the army that was then at the places of rendezvous, or on their march, and the alacrity with which they left their farms and their merchandize, in order to ſupport the government, and laws, when called on for that purpoſe, and ſaid that it was found neceſſary to ſend repeated expreſſes to prevent too great a number from marching from ſome of the ſtates, particularly New-Jerſey, and that all the ſtates that had been called on, appeared to have ſent forward the quota required.

He lamented the ſacrifices that the farmer and merchant were under the neceſſity of making, and the great expence that would be incurred to the government by the expedition. He expreſſed his aſtoniſhment, that the people were ſo blind to their own intereſt as not to have prevented the neceſſity of it by giving to the commiſſioners ſuch aſſurances of their ſubmiſſion to the laws, as would have ſheltered them from puniſhment and ſecured the reſtoration of order, and that we and other well diſpoſed citizens

had not been more fuccefsful in perfuading them to
take that falutary courfe.   He concluded his obfervations on this fubject, by giving his opinion, that the
refolutions which we had prefented were not fufficiently unequivocal to juftify him in difmiffing the army,
now when they were rendezvoufed, and the greateft
proportion of the expences incurred, and the facrifices
of the merchant and farmer already made.   He appealed to our own knowledge, that the preparation for
an expedition was the greateft part of the expence, and
obferved,   that being thus far advanced, it would be
neceffary to obtain further and more ample affurances
of fubmiffion, before he could difmifs the army, than
perhaps would have been required at an earlier period;
That the objects to be obtained by the expedition were
unequivocal affurances of fubmiffion to the laws, and
protection to the officers of the revenue for the future ;
and that the good difpofitions of government, expreffed
by the commiffioners, being rejected, and the march of
the army rendered neceffary, fome atonements would
be required for the infractions committed againft the
laws.   Obferving that the refolutions referred him
to us for further information, he invited us to proceed
in giving it to him.

We, in reply, expreffed our unfeigned fatisfaction
at difcovering that the authority of the United States
could call forth fo refpectable and well equipped an
army, to fupport the government and laws, when fuch
a meafure became neceffary, and at the patriotifm difplayed by thofe who had made fuch facrifices for that
purpofe ; but expreffed our fincere grief for the occafion that had rendered fuch a difplay of power and

patriotifm neceffary. We expreffed our opinion, that
a militia army was the moft congenial to a republican
government, and the moft favourable to liberty, but fuggefted ferious apprehenfions that from fome peculiar
circumftances the prefent militia army, though fo very
refpectable, had a more threatening afpect to the people
of the weftern country than even a mercenary army;
and fuggefted that their irritation and fenfe of infult
might be in proportion to their wealth, refpectability,
and the facrifices which they had made, and that from
thefe circumftances the difficulty of introducing difcipline, and preferving fubordination to the laws in the army, might be increafed. We acknowledged the wifdom
and humanity, difplayed by the Prefident, in fending
commiffioners, vefted with fuch ample authority to
reftore order, by granting fo liberal an amnefty to the
infurgents, and our grief that this beneficent meafure
had not rendered coercive meafures unneceffary, and
then proceeded to relate the circumftances which contributed to prevent that falutary meafure from being
completely fuccefsful.

In doing this, we ftated briefly the unforefeen and
untoward circumftances, that rendered it impoffible for
the well difpofed people to prevent the commencement
of the infurrection; fuch as their diftance from each
other, the hurry of the feafon, and the fecrecy of the
marfhal's arrival and progrefs, which put it out of the
power of the friends of order to make any arrangements for his protection, and to preferve the peace of
the country; that it required time for the well difpofed
people to know in whom they could confide, and the
unexpectednefs and rapidity of the outrages at firft

struck people with such astonishment, as required time for reflection before exertions could be made. The backwardness of well disposed people, who were innocent, to expose themselves, the terror that was spread abroad by those who became leaders among the insurgents, and the disapprobation of the excise law, even by many, who, though they were disposed to submit to it, hesitated some time before they would put themselves to risk for its support, rendered it impossible to put a stop to the disorders without time and labour. We detailed the imperious and unforeseen circumstances, that in a great measure frustrated the intention of the meeting of the committee of 60 at Redstone old fort, and the motives by which the innocent citizens were actuated in declining to attend the meetings, or refusing to sign the instrument of assurances submitted to them by the commissioners. We gave a candid account of the violent opposition that was given at some township meetings, and asserted, that this violent opposition, as far as was within our knowledge, was, with very few exceptions, made by the most ignorant and obstinate class of people, some of whom are to be found in all countries; that few of these having either character or property to lose, availed themselves of this season of disorder to insult judges, magistrates, and generally those people to whom they, on other occasions, had recourse for sustenance, or to whom they usually resorted for advice in their difficulties: And in the few places, where these gave disturbance, that their success was owing to their desperation, and not to the greatness of their number; that from the very circumstance of their having little or nothing to lose, their threats of burning, and other acts of violence, were the more dreaded; yet that notwithstanding their threats, there had not been a single instance of their having been put in execution on this occasion. We stated, that these were not the people that ever could give trouble to government in settled times, and that most of them had come in, some of them in tears, within a few days, and requested to be permitted to sign the assurances; and that in many places they had been permitted to sign, with certification, however, that though it might go in abatement of their offence, yet it gave them no claim for an amnesty. We assured the President, that but few of those who opposed the signing had been guilty of other offences, except, perhaps, where the riots originated.

We also assured him, that in all the counties prosecutions had been commenced against such of them, as it was thought necessary and prudent for the present peace of the country to prosecute; and that what had been done in this way rendered it certain, that the public peace could be preserved, and atonements procured for infractions committed on the laws by the ordinary proceedings in the courts of justice; and gave it as our opinion, that if the powers of the commissioners had not expired so soon, order would have been perfectly restored, and satisfactory assurances of submission to the laws obtained. We informed him, that the newspapers, containing the orders to the militia to hold themselves in readiness to march, coming to Parkison's ferry meeting on the morning after the arrival of the commissioners had been announced, excited an inflammatory agitation of mind with many, which tended, for a time, to

Efface the favourable impreffions, that had been previoufly made, by the approach of the commiffioners being announced, the extent or nature of whofe powers was not yet generally known, and that in fact this circumftance irritated fome who had been heretofore well difpofed. That, generally, all who had been difaffected to independence, either among the Englifh or Germans, countenanced the diforders, and were oppofed to the reftoration of order ; that among thofe, ftrangers were known to be entertained, who were fuppofed to be emiffaries from places at a diftance. That though the fpirit of diforder fpread like an epidemic from place to place, yet at every attempt to reftore order, fome progrefs had been made, and many induced to forfake the caufe of oppofition ; that after the Redftone meeting, few, if any citizens, otherwife fenfible and difcreet, adhered to the infurgents; that in confequence of this, thofe who continued obftinate became the more defperate in proportion to the fmallnefs of the number of men of difcretion and property that countenanced them, and as their laft hopes of fuccefs in their oppofition depended on their preventing the fuccefs of the meetings for giving affurances on the 11th of September, the agents of Tom the Tinker made their laft effort to defeat the falutary intentions of thefe townfhip meetings, yet with all their induftry, it was but in comparatively few places that they had any fuccefs, or produced any difturbance.

We affured him that the greateft caufe of fo fmall a number figning the declaration of fubmiffion, was the reluctance of the innocent to give fuch affurances as might imply an acknowledgment of guilt, have the appearance of giving a new teft not required by law; or (as they thought the words indirectly meant) prevent them from petitioning for a repeal or revifion of the excife law. That it was this principle that influ. enced the whole county of Fayette, the greater extent of Weftmoreland, and the frontier parts of the other counties, to withhold their fignatures from thefe affurances prefcribed by the commiffioners.

We ftated that from the meeting at Redftone, but efpecially from a view of the charaders who in fome places oppofed the giving affurances to government, the well difpofed people had become convinced that it was their duty to ftand forth with greater vigour in fupport of the laws; that they, having come to know, and have confidence in, each other, had very generally entered into affociations to fupport the laws, and that thefe affociations in favour of government were generally entered into within a few days after the 11th of September, and had every appearance of being fo fuccefsful, that the people, who had been the moft troublefome, folicited permiffion to fign the affociations as a matter of favour, and that fince that time there had neither been difturbances nor threats.

We alfo ftated, that on the whole a much greater proportion of ufeful information had been diffeminated among the people, refpecting their political duties and interefts than formerly, that the number of thofe who had qualified themfelves for giving information, and who were induftrious in inftruding their neighbours, were greatly encreafed in the country, and that many of the clergy were particularly ufeful in this way, and had been induftrious in promoting fubmiffion to the

laws, that the infolence of the moft ignorant and turbulent perfons had fully convinced all men of difcretion
and intereft in the country, that if they permitted government to be violently oppofed, even in the execution of an obnoxious law, the fame fpirit would naturally lead to the deftruction of all fecurity and order; they
faw by experience that in a ftate of anarchy the name
of liberty would be prophaned to fanction the moft
defpotic tyranny, that for fome time after the commencement of the infurrection, the extreme agitation
of mind that prevailed operated as a repulfive principle againft receiving information, but that, that temper
having fubfided, there was now a folicitude to be informed, and that in fact many who had been active in
fome of the diforders, being fince convinced of their
folly, were now among the firmeft friends of order, and
active in promoting that difpofition among their neighbours. This circumftance, together with the leaders
having generally figned the amnefty, and left the more
ignorant and obftinate to fhift for themfelves, we faid
would for the future deftroy all confidence among
thofe who might be difpofed to commit diforders; that
added to this the general conviction now prevailing
among all men of property and difcretion, that it is
their intereft as well as duty to preferve order, afforded
the ftrongeft ground of rational confidence, that in future the laws would be obeyed and the officers protected.

With refpect to atonements, we fuggefted, that if
the army marched into the country in order to procure
them, the moft proper objects having already fheltered
themfelves under the faith of government, thofe who

Y

were guilty and had not figned the amnefty would have
time to efcape while the army was advancing. We
propofed to carry up with us in confidence fuch in-
ions as the Prefident would tranfmit to any perfon,
whom he would appoint to commence profecutions,
that in that way alone proper fubjects for
punifhment would be procured, and that doing
this would afford a decifive teft whether the execution
of the law would be fupported or not. We concluded
by requefting the Prefident to inform us if time would
be allowed to procure more certain and unequivocal affurances, and if this was granted, in what manner
the affurances fhould be obtained, and how, or where,
it fhould be communicated to him.

The Prefident, in reply, affured us that it would
have been his wifh to have authorifed the commiffioners to have given the people fufficient time for the
agitation to fubfide, and to be informed of the terms
and to deliberate on them, without ordering the militia
to be in readinefs for marching, if time and other circumftances would have permitted, but that the time
the infurrection commenced was not of his choofing,
and was too near the winter to enable him to afford the
time he wifhed to have given, and that the flame having
caught in Maryland, and fymptoms of it having been
difcovered in fome other places in Pennfylvania, rendered it improper to delay the expedition till the
fpring, left the flame fhould fpread further.

He faid there were fome diforderly corps in the
army, that fome diforders had been committed on the
march to Carlifle, and that two men had been actually
killed, he defcribed, circumftantially, the manner in

which they were killed, and faid that though from the information he had received neither cafe appeared to have been murder, yet he had given up the authors of both thefe offences, to the laws of our own ftate, and would do fo in every inftance, where the laws required that this fhould be done, and he affured us that he would provide by difperfing the diforderly corps among better troops, or otherwife, that they fhould be kept in ftrict fubordination, that in every inftance, where infractions were made on the laws by any of the army, they fhould be fubjected to punifhment. He affured us further, that the army fhould not confider themfelves as judges or executioners of the laws, but as employed to fupport the proper authorities in the execution of them. That he had been obliged to leave Virginia, before he tranfacted fome neceffary bufinefs, which he had intended, and to come in hafte to Philadelphia on account of the infurrection, and that he had left Philadelphia, where we knew his prefence was neceffary to prepare for the meeting of Congrefs, in order to come to the army; that he mixed and converfed daily with the officers, and that his great object in all this was to imprefs the army with a proper fenfe of the importance of fubmitting to the laws, and that unlefs they did fo, the laft refort of a republican government would be defeated. He added that he would go to the Maryland Brigade, then rendezvoufed at Williams-port, and from thence to the Virginia troops at fort Cumberland, and return by Bedford, where the troops now on their march from Carlifle would encamp for fome time, and that his great object would be to imprefs on

the army, in thefe different places, a fenfe of the neceſ-
fity of its fubordination to the laws.

With refpeᶜt to the expence, &c. of the expedition,
he faid there might fome good grow out of it to confole,
if not compenfate us. That though we had made a republican form of government and enaᶜted laws under it,
yet we had given no teftimony to the world of being
able, or willing to fupport our government and laws,
that this being the firft inftance of the kind fince the
commencement of the government, he thought it his
duty to bring out fuch a force as would not only be
fufficient to fubdue the infurgents, if they made refiftance, but to crufh to atoms any oppofition that might
rife in any other corner; that this would operate in favour of humanity, by effeᶜtually difcouraging any, that
might be otherwife fo difpofed, from provoking bloodfhed; and that in the refult it might teach the citizens
to be more cautious of writing or fpeaking in fuch a
manner of the meafures of government, as might have
a tendency to inflame the citizens, and would alfo convince other nations that we could defend ourfelves. He
faid that the queftions we had afked, refpeᶜting further
affurances, would require fome time for confideration,
and appointed us to wait on him again at five o'clock in
the evening.

In the evening interview, the Prefident declined
fending forward with us or others, orders for fecuring
offenders. This we expeᶜted. He told us that we ought
to know among ourfelves who were guilty, and profe-
cute them. He encouraged us to take more unequivocal affurances from the people, but made no promife of amnefty on the account of thefe affurances, but

repeatedly faid that they might do good, and could do no harm, and he on this and every other occafion preffed it on us to take the utmoft care that one gun fhould not be fired, and added that if one gun was fired, he would not be refponfible for the confequences; we affured him that there was no defign of making refiftance, but on the caution being repeated, we remarked that if a fool or defperate man, to prevent himfelf from being taken, fhould fire a gun, that it would be a great hardfhip if the whole country fhould be implicated in his guilt; he anfwered that he did not intend that they fhould, but that we did not know what might be the confequence of firing one gun. He told us that he did not command the army, in perfon, but had appointed governor Lee commander in chief, and mentioned who were to command the militia of the different ftates, and directed the orders he had prepared, to be read to us, as far as they refpected the fubordination of the army to the laws.

' We had free accefs to converfe on every topic that we thought might be ufeful, as long as we judged in convenient to ftay, and in the courfe of the converfation fecretary Hamilton, who was prefent and took a part in the general converfation, afked us what were the grounds of our own confidence of fubmiffion to the laws, and the protection to be afforded to officers in the different parts of the country.

In anfwer to this we related the particular inftances of coercion that had recently been given in the different counties, which difcovered that there was both a difpofition and ability to put the laws in execution in all the four counties. We mentioned as another ground of

our confidence, the induſtry of the clergy in promoting
ſubmiſſion to the laws, and ſtated ſeveral inſtances of it,
ſuch as Mr Mꞌ Millin of Waſhington county refuſing
to adminiſter the ſacrament of the lord's-ſupper to his
congregation, until they would ſubmit to the laws, and
Mr. Porter of Weſtmoreland, who laboured publicly
and privately with ſucceſs from the beginning, to prevent the ſpirit of diſorder from ſpreading in his congregation ; that many other clergymen had diſtinguiſhed
themſelves, and, that as ſoon as the agitation of mind
had ſubſided which in ſome places rendered men deaf to
inſtruction for a time, they had great influence with the
people in bringing them to a ſenſe of their duty. We
alſo ſtated that all the judges of the court in the different counties, without exception, the juſtices of the
peace, and all who ever had been, or then were, Members of Aſſembly, with a few exceptions, chiefly in one
county, were, and always had been well diſpoſed, and
that in general all who had been diſtinguiſhed for un-
derſtanding, to whom their neighbours in ſettled
times had looked up to for counſel, were the friends of
order.

We obſerved that during the agitation a remarkable change appeared to have taken place in ſociety,
that an unuſual number of falſehoods, aſſerting that a
vaſt variety of unuſual and oppreſſive taxes had been
laid by Congreſs, that the wages of the members had
been raiſed to eight dollars a day, &c. and that
in conſequence of theſe reports, men who held
offices either in the Federal or ſtate governments,
were conſidered as combined againſt the people,
and diſcredited in contradicting thoſe reports, while
at the ſame time every traveller or vagrant was credi-

ted in aſſerting them, but that now, people having been
generally undeceived, would never ſuffer themſelves to be ſo milled for the future by crediting ſuch
ſtories.

On being aſked by the ſecretary, what ground of
confidence we had with reſpect to the country adjacent
to the Monongahela, we anſwered that not having
been preſent at the laſt meeting at Parkiſon's Ferry we
had not perſonal knowledge reſpecting that country,
but that Alexander Addiſon, Preſident of the ſtate courts
in that diſtrict, who had been ſecretary of the meeting
at Parkiſon's Ferry, had informed us by letter, that he
had converſed with the principal diſtillers who reſided
there, and that they had aſſured him that they would
all ſubmit to the law. We added that Mr. Andrew
M' Farlane, who reſided in the ſettlement, where the
oppoſition had been the moſt violent, and who had
himſelf been obnoxious to the rioters, had travelled
down the road with us, and aſſured us, that he would
be reſponſible with all his eſtate, which was conſide-
ble, for ſubmiſſion to the law, and protection to the
officers in that ſettlement; and that he would even permit the office to be held in his own houſe, and be reſponſible for its ſafety; that on aſking him if he would
permit an office to be kept in his houſe, ſuppoſing the
officer to be very unpopular, he replied, that if that
ſhould be the caſe, it might be more prudent for the officer to hold it for ſome time in Pittſburgh; where the garriſon was; but that a perſon who was not otherwiſe obnoxious would be in no danger from holding the office.
Mr. M' Farlane's houſe is in Allegany county, but part
of his land is in Waſhington *.

* See Note A. end of r lume.

We acknowledged that a number were backward to believe that the militia would march out against them; but that this was occasioned by the reports they heard almost every day, of liberty poles being erected in the old counties, of the militia refusing to turn out, or determining to join the Insurgents, when they did come; that hearing of the threats of violence that had been uttered by some, and greatly magnified by report, deterred waggoners and other travellers from telling the truth, unlefs they were certain of the company they were in ; but that this deception no longer existed, and had generally prevailed only with a very ignorant set of people who were almost the only ungovernable persons, that we had any trouble with towards the last: That the agitation of mind, anxiety, and apprehensions of danger, false alarms and suspicions, which perplexed society for a few weeks, had rendered the citizens generally extremely defirous of having order restored, and that before it had been so far accomplished, every man of influence and understanding was fully convinced that it was for their own interest to have the laws supported, and officers protected, in the discharge of their duty. The state officers themselves conceiving that the transition, from supprefling excisemen to that of insulting judges and other state officers, was very eafy, felt themselves particularly interested in restoring order, and then we observed that from this general apprehension of danger and anxiety for order, there arose a greater security to government, than the most solemn declarations could possibly have otherwise given.

We fuggefted that the affurances which might be procured by the march of the army, and making fevere examples by way of atonement, might not be unequivocal, that it might poffibly rather increafe animofity and change the direction of refentment from public outrages to private revenge, which was the more dangerous, as it would be more difficult to guard againft it.

The Prefident had informed us, that it was the opinion of a number of the moft refpectable of our own citizens, that the march of the army would be neceffary, not only for the reftoring fubmiffion to the revenue laws, but for the protection of well difpofed citizens. We acknowledged that appearances about the time that the commiffioners went away; and at fome places on the day of figning the declaration, were fuch as to juftify that opinion, but affured him that from the change of temper, which had been evidenced, fome of the beft informed of thofe who gave that opinion had changed their fentiments, that probably all had, that though fome citizens had received infults, yet they did not wifh for an army to revenge their caufe; that the courts having been held through the whole circuit without infult or oppofition, there was no room to doubt but they were fully competent to the protection of the citizens.

We enquired whether advantage would be taken of want of form in figning the declaration? The Prefident faid he could not inform us unlefs he knew the circumftances. We explained to him, that we meant only fuch want of form as did not arife from any fault in the perfon claiming the amnefty, but from the con-

Z

duct of others, such as the papers being torn by a defperate banditti after they had been figned; to this it was replied, that no advantage fhould be taken of want of mere matter of form.

At this and all the other interviews, the Prefident authorifed us to affure the citizens who had fheltered themfelves under the faith of government, that one hair of their head fhould not be injured, let their crimes have been ever fo great.

We undertook to procure more general and unequivocal affurances, and to tranfmit them to the army, and were affured that the army would halt fome time at Bedford, fo as to give an opportunity of procuring the affurances, and that they would be well received. We then withdrew with a view of returning homewards next morning, but the Prefident fent his private fecretary early next morning to our lodging, to afk us to wait on him again before we left town, but having rode out a few miles to fee relations, the Prefident was gone out to the army before we returned; but as he returned from feeing the laft divifion of the army begin their march, he ftopped his horfe before the door of our lodging, and calling us to him, converfed fome time with us in the ftreet, and appointed us to wait on him again in the evening, and to bring fome affurances which we had informed him we had with us, that had been fubfcribed after the 11th of September. We fpent that evening converfing in the fame manner, as we had done the former, and chiefly on the fame fubjects, till we thought it convenient to retire. We were difmiffed as politely as we had been received, and in all the opportunities we had of converfing with the Prefident, we were treated with that candour and politenefs which have at all times diftinguifhed his character.

At parting, both on this and a former interview, we expreffed a wifh that the Prefident could accompany the army to its fartheft deftination, and acknowledged that he had given every poffible affurance of the army being kept in fubordination, fhort of what his own prefence and authority along with it would produce. He replied on this occafion, that if when at Bedford he difcovered that his prefence would be neceffary, and he was not under the neceffity of returning to Philadelphia, he poffibly would flay with the army, if it advanced into the weftern country.

I do not pretend that we were treated with attention, from any peculiar attachment to us, whether that was fo or not is a matter of no importance in this cafe. The attention however that he paid to us was the refult of found difcretion. He was anxious to prevent bloodfhed, and at the fame time to enforce due fubmiffion to the laws, with as little trouble as poffible, and by encouraging us to procure more explicit affurances, he was accomplifhing a principal object of the expedition, before the army arrived. And in fact, fuch explicit affurances were procured before they arrived, that nothing remained to be done by them but to fupport the civil magiftrate in procuring proper fubjects to atone for the outrages that had been committed.

The Prefident was very fenfible of the inflammatory and ungovernable difpofition that had difcovered itfelf in the army before he arrived at Carlifle, and he had not only laboured inceffantly to remove that fpirit and

prevent its effects, but he was folicitous alfo to remove
our fears.   As often as we fuggefted apprehenfions of
danger from that quarter, he confoled us with affurances of good difcipline and fubordination to the laws being enforced, and of the diforderly corps being difperfed
among fuch as were more orderly, or if that would not
do, that they fhould be difcharged with infamy.   Orders were actually given to this effect, and at leaft in
fome inftances punctually executed.

   The Prefident's attention to promote fubordination to the laws, and curb the difpofition to licentioufnefs, which was too evident, and to give us fufficient
confidence to encourage the people in the weftern
country, was found policy ; for though nothing could
be conceived more diftreffing to us than the very
thoughts of hoftile oppofition to the authority of the
United States, and though it was well known that we
had made every exertion in our power to prevent it,
yet if the army had marched to the weftern country
under the prevailing influence of that inflammatory
and licentious fpirit, which difcovered itfelf among a
part of them for fome time at Carlifle, we muft have
thought it our duty to have returned with all hafte, and
told the people what they had a right to expect; and
in that cafe defperation muft have fupplied the want
of refources, and the innocent muft have made a common caufe with the guilty ; for there is no law, divine
or human, to oblige people tamely to fubmit to be
fkewered, hanged or fhot, in cold blood, and this was
for fome time the declared object of fuch as made moft
noife, and even of fome who laid claim to the character
of gentlemen ; and it was a fingular circumftance, that

fuch citizens of the weftern country, as had made the greateft exertions in preventing the fpread of the dif-.orders, and refloring fubmiffion to the laws, were deftined to be the firft victims of this lawlefs rage.

The Prefident was happily fuccefsful in reducing the licentious part of the army to fubordination to the laws, and in infpiring the people in the weftern counties with fuch a meafure of confidence, as prevented any conduct on their part, that could give the army any juft caufe of irritation.

Information that there were many officers of difcretion and experience in the army, as well as a great many orderly citizens, who come out in their proper clafles, on militia duty, had alfo a tendency to abate the fears of the people of the weftern counties.

C H A P. XV.

M R. Redick and I, returning with all
convenient fpeed, feparated at Greenfburgh in Weftmoreland county, after preparing an advertifement to
be publifhed in the Pittfburgh gazette, calling for a
meeting of the delegates of townfhips, which had been
elected for the firft meeting at Parkifon's ferry, and requefting alfo the attendance of as many difcreet citizens
befides, as could conveniently attend.   Knowing that
the gazette would be put to prefs before the advertifement could reach the editor, we were obliged to make
it too fhort for conveying fuch information as we wifhed to communicate ; conceiving alfo that the gazette
was too flow a method of warning the citizens in the
four counties, I undertook to give information by circular letters to the counties of Weftmoreland and
Fayette, and with the affiftance afforded by others, thefe
letters were fent to proper perfons without delay. The
extent of the country over which the people were fpread,

and the importance of having the general fense of the
country, unequivocally understood at the meeting, induced us to delay it some days longer than we had contemplated at Carlisle, rather than that the assurances to
be obtained should be doubtful. This, however, rendered it impossible to have the assurances forwarded to
Bedford before the army had left it. The President
had found it necessary to return to Philadelphia, some
days before the army left Bedford.

An excellent opportunity offered for taking the fense
of the citizens, at the regimental musters, which happened on the week previous to the meeting. In Westmoreland and Fayette counties, the brigadier-generals
and inspectors of both counties, without mutual confultation, proposed to those who attended the musters,
that they should sign assurances engaging themselves,
personally, to submit to the laws, protect the officers,
&c. and before the end of the week, on which the musters were held, all the citizens of those two counties,
whose names were in the muster rolls, and could attend, had signed explicit assurances. A number of them
had done so before, on the day appointed by the commissioners, or within a few days after it.

Mr. Redick having to go by Pittsburgh with the
advertisement; it was two days after the letters had
been circulated in the other counties, before he arrived
at Washington town, so that he had not so early an opportunity of communicating information as I had, and
the news-paper circulating slowly, the people south of
the Monongahela not having encouragement for giving
new assurances, neglected the opportunity of the musters,

though many of them had figned in their refpective townfhips before the Parkifon ferry meeting.

On the 24th of October, the meeting convened; great indeed was the difference between the complexion of this meeting, and that which met at the fame place on the 14th of Auguft preceding, and this difference was in a great meafure owing to a few men. Bradford, Fulton, Parkifon, Marfhal, and others, who had contrived and promoted the meeting at Braddock's field, had either fecured an amnefty by fubmitting in due time, or fled out of the country, and others who, perhaps, had done neither, were afhamed to appear at this meeting, though the terror of them and their friends had overawed the firft; and a great number of refpectable citizens attended at this meeting, who did not think it prudent to countenance the firft. The citizens did not act here as delegates, nor produce credentials, and the greateft harmony and good order prevailed. James Edgar was appointed chairman, and Albert Gallatin fecretary.

When the meeting was opened Mr. Redick and I gave an account of the difcharge of our truft at Carlifle, and ftated the propriety of giving more unequivocal affurances than had yet been obtained, and the encouragements given for doing fo, as nearly in the Prefident's own words as we could exprefs them. We alfo ftated the importance of preventing any headftrong foolifh people from irritating the army, if it advanced into the country, either by firing a gun at them, or any other conduct that might be conftrued into a pretence by any in the army to break through the rules of difcipline, &c. and in order to render them the more cautious, we

Informed them that the fame inflammatory fpirit appeared to pervade fome part of the army, that had fo recently prevailed in this country. We alfo, according to the Prefident's inftructions, affured thofe who had fheltered themfelves under the faith of government, that they would not be difturbed, let their crimes be what they might, and that no advantage fhould be taken of want of mere matter of form. We added fuch other information, and made fuch obfervations, as we thought fuitable to the occafion ; but many obfervations were not neceffary, the people were willing to do every thing that was judged proper, indeed if the fame people had attended and voted at the firft meeting that did at this, and if thofe who governed the paffions of that day, and were abfent from this meeting, had alfo been abfent from that, an army would not have been marched into the country. At this meeting, the following refolutions were unanimoufly adopted :

1ft. Refolved, that in our opinion, the civil authority is now fully competent to enforce the laws and to punifh both paft and future offences, inasmuch, as the people at large are determined to fupport every defcription of civil officers in the legal difcharge of their duty.

2d. Refolved, that in our opinion, that all perfons who may be charged or fufpected of having committed any offence againft the United States or the ftate, during the late difturbances, and who have not entitled themfelves to the benefits of the act of oblivion, ought immediately to furrender themfelves to the civil authority, in order to ftand their trial, that if there be any fuch perfons among us, they are ready to furrender

A a

themfelves to the civil authority accordingly, and that
we will unite in giving our affiftance to bring to juftice
fuch offenders as fhall not furrender.

3d. Refolved, that in our opinion, offices of infpection may be immediately opened in the refpective
counties of this furvey, without any danger of violence
being offered to any of the officers, and that the diftillers are willing and ready to enter their ftills.

4th. That William Findley, David Redick,
Ephraim Douglafs, and Thomas Morton, do wait on
the Prefident with the forgoing refolutions.

That these refolutions were unequivocal was not
only teftified by the unanimity of the vote, but by the
papers that had been figned by the people at the mufters,
and otherwife. The citizens fouth of Monongahela, who
had not had the opportunity of figning at the mufters,
exprefled great regret that they had not known in time
that fuch a meafure would have been acceptable, and
affured the meeting, that thofe who had not yet figned
affurances would do it without delay. Affurances
figned by a number of them, a few days after that
appointed by the commiffioners, had been prefented
to the Prefident at Carlifle.

The four commiffioners appointed to carry the
affurances to the Prefident, could not do it without
fome delay, as they refided in the four different counties, and when they met together at Greenfburgh, they
were informed that the Prefident had returned to Philadelphia, and that the army was on its march from
Bedford and fort Cumberland to the Weftern counties; we therefore concluded to halt, till the army would
advance, and to prefent the affurances to the comman-

der in chief, but as fecretary Hamilton was with the left wing of the army, and as we believed that he would influence whatever meafures might be adopted in confequence of the affurances we had to prefent, we waited fome days for his arrival at Bonnet's camp, in the fouthern extremity of Weflmoreland county, and prefented them firft to him, who when he had examined them, returned them to us, after telling us, that for the fake of decorum, it would be beft to prefent them to the commander in chief. This was what we intended to have done.

The next day we arrived at Union town, in Fayette county, where the head quarters then were, and prefented the affurances to the commander in chief, who fent for the other general officers, and he and they treated us with civility. The commander appointed us to wait on him the next morning. Secretary Hamilton arrived at Union town the fame evening, and the main body of the left wing of the army arrived at Union Town, the fame day.

The next morning, fome hours later than the time appointed, the commander in chief prefented us with an addrefs to the people, in anfwer to their affurances.

We had, in converfation with him on the preceding evening, ftated fubftantially, though much more concifely, the fame reafons, for our confidence that the people would fubmit to the laws and protect the officers, as we had done to the Prefident, with this difference however, that being better informed, our confidence was more perfect. We admitted indeed, that it was true, that fome of the ignorant people in fome

places believed the falfehoods that had been propaga-
ted, and did not believe that the army was approaching,
until they were on their march.   One of our number
admitted, that fome young headftrong boys, who had
got arms in their hands, were not willing to give affurances of fubmiffion, until they were convinced that the
army was approaching, and that with them thefe fears
might have been a prevailing motive to fubmiffion, but
we denied that this was the general principle of fubmiffion, and affured him that the fubmiffion had been
very general before it was known that the army would
march, that it was from a conviction of this, that men
of the beft difcernment, who had an opportunity of
learning the fentiments, and obferving the temper of
the people, at the courts which had been held in all the
counties, called the meeting at Parkifon's ferry, who
adopted the refolutions of fubmiffion that had been
tranfmitted to the Prefident at Carlifle.   That this
conviction was obtained, and a call of the Parkifon
meeting delegates agreed on, as early as the report of
the commiffioners to the Prefident, on which the orders to march were founded, was made.   That this
change of temper was founded on a general conviction,
that it was their own intereft to have the laws fupported, and was promoted by the induftry of thofe citizens
who had been always well difpofed, but who had lay
by during the height of the difturbances, till they were
convinced of the neceffity of ftanding forward for the
reftoration of order, and entertained hopes that reafon
and argument would be attended to.   We affured him
alfo that thofe who had taken a lead in difturbances,
had either fubmitted in time to fecure themfelves

under the amnefly, or were fled, and that confequently the ignorant and obftinate, who had oppofed fubmiffion to the laft, finding themfelves forfaken by all in whom they had confidence, would have no encouragement to be troublefome for the future, and that their confidence in each other would be fo deftroyed as to leave no ground for fufpecting their being able to form any new dangerous combinations. Notwithftanding that we affigned thefe and other fuch reafons as grounds of confidence in the reality of the people's fubmiffion, the commander in chief in his addrefs to the inhabitants of that country through us, did not acknowledge that we had affigned any other reafon, but the panic occafioned by the advance of the army. When we objected to this ftatement, and alleged that we had candidly given other and more fubftantial reafons, and that this reafon would apply to only a few of the moft ignorant and obftinate, he ftruck out the words which fixed this charge on all the people, and interlined, *the lower order of the people*, words which we had never fpoken; for though we mentioned a difference of character, we had not thought of a diftinction of orders in fociety. We have few flaves and no nobles.

Near the conclufion of the addrefs, he recommends it to thofe focieties, who had poifoned the minds of the people with falfehoods, to continue with their ufual formalities, to counteract the falfehoods they had circulated, and that thereby, they would make fome atonements for the mifchief they had done; we returned it to him again, and requefted to know to what meetings he alluded. He anfwered, that it was the Par

kifon meetings, and fuch as them. We replied, that
the Parkifon meetings and others of that kind, were
held for the exprefs purpofe of reftoring order, that
the firft Parkifon meeting, in a great meafure put a flop
to the outrages, and that the fubfequent meetings, had
completed the reftoration of fubmiffion to the laws,
but he feemed not to underftand the diftinction between thofe and other meetings. The denunciation
of felf created focieties however, that foon followed,
indicated that his advifers had other meetings in view.
Indeed from his underftanding fo little of the fubject
of his own addrefs, and difcovering fo little candour
in it, we fufpected, at the time, that it did not originate with himfelf. When we withdrew, it was propofed to accompany the publication of it in the news-
papers with remarks, containing a candid ftatement
of the reafons we had affigned for the confidence that
might be placed in the affurances of fubmiffion, which
we had prefented ; but on conferring together, we
agreed rather to fubmit to an uncandid ftatement of
our own conduct, which was evidently calculated to
give the beft difpofed people in the country juft caufe
of offence againft us, than to do any thing that might
give the army a pretence for irritation, we plainly difcovered that the addrefs was calculated to give a bad
impreffion of us to the people, and of the people to
the army, and the world. It was alfo calculated to
afford reafons for continuing the army longer in the
country, and convinced us that thofe, who then gave
the fupreme direction to the proceedings, did not defign
to pay much refpect to the unequivocal affurances,
which the Prefident feemed folicitous that we fhould

procure. Indeed though we were treated politely in other refpects, and employed to affift in fixing the prices of neceffaries for the army, and confulted about the ground on which it fhould encamp, when it advanced further into the country ; yet we did not meet with that candour and franknefs, with which we had been treated by the Prefident at Carlifle. On reading fome of the preceding Chapters, it will occur to the reader that either governor Lee was not the author of the addrefs he prefented to us, or that he did not underftand the fubject, when he afcribed the circulating of falfehoods, to poifon the minds of the people, to the meetings held at Parkifon's Ferry.

C H A P. XVI.

THE firſt orders, that appear to have been executed under the authority of the federal judge, were at Bedford, from whence the four men mentioned already were eſcorted to Philadelphia under a military guard. As far as it was in the power of the parties employed to eſcort them, theſe priſoners were treated with propriety.

Some few were taken without legal orders, when the army entered the weſtern counties, but were ſoon diſmiſſed. One of theſe had ſigned aſſurances in due time ; but no general attempt was made to take priſoners, until the army had encamped a conſiderable time in the vicinity of Monongahela, and were apparently preparing to return home ; arrangements were then made to have the priſoners taken in all the different parts of the country, on the 13th of November. For this purpofe, different detachments were deftined to various routs, who in moft inftances fecured thofe that they had orders to apprehend. The orders were executed with promptitude and addrefs, but not with equal humanity by all the parties.

To drag men unexpectedly and unprepared, from their wives and children, from bed time till morning, is an exertion that fhocks humanity, and yet in fome imperious cafes the interefts of humanity require that it fhould be done. When it becomes expedient to make prifoners of bold and intrepid men, accuftomed to danger, it is neceffary, in order to prevent bloodfhed, to take them by furprife; nor is this the lefs expedient when they happen to be innocent, for in that cafe, they might be difpofed to make the more defperate defence; and every thing that would lead to a conteft, was to be avoided on this occafion with peculiar care, as it was apprehended that fome inflammatory fpirits in the army wifhed for a plaufible pretext to burft the bonds of difcipline, and fatiate their vengeance on a defencelefs country.

Though it appeared, in the refult, that but a fmall proportion of thofe that were taken in this manner had done any thing for which they could be punifhed, yet thofe who were employed to take them, had no right to examine, or difcriminate between the innocent and the guilty. But though the rigid duty muft be performed, no man of honour or humanity would add infult or cruelty to unavoidable feverity. I rejoice at having it in my power to flate that, in moft inftances, care was taken to employ men of character and difcretion in taking prifoners.

Captain Dunlap of Philadelphia, and his company, were fent to Muddy creek in the upper end of Wafhington county, they took colonel Crawford and fon, Mr. Sedgwick, a juftice of the peace, Mr. Corbly, a clergyman of the Baptift perfuafion, and others. They were taken early in the morning, and had no opportunity of making refiflance. Captain Dunlap and his party, while they behaved with the greateft dexterity in taking the prifoners, treated them with as much politenefs and attention as their fituation would admit of, and engaged their gratitude by accompanying unavoidable feverity with humanity.

Thefe prifoners affert, that they had not the opportunity of figning the terms of the commiffioners until the appointed day was paft. They were admitted to bail, after feveral months imprifonment, and though two of thofe perfons were reported to have been a good deal inflammatory, there was no bill found againft any of them on their trial. They were not engaged in the outrages againft excife officers, or at the rendezvous at Braddock's field. I cannot find that Sedgwick, the juftice of the peace, had done any thing to lay a foundation even for fufpicion. Crawford, the younger, had been one of the armed party, who appeared at the Redftone meeting with a defign to punifh Jackfon, but he was difmiffed at Pittfburgh.

General Irwin had been ordered to march to the neighbourhood of Pittfburgh with a divifion of the army, and was directed to take a number of the citizens of Pittfburgh prifoners on the fame night on which the general feizure was made. It appears that two

lifts were defigned for him, but one * only was delivered, without any diftinction made in it between criminals and witnelfes, or any difcretionary power
of difcrimination intrufted to him. The lift contained the names of eighteen citizens of Pittfburgh,
of whom one perfon, on receiving fome private
hint of the defign, delivered himfelf up to the judiciary, then fitting in his own houfe. The general, it
has been faid, was inftructed to ftrike two other perfons out of the lift,

Thus, agreeably to orders, a number of citizens were
dragged out of their beds in the night, and marched to
the camp, with fcarce fufficient time to put on their
neceffary cloathing. The camp affording no better
accomodations, they were obliged to lay that night on
the wet earth, under fnow and rain, and to add to their
mifery they complain that they were barbaroufly infulted by fome of thofe, by whom they were taken, and
alfo by fome of the guards in the camp. Next day
they were empounded in a wafte houfe, where they
were detained for feveral days ; no better lodging could
be procured in the camp. Whatever infults, they may
have received, were contrary to the orders of the general.

On the reprefentation of general Irwin, they were
removed from the camp to the garrifon, and put under
the direction of colonel Butler ; they were then confined in a new houfe, without fire, for five days more.
So many prifoners, from various parts, were then con-

---

* This lift is publifhed at length in Mr. Brackenridge's Incidents ; but general
Irwin does not know how it was procured, and fays, that he had no means of dif-
pugnifhing between criminals and witnefles.

fined in Pittſburgh, that proper accomodations could not be procured.

When the time arrived, that they were to appear before the judiciary, though the priſoners were in the cuſtody of the officer of the garriſon, general Irwin was called on, perhaps in compliment to his rank, to iſſue orders for releaſing them individually from the garriſon in courſe as they were demanded by the judiciary. It was by the call of the judiciary for their appearance, that he, to his ſurpriſe, firſt diſcovered that a number of thoſe whom according to orders he had taken and treated as criminals, were only called on as witneſſes; but how much greater muſt his ſurpriſe have been, if he had known that a number of them had ſigned the amneſty in due time, and conſequently were ſo ſheltered under the faith of government, that according to the Preſident's declaration at Carliſle, they were not to have been diſturbed, let their crimes have been ever ſo great.

I confeſs, when in Philadelphia, I found ſome in the priſon who had ſigned the amneſty, and was informed of the treatment others received on this occaſion at Pittſburgh, I regretted that I had been an inſtrument in encouraging thoſe who had done ſo, to exerciſe unlimited confidence in the faith of government, and on that ground, I demanded the releaſe of a priſoner of that deſcription, from the attorney of the diſtrict and the attorney general, and he was admitted to bail, but had to appear at the court as a witneſs; an apprehenſion that ſomething of this kind would happen, was one reaſon which induced me to ſuggeſt twice to the Preſident at Carliſle the importance of his croſſing the mountains with the army, and I am still perfuaded, that if he could have done fo, fuch miftakes would not have been fo numerous.

The agonizing diftrefs of thofe citizens and their families, who were made the victims of, perhaps, private refentments, on this occafion, can be more eafily concieved than expreffed. The confternation of others, when they oblerved the innocent, thofe who had figned the amnefty, witneffes and criminals, treated with fuch undiftinguifhing feverity, was inexpreffible. They juftly apprehended, that no man was fafe, let his conduct have been ever fo innocent, or his affurance of protection from government ever fo great, if thofe who influenced the judiciary had enmity againft them.

I have already ftated that many of them had figned the amnefty, others had refufed to fign from the pride of innocence, or an averfion to an implied acknowledgement of guilt. A number of them were men of unimpeachable behaviour through the whole period of the infurrection. Though there had been a good deal of heat and irritation among the moft ignorant clafs of people at Pittfburgh, yet there was no higher crime committed, even by them, than erecting a liberty pole, but a proportion of the prifoners were not of that clafs, one of them was a refpectable and well behaved magiftrate of the Town.

A captain, with a detachment of the army who took a number of prifoners in the fouthern parts of Wafhington, is afferted to have driven the prifoners under his care, like cattle at a trot, through muddy roads, and through creeks up to their middle in water, and to have empounded them in a wet ftable at night, and otherwife to have maltreated and infulted them ; though this fact has been confidently afferted, and never contradicted, yet not having vouchers for it before me, I fhall pafs it over without being more particular.

The greateft outrage, however, againft humanity and decency was committed by general White in the Mingo-Creek fettlement.

It is faid that he had been folicitous to have the command of the New-Jerfey militia on the weftern expedition, but that from an apprehenfion of the peculiarity of his temper rendering him unfit for fuch a truft, arrangements were made that prevented him from attaining that rank; but being determined to be employed in the expedition, and holding the rank of brigadier general in the militia, he marched to Carlifle with the light-horfe volunteers and after a part of them were incorporated with the legion, he continued to command the Jerfey light-horfe until the return of the army ; when governor Howell taking the horfe, all but a very fmall corps, which he left with general White, he gladly accepted of the charge of taking down the prifoners, after that truft had been folicitioufly declined by others. Governor Howell returned with the horfe by the way of Northumberland, and behaved in fuch a manner as to do honour to himfelf, and the corps he commanded, both in the weftern country and on the return. Though there feemed to be a general conviction, that general White was not poffeffed of fufficient difcretion to be intrufted with the delicate charge of arrefting prifoners, yet by fome means, I never could learn, from any officer of whom I have had an opportunity of enquiring, how, he was intrufted to fuperintend the taking of prifoners in Mingo Creek fettlement, on the 13th of November, before mentioned, which, from his conduct, more than that of any other officers in that country, was known by the name of the *dreadful night.* I fhall ftate his conduct, on that occafion, nearly in the words, by which it is exprefled in a voucher now before me.

On Thurfday, the 13th November, there were about forty perfons brought to Parkifon's houfe by order of general White; he directed to put the damned rafcals in the cellar, to tie them back to back, to make a fire for the guard, but to put the prifoners back to the farther end of the cellar, and to give them neither victuals nor drink. The cellar was wet and muddy, and the night cold; the cellar extended the whole length; under a large new log houfe, which was neither floored, nor the openings between the logs daubed. They were kept there until Saturday morning, and then marched to the town of Wafhington. On the march, one of the prifoners who was fubject to convulfions, fell into a fit; but when fome of the troop told general White of his fituation, he ordered them to tie the damned rafcal to a horfe's tail, and drag him along with them, for he had only feigned having the fits. Some of his fellow prifoners, however, who had a horfe, difmounted, and let the poor man ride: he had another fit before he reached Wafhington. This march was about twelve miles. The poor man, who had the fits, had been in the American fervice, during almoft the whole of the war with Great Britain.

Having heard much about this inhuman bufinefs, and having occafion laft fummer to go to Wafhington, I travelled that road for the firft time that I had ever been in that fettlement, and lodged a night at the place. The plantation is the property of Benjamin Parkifon, but rented by him to a Mr. Stockdale, who keeps tavern at it, and who feems to be a decent man, and one againft whom there was no charge. He not only confirmed what I have ftated above, but added a variety of other particulars equally fhocking. Stockdale was forbid on the peril of his life to adminifter any comfort to his neighbours, though they were perifhing with cold and famifhing with hunger. The general treated the prifoners, as they arrived, with the moft infulting and abufive language, caufing them all to be tied back to back, except one man, who held a refpeclable rank, and who however was faid to be one of the moft guilty in his cuftody. One of the neareft neighbours, who had a child at the point of dying, and obferving that they were bringing in the whole neighbourhood prifoners, without regard to guilt or innocence, went and gave himfelf up to general White, expecting that as he was confcious there was no charge againft him, he would be permitted to return to his family on giving bail, but he alfo was inhumanly thrown into the cellar, tied with the reft, and refufed the privilege of feeing his dying child; nor was he permitted to attend its funeral, until after many entreaties he obtained that liberty, accompanied with the moft horrid oaths and imprecations.

The moft of thefe prifoners were found to be innocent men and were liberated. There were but, three fent to Philadelphia for trial ; one of them after having been difmiffed at Pittfburgh, and perhaps having taken a hearty grog, through joy at regaining his liberty expreffed himfelf unbecomingly to fome of the light horfe men. He was afterwards purfued near thirty miles, and taken to Philadelphia, but there was no caufe of action found againft him at the court. He had ferved with approbation in the army during the war ; his name was Samuel Noy.

Whether general White had a lift given him by the judiciary or not, I have not been informed, but he certainly had no orders to torture them with hunger, cold, and infults. Capt. Dunlap had a difcrimination made in his orders between witneffes and fuppofed criminals, and treated them all with humanity, and had them comfortably lodged, and provided with victuals and drink, previous to his taking refreshments himfelf. By the orders given to general Irwin, he was obliged to take and treat all as criminals, but he did not infult any of them himfelf, nor permit them to be infulted by others in his hearing, and he provided for them as well as the camp would permit, and that being a very uncomfortable fituation, he had them removed from it as foon as he could. That they were innocent perfons, had fheltered themfelves under the faith of government, or were only called as witneffes, was not known to the general, till it was difcovered in the refult ; but general White was himfelf the leading or perhaps the only man; of his corps, who infulted the prifoners with the moft approbrious language, and pu nifhed them in the moft fhocking manner, fhort of inflicting death. It is an approved maxim, that every man fhould be treated as innocent till found guilty. An adherence to that falutary maxim was never more neceffary than on this occafion, for the prefumption was that every man who was confcious of guilt had either figned the amnefty or fled, having had fo favourable an opportunity to provide for their fafety by flight, and in the iffue it became evident that they had availed themfelves of one or other of thofe modes of efcape, with very few exceptions. This was in fact the cafe with moft of thofe taken by general White, and of all that were taken by the different parties, on that *dreadful night*, as it is ftill called. Only eighteen were fent to Philadelphia, and none of thefe were convicted on trial. Two or three of them, however, might probably have been found guilty on a charge of mifdemeanour, but the charge on which they were tried being *treafon*, two witneffes were neceffary to prove the fame fact, and this requifition could not be complied with.

When the facts had been fully examined in the court, it was the opinion of fome of the moft able lawyers that there was no treafon in the cafe. Though as it happened that they were not convicted, the charge of treafon was moft favourable to the prifoners that had been guilty of mifdemeanours.

As the army returned through Weftmoreland, two prifoners were taken in the fouthern extremity of that county, and one in the neighbouring parts of Fayette county. They were taken to Philadelphia, the laft had been in Kentucky during the infurrection, and did not return till after the riots had ceafed. Ifaac Meafon, a judge of Fayette county, followed judge Peters near forty miles into Bedford county, and offered himself and judge Wells of Bedford county, both of them acknowledged friends of government, as bail for the prisoner, but was absolutely refused. As Mr. Meafon knew that the prisoner was guilty of no crime, which evidently appeared to be the cafe by no bill being found against him on his trial, he and Mr. Wells complain of the judge for not admitting him to bail on their application. Judge Peters, being well known to be a man of feeling and humanity, his conduct in this and several other instances can only be accounted for from his apprehenfion, that it was necessary that a considerable number of prisoners should be brought down, in order to prevent the inflammatory part of the army from committing outrages at leaving the country. His mind was tortured at being obliged to bring down fo many prisoners, and his peace was disturbed by being teafed for difmiffing fuch numbers of them.

One of the two prisoners taken from Weftmoreland was found guilty of letting fire to the houfe of Wells, the collector, and condemned to be hanged ; but was afterwards reprieved, and then pardoned by the Prefident of the United States. He is a very ignorant man, faid to be of an outrageous temper, and fubject to occafional fits of infanity. The principal witnefs against him was a perfon, who is faid to have been the principal leader in the riot, but he was pardoned by the commander in chief ; the other was a young man, who had come lately from Maryland, and had no family or friends in the country. No bill was found against him on trial.

I have mentioned before, that four prisoners were sent from Bedford, as the army advanced; one of them, Herman Husbands, was a very old man, extensively known on account of some singularities in his character. After suffering four months imprisonment, no cause of action was found against him, but though he was liberated, with others by the court, his constitution had received such a shock that he died before he left the city. Another of them, Mr. Filson, who kept a large store thirty miles above Bedford, was refused to be admitted to bail, though this favour was warmly solicited by several reputable merchants in Philadelpia. The prosecution against him was conducted with unusal severity; being first acquitted on a charge of treason, he was tried for a misdemeanour, and in this the verdict also was, *not guilty*. He is now a member of assembly for Bedford county.

Of the two others taken near Bedford, one was an old inoffensive German, named Wisegarver; he was taken to Philadelphia, and after being imprisoned four months he was admitted to bail, and no bill was found against him at court. The other, whose name is Lucas, had been a sergeant in the army in the time of the war, and was well known at the time of the revolt of the Pennsylvania line; and though he was one of the leaders of that revolt, yet in that situation he rendered such essential services to the public as to have a special reward assigned to him. After near four months imprisonment, he was admitted to bail on the intercession of a general officer, who was well acquainted with his services. When he attended the court to stand his trial nothing was found against him. He has a numerous family of small children, and like too many, who ferved in the late war, he is poor.

No crimes had been committed in Bedford county of a more outrageous nature, than erecting some liberty poles, except an attempt on Webster, collector of excise; this, however, being conducted with greater mildness than other instances of the kind, and he having provoked it by transgressing the law himself, no person was profecuted for it. The greatest number of those concerned were from Weftmoreland. Hufbands and Filfon had attended the firft meeting at Parkifon's ferry; as no riots had taken place in the fettlement in which they lived, this was probably conftrued to indicate a bad defign, but they did not propofe any thing at the meeting that was offenfive. Wifegarver and Lucas had only been present or affifted at erecting a liberty pole in the town of Bedford, with a mixed multitude of others. I have already mentioned the bad effect, which the erecting of liberty poles had in encouraging the infurgents, yet the act of erecting them was no furthercriminal, than the correfpondent conduct expreffed a feditious defign.

A certain John Mitchel who, with the affiftance of another perfon, had robbed the Pittfburgh mail, gave himself up to general Morgan, after the judiciary had left the country. This man's evident fimplicity induced the general to wifh him to escape, and to difcredit his being the perfon; but Mitchel infifting that he was one of the perfons who robbed the mail, the general, inftead of confining him, gave him a pafs to go to Philadelphia, thereby putting it in his power to reflect on his fituation, and make his efcape; but he went to Philadelphia, furrendered himfelf to be committed, and being found guilty on his trial, he was condemned to be hanged. This refult was unavoidable on the fact being eftablifhed; but the Prefident, with great propriety, firft reprieved for a time, and then pardoned him.

Thus an oppofition to an excife fyftem, which began with only clandeftine attacks on fome of the officers, and which, by the timely attention of thofe intrufted with the execution of the law, might eafily have been checked, the revenues fecured, the peace of the country preferved, and the credit of a republican government faved, was, by inattention or defign, treated with neglect, or tampered with in a manner, that was more cenfurable than neglect, until it produced fuch an effect on the folly and prejudices of the people in a fmall part of a diftrict, or rather a fmall part of a county, as, aided by the diftraction or wickednefs of a few others, broke fuddenly out into fuch alarming diforders as agitated the whole United States, and occafioned the levying and marching of one of the beft provided, moft formidable, and in fome refpects, the moft refpectable army that ever marched under the banners of the United States; and yet the whole of this ftupendous fcene was wound up, without any perfon being killed, except in the attack on the infpector's houfe at the commencement of the infurrection, and the two men who were, perhaps, too wantonly killed by fome of the army, before there had been an opportunity of introducing difcipline into it. Several, however, died by ficknefs, efpecially in the left wing of the army.

When the judiciary had finished the examinations, and made a selection of those who were to be sent to Philadelphia, the army returned with rapid marches to the different counties from whence they were draughted, or had turned out volunteers. The quickness of their march prevented even the most disorderly corps from injuring the settlements so much as was apprehended, though it is certain several families, near where they encamped, did sustain considerable damages, chiefly occasioned by the troops in the rear. Assurances were given by secretary Hamilton, that the damages should be paid on their presenting appraisements to Congress. The appraisements were made out, and given to the proper officers, but have not been presented to Congress, nor otherwise provided for.

_____

CHAP. XVII.

THE fituation and circumflances were not convenient for deliberate and impartial examination. The multitude of informations, and declarations of affurances, neceffary to be perufed, and the panic and embarraffinent of witneffes, who were interrogated in a manner at the point of the bayonet, many of whom were more guilty than thofe againft whom they gave teftimony, and the unavoidable confufions of a camp rendered it very difficult for the civil magiftrate to conduct the bufinefs with precifion. Such witneffes were inevitably influenced by a fenfe of their own danger, and the hopes of obtaining pardon from the commander in chief ; for the pardon from the commander was not irrevocably fecured, before the expectant had given his teftimony, and in fome inftances, fear was added to hope, to draw from the witneffes fuch teftimony, as was thought beft calculated to fecure the object they had in view. Perfons who had been ill-treated by the infurgents, and who of courfe were too much under the influence of refentment to give impartial teftimony, were alfo interrogated as witneffes. Their teftimony was doubtlefs admiffible in law, though not entitled to fuch credit, as if they had been difinterefted. In confequence of thofe untoward circumftances, it happened that in many inftances the teftimony was inconfiftent or directly contradictory. Where this was evidently the cafe, the judge fet both afide.

After a full inveftigation of the whole bufinefs it appears that a very fmall proportion of thofe who had been guilty fuffered imprifonment. Thofe who had been moft influential in oppofition to the laws, had either complied with the terms of the commiffioners, or, had fled when they found the army was approaching. Indeed many had fled who were guilty of no crime, but were fo ill informed as to apprehend that their declining to fign the declaration of affurances would be conftrued into one. No attempt having been made to arreft or difturb any perfon all the time the army lay in the country, till it was apparently preparing to return, and the few that had been apprehended being difmiffed, emboldened fome who had fled or concealed themfelves to return, and appear in public again, no doubt concluding that the affurances they had figned after the day appointed by the commiffioners had been accepted as evidence of their repentance. This circumftance put many in the way of being taken, who would have efcaped if the orders had been iffued foon after the arrival of the army, but withal, there was not a fingle perfon fent to Philadelphia, who had been an influential leader in any of the outrages ; feveral however were in cuftody and difmiffed, who are declared to have been much more guilty than moft of thofe that were detained I have already faid that feveral were taken down prifoners who were innocent, and fome of them meritorious. Some circumftances that influenced this irregular diftribution of juftice naturally arofe from the fituation of the bufinefs ; others will be accounted for in the fequel.

The commander in chief was authorized to exonerate thofe who gave fuch evidences of their repentance as were fatisfactory to himfelf, as well as thofe who had agreed to the terms propofed by the commiffioners ; confequently thofe who had the greateft addrefs or the moft influential friends would of courfe obtain an amnefty, whilft the bafhful, the ignorant, and the friendlefs were neceffarily left to be the fubjects for atonement. In this cafe the interceffion of the excife officers who were the parties injured could not fail of fuccefs ; I wifh I could fay that their private refentments had not been influential alfo. Thefe evils arofe naturally out of the ftate of things. There are no complaints of governor Lee having been inexorable or inhumane, but he had no rule to direct his judgment as to the manifeftations of repentance, but the reprefentations of thofe in whom he had confidence, and thofe reprefentations were often unavoidably influenced by favouritifm or refentment.

Comparatively few indeed were tranfported to Philadelphia for trial, and it was a hardfhip that moft

of thefe few were innocent, and that others were difmiffed who had been more influential in the riots
than any of thofe who were brought to trial. I do
not complain that many guilty perfons were pardoned,
nor do I call in queftion their repentance. I believe
there were few, if any, but what had given every evidence of repentance that was required before the army
croffed the mountains, unlefs giving teftimony liberally againft others was fometimes confidered as an
evidence of repentance.

From thefe circumftances it is evident that the
judge of the diftrict had an arduous tafk to perform.
The felection of proper characters for making atonement was rendered difficult by the exercife of the pardoning power of the commander, which in numerous
inftances interfered with the opinion of the judge.
The commander not being bound by ftrict rules of
law in the exercife of his difcretion, and the judge,
and attorney, conceiving that they were authorifed only to act according to fuch rules, contributed to the
refult I have mentioned ; but there were other caufes.

When fo great a number of thofe who had been
taken prifoners by the detachments were releafed, many of the army became clamorous againft the judge,
and complained of having marched fo far, fuffered fo
many hardfhips, and taken fo many prifoners, and that
after all, thefe prifoners were likely to he difmiffed
without atonements being made ; on the difcovery of fo
much hot blood in the army, the judge became afraid
that it might mutiny, and take indifcriminate vengeance
on the country, and juftly confidered fuch an event to
be the greateft of all poffible evils, not only to the

western counties, but to the government of the United States. In this dilemma he thought it was advisable to take down a greater number of prisoners than he otherwise would, and consequently conceived himself under the necessity of taking some who were innocent, or at least such as against whom there were no strong presumptions of guilt, trusting that the necessity of the case would justify the measure. He also considered himself as justified in law in committing such as had been present at, or members of, such meetings, as might from any special circumstances be deemed treasonable or seditious, and this construction was given not only to the riotous assemblies which committed outrages, and such as erected liberty poles, but even to the Parkison's meetings, &c.; for though the intention, of the great majority of those who were members of those meetings was to restore order, and though they had in every instance been considerably successful, and were in the issue completely so, yet the first appointment, as it grew out of the attack on the house of the Inspector, was considered as criminal, and such as were most influential in making that appointment had endeavoured at the first Parkison's meeting to promote measures for consolidating the opposition to government, supported by these reasons. The district attorney in the charge, which he exhibited at Philadelphia against the prisoners, exhibited the attendance on these meetings among the acts of treason which had been committed.

This charge of treason against the meetings at Parkison's, was possibly calculated to be an apology for having brought down prisoners, against whom no other offence was alleged. It was acknowledged by the district judge and attorney, that a large proportion of those, who not only attended at these meetings, but even at the Braddock's field rendezvous, which undoubtedly assumed the appearances of an insurrection, were not only innocent, but meritorious persons, and that it was not the assisting at those meetings, but the conduct when there, that should determine the criminality of the prisoners. If, by attending those meetings, a person became involved in criminality, the most decisive and useful patriots in the western country would have been liable to prosecution, as well as the most outrageous, but this rule of conduct was only pursued to a small extent as to numbers, and perhaps would not have been pursued at all, but in complacence to the inflammatory part of the army.

I know this circumstance is denied by a number who were in the army, and had a good opportunity of being acquainted with its prevailing temper; but it is suggested by the judge, and it may be reasonably admitted that a few inflammatory characters teasing the magistrate, and not only discovering their own ungovernable temper, but asserting that this temper was general in the army, was fully sufficient to give ground for these apprehensions. I have had occasion several times to mention, that a few noisy and restless spirits have it in their power, on particular occasions, for a time, to fix the character of the whole mass of either an army or a country; and this was undoubtedly the case with the army on this occasion. The sentiments of those, who were virtuous enough not to attempt to influence the decisions of the magistrate, were not known, as they made no noife, while the inflammatory few, not only were fo impertinent, as indirectly to interfere with the decifions, but in fome inftances, with the examinations. There was but one general officer, who difcovered a difpofition to promote diforders, and his influence was fmall.

I have faid that fome were brought prifoners to Philadelphia, againft whom there was no caufe of action, and others, without having been examined. I have already affigned the reafons why fome were brought who were innocent. That any were brought without examination arofe in part from other caufes. Owing to the hurry and confufion of the camp, the judge could not attend to the examination of them all himfelf; fometimes the fecretary of the treafury examined, and decided himfelf; on other occafions, the prifoners were examined by the diftrict attorney, or by fome of the ftate judges. Thus through the multitude of examiners, fome were committed without being examined at all. It has been alfo fuggefted that fome perfons were fent down in confequence of the predetermination of the fecretary of the treafury; inftances might be given if it was neceffary, and fome will be offered in the fequel.

CHAP. XVIII.

PERHAPS the moſt myſterious circumſtance attending the weſtern expedicion, was the character ſuſtained by the ſecretary of the treaſury. Frequent enquiries have been made from me, and I have often enquired of others, what ſtation he held, to which his reſponſibility was attached, but without any ſatisfactory anſwers. But as it was generally believed that he gave the ſupreme direction to the meaſures that were purſued, and as the praiſe of all that was laudable, and the blame of what was cenſurable, has been by a kind of tacit conſent aſcribed to him, it will, for want of better ſources of information, be neceſſary to examine ſuch inſtances of his paramount influence, in the previous plans and ſubſequent conduct of the. expedition, as have tranſpired.

That he was the reſponſible head of the revenue department, and had the direction of the meaſures relative to the execution of the excife law, is evident from the powers vefted in him by law for that purpofe. That he originated not only the excife fyftem, and the other revenue laws, which were enacted by Congrefs, previous to the infurrection, and the arrangements for carrying them into execution, is evident from the journals of Congrefs; and his own reports to the Houfe of Reprefentatives. The manner in which the coercive part of the excife law was executed, or rather, in which the execution of it was neglected, and the influence which that neglect had in promoting the oppofition to the law, which finally burft forth into an infurrection, has been ftated in Chap. VI.

That a government could never be confidered as eftablifhed, till its power was put to the teft by a trial of its military force, is a fentiment that has been often afcribed to him, and never that I heard of contradicted; and that in perfect correfpondence with their principle, he even in the cabinet expreffed his forrow that the town of Pittfburgh had not been burned by thofe who rendezvoufed at Braddock's field, that fo a trial of the military force of the government might have been rendered the more neceffary and juftifiable, has been afferted by authority that cannot be reafonably doubted. This affertion, which leaves no doubt of the principle from which it proceeded, perfectly coincides with the manner in which the excife law was executed in the weftern counties, and fully accounts for not holding fpecial feffions of the court nearer the places where the crimes were committed, after a law had been made for that purpofe, and may alfo without any forced induction account for iffuing the proceffes cut of the diftrict court fo early in the winter. When it was known that a law was about to be paffed to veft the ftate courts with powers for that purpofe, and alfo for delaying the execution of the procefs, till fo long after the ftate courts were competent to decide on the cafe, and until the throng of harveft, which is confeffedly the moft inconvenient feafon in the year for farmers to attend at a diftance of above 300 miles, and which, from other circumftances, was the moft likely to excite refiftance. It is worthy of remark that when the diftillers of Fayette county, without delay, fent to enter their appearance at Philadelphia, the writs were found to be erroneous, and therefore null. What a pity it was, that this had not been difcovered before they had been made the inftrument of promoting an infurrection.

If all thefe circumftances happened through inattention, that inattention was highly culpable ; if they were the refult of cool defign, the connection of all the parts of the plan, and its eventual fuccefs, while they afford a ftriking evidence of dexterity and addrefs, reprefent the morality of the conductor in a very queftionable point of view. The exertions made by fome of his friends in the Houfe of Reprefentatives, about the fame time, in the winter in which the irregular proceffes were iffued, which in the following harveft produced the infurrection, to have a law paffed for raifing an army of 25,000 men, and the evident indignation with which that plan was rejected by a decided majority of the Houfe, is well remembered. While this meafure difcovers a perfect correfpondence with the general conduct which led to the infurrection,

E e

the rejection of it gave a testimony that the Representatives would not employ an army without a sufficient
cause.   The burning of Pittsburgh, if it had happened, would have afforded an argument for such an army
as had been urged the preceding winter.

That when the outrages against the excise officers
came to a violent height, the secretary should report to
the President on the subject, was to have been expected, and that, when this report was to be published in
the newspapers, as an address to the citizens, to convince them of the necessity of turning out in support
of the government and laws, that the facts should have
been represented with pretty high colouring, was not
at all surprising, but that that conduct which was lawful should have been represented as criminal, and that
charges should have been insinuated against the whole
people of the western counties which were not founded in fact, could not be justified on any honest principle.   These remarks will be better understood when
I come to examine some parts of the report itself.

How the important duties and legal arrangements
of the treasury could admit of the head of the department to attend on the western expedition to its fur-
thest destination, is no part of my enquiry.   While
the President was with the different wings of the army,
the secretary accompanied him, and appeared to act as
his official secretary.   When I was at Carlisle, he
took a part in the conversations between the President
and the commissioners from the western counties, and
behaved with propriety in them ; he signed officially
the President's instructions to the commander in chief
of the army.

When the Prefident returned to Philadelphia, the fecretary of the treafury remained, and marched with the right wing of the army, and on the march, and at the different encampments, in the Weftern country, was extremely attentive to the wants of the army, and was looked up to by many in it, as fomething more than even the commander in chief. The fuperb marque, which he accupied, and which was by far more extenfive and elegant than that of the commander in chief on that expedition, or as the officers fay, in the war with Great Britain, contributed to draw the attention of the army and of the country people to him, as a man of more than common authority.

In what character he affumed this fuperior ftate and influence, or to what extent he carried his authority, I have not been informed. It is well known, however, that orders were fometimes iffued by him, and that he confidered no officer in the army, as beyond his controul, though much of this authority was probably exercifed through the inftrumentality of others; fome pretty high inftances of this were not concealed. It is well known, that by his own authority, he wrote a fevere reprimand for fuppofed mifconduct to the commander in chief of the right wing of the army, in confequence of which, that officer was treated in a manner not becoming his rank; but it is of no importance to trace the character he affumed, or the authority he exercifed, in the army; for to him has been afcribed, by fome in the army, the meafure of difcipline that was preferved in it, and the regularity of the fupplies they received; though this was undoubtedly afcribing too much to him, as a num-

ber of valuable officers occupied the various ftations in
the army. There is no doubt, however, but his attention and induftry, were of great fervice. It is the
fecretary's connection, however, with the judiciary, that
is of the greateft importance to examine. In this he
was generally taken, or perhaps miftaken to be, the
principal director. To mention all the inftances of
the authority he exercifed as a civil magiftrate, would
lead me beyond the intended compafs of this work; a
few inftances, fhall only be felected.

The commander in chief had his quarters for fome
time at the houfe of major Powers, between Youghiogany and Monongahela rivers, and the quarters of
the judiciary were at the next plantation. Major Powers had not only behaved well through the whole of the
troubles, but had been zealoufly employed in endeavouring to reftore order from an early period, till it
was finally eftablifhed. He had been a member of feveral meetings for that purpofe, and was one of the
committee of twelve who fettled the terms of amnefty
with the commiffioners at Pittfburgh, and took an active lead in his neighbourhood, in procuring a compliance with thofe terms, his fervices were acknowledged
while head quarters were at his houfe, and he was paid
a larger fum than he demanded for his trouble and expences.

After the judiciary and part of the army had gone to
the town of Wafhington, major Powers was invited
by a polite letter, to wait on the fecretary at that place,
which was above thirty miles diftant. When he arrived the fecretary examined him about the conduct
of certain characters, with fome of whom he was not

even acquainted, but particularly about the conduct of Mr. Gallatin, at the meeting at Parkison's ferry, &c. On major Powers not anfwering to his fatisfaction, he complained of the difficulty of obtaining information, and advifed major Powers to retire an hour, to refrefh his memory, in order to be re-examined, and fpoke to an officer prefent to conduct major Powers into another chamber; in all this, the fecretary appeared to treat him politely, but he was not a little furprifed when he found himfelf thruft into a room among other prifoners, and there confined, under the point of the bayonet. This he thought an odd fituation for cool recollection, if he had needed any. At the time appointed he was taken again into the prefence of the fecretary, who afked him if he had recollected himfelf fo far as to give more fatisfactory information; on being anfwered that he had nothing further to recollect, having already related all he knew, the fecretary then fuddenly afluming all his terrors, told major Powers that he was furprifed at him, that having the character of an honeft man, he would not tell the truth, afferting, that he had already proofs fufficient of the truth of what he knew he could teftify, if he would. After fome further infulting language and threats, major Powers was committed clofe prifoner under a military guard; and though the moft unexceptionable bail was offered for permiffion to go to his family, it was refufed, and he was marched under a military guard to Pittfburgh, and there detained till the eighth day after he was taken into cuftody. The fecretary being gone, the judge fent for major Powers, and when he was brought into his prefence, invited him politely to fit down, affuring him that he had no charge at all againſt him.

It will appear in various other inſtances, that it was uſual with the ſecretary to aſſert to thoſe whom he was examining, that he was poſſeſſed of ſufficient proofs already of the facts to which he endeavoured to extort teſtimony. The ſpring following, major Powers was much diſpoſed to bring an action againſt the late ſecretary, for the treatment he had received. He thought this neceſſary for the vindication of the government, as well as to obtain ſatisfaction to himſelf, but finding that he would be obliged to go to New-York to proſecute, on the advice of his friends he relinquiſhed the deſign.

John Hamilton of Waſhington is high ſheriff of that county, and colonel of a regiment of militia, in the Mingo-Creek ſettlement; though a number of this regiment were known to have had an active hand in the attack on the inſpector's houſe, and were in fact conſidered as the greateſt promoters of the inſurrection, yet he not only kept himſelf free from thoſe outrages, but endeavoured, as ſoon as he heard of the deſign, to prevent the rendezvous at Braddock's field. It was he who informed Bradford that the arms and ammunition in the garriſon at Pittſburgh were deſigned for general Scot's expedition againſt the Indians, and with the aſſiſtance of ſome others perſuaded him to countermand the orders, and procured his promiſe to prevent the march. (See Chap. VIII.)

When he could not prevent the march to Braddock's field, he put himſelf at the head of his regiment, and was very inſtrumental in preventing further outtages from being committed. At the court that was held for the county of Wahington, a short time after the commissioners left the country, he proposed to take any twenty of the leading insurgents, and lodge them in the county jail, if writs were issued for that purpose, but it was not thought adviseable to issue the writs, until it should be known what measures the commissioners would recommend to the President; and until the inflammation would be more effectually cooled down. The sheriff however, to give testimony that he could have accomplished what he proposed, executed every writ of *cap as* that he had in his hands without difficulty. He attended all the meetings for restoring order with a view to prevent outrages. His being a friend to order, and living where he did, merited higher approbation, than if he had resided where the citizens generally were less disposed to riot.

Yet it has been asserted, that this man was by the predetermination of the secretary of the treasury doomed to be sacrificed as an atonement; to justify this determination by motives of humanity, the secretary suggested that colonel Hamilton had no family to lament his loss; and as he understood he was a man of considerable influence in the country, he did not doubt but though it might be difficult to find proofs against him, he was as guilty as any of them.

Colonel Hamilton was informed by a friend of designs against him time enough to make his escape, but conscious of his innocence he preferred travelling above thirty miles to where the judiciary then was, and presenting himself to Judge Peters informed him that

he had heard there was a charge againſt him, and requeſted to have it examined. The judge ſaid he was
then too much engaged, but would call on him pre-
ſently ; that day, however, paſſed, till evening, when
major Lenox, the marſhal, in the moſt delicate manner
he could, told him he muſt put him under guard, but
afterwards diſpen´ed with arreſting him, and only took
his promiſe that he would not depart till judge Peters
would converſe with him ; but the next day the marſhal informed him that he had ſpecial orders to put him
under guard, which he did accordingly, though with
evident regret. The ſheriff here remarks that major
Lenox treated him with as much friendſhip and politeneſs as the nature of the caſe could poſſibly admit,
and let me add that that officer's politeneſs is generally
well ſpoken of.

On the third day after he demanded an examination,
and the ſecond after he had been put under guard, he
was ſent back to Waſhington town, from whence he
had come, in cuſtody of a ſmall party of horſe. The
judiciary having arrived at Waſhington, the ſheriff
applied to judge Peters again to have his caſe examined,
who told him he would in half an hour, but on the
ninth day after he firſt applied to the judge, he was ſent
cloſe priſoner to Pittſburgh, and from thence to Philadelphia, paraded through the ſtreets with an igno-
minous badge in his hat, and thrown into the cells
without his caſe having ever been examined. After
an impriſonment of near two months and a half, he
had his caſe brought before the ſupreme court on a
writ of *habeas corpus*, and on examination nothing
being found againſt him, he was admitted to bail. At

the circuit court, held in Philadelphia, in June following, a bill for misprison of treason was sent to the grand jury against him; but every witness that was sworn testified largely in his favour. There was not even a suspicious circumstance found against him.

Thus a man, who was at the time sheriff of the county, and a colonel of militia, and who, in a part of the country, and in circumstances where temporizing might have been excuseable, was not only clear of any charge, but had merit; was selected by the secretary for a victim, and without being examined, illegally taken from the exercise of an office, at that time of importance to the peace of the country, and dragged down to Philadelphia in the winter, paraded in a barbarous manner through the streets, thrown for some time into the cells, and though, after a long confinement admitted to bail, yet obliged to attend again at Philadelphia to stand a trial apparently because the secretary of the treasury had determined on his destruction. It is probable, that it was only motives of humanity that operated to prevent major Powers from being also sent to Philadelphia, for he has a wife and family, and we are informed that the sheriff of Washington, having no family to lament after him, was assigned by the secretary as one reason why he was selected as an object of atonement.

It is not easy to assign probable reasons for selecting these two men as objects of vengeance. They had both been friends of order during the continuance of the disturbances, though they were naturally quiet, and never had distinguished themselves in political contests, nor taken any lead in the discussion of pub-

F f

lic meafures. Perhaps the principal motive for treating
major Powers with fuch unjuftifiable feverity, was to
extort teftimony from him, and to teach others what
they might expect, if they did not give fuch teftimony
againft certain characters, as the fecretary required.
As colonel Hamilton was the fheriff of the county,
and colonel of the battalion, where the infurrection
originated, his rank and the relation he ftood in to that
county, were probably the reafons of his being felected.

My firft perfonal acquaintance with either Powers
or Hamilton, was at the meetings for reftoring order,
on which occafion their conduct was that of good
citizens, and fuch as entitled them to my efteem.
Hamilton was not a member of any of them, more
than myfelf.   I was much furprifed, when I faw him
in Philadelphia gaol, but efpecially when I found
that he had been committed without charge or examination.

.When he was admitted to bail, he told me he was
about to put a ftatement of his cafe in the newfpapers,
but I advifed him not to do it at that time, alleging
that with the means that were ufed to procure teftimony againft him, it was probable, that fome plaufible
charge might be produced on the trial, and that as
fome others were committed without examination, who
were probably equally innocent, it was beft to publifh
nothing till the final refult of the trials would be known.
This narrative is taken from colonel Hamilton's own
ftatement of the cafe, and from my own knowledge.

I have ftated, that undue influence was ufed to procure teftimony againft certain individuals, and given an

inftance of it in the cafe of major Powers; I will add another inftance in relation to fheriff Hamilton.

During the time fheriff Hamilton, was waiting to have his cafe examined, and before he was put into clofe confinement, a certain John Baldwin was under examination. He was interrogated alternately, by fecretary Hamilton, judge Peters, the diftrict attorney, the infpector, and Mr. Vaughan, a light horfe man, from Philadelphia; the two laft of whom treated him with the greateft indecorum. In the courfe of the examination, every means were ufed to induce him to teftify againft the fheriff. Baldwin had candidly informed them of himfelf being one of the committee at the burning of Nevil's houfe, and of the perfons concerned in that riot, &c. and affured them that the fheriff was not concerned in the bufinefs. He was then urged to teftify that the fheriff had notified his regiment, to affift at that riot, &c. and when he refufed to give teftimony to that purpofe, becaufe it was not true, he was infulted, and told that he equivocated, and evaded fwearing the truth, and was affured that by his conduct, he had forfeited the benefit of the amnefty to which he was otherwife intitled, and alfo his life and property, in not teftifying to what they demanded of him (and of which, he adds, he was confcious it was not true,) and told that he could only fave himfelf by giving fuch teftimony.

David Hamilton and others were treated in much the fame manner, in order to extort teftimony againft fheriff Hamilton, and though no teftimony could, even by thefe means, be extorted, yet this innocent man was fubjected to the infults and fufferings already related.

I have been informed of various other cafes, wherein improper methods were ufed, to influence witneffes, but as a recital of them would fwell thefe fheets to an improper length, I fhall decline mentioning them at prefent, and conclude this chapter with an extract from Mr. Brackenridge's Incidents, page 78.

"In collecting evidence againft me, there was no pains fpared——In the examination of witneffes, when brought forward, there was no boot nor other inftrument of torture in the hands of the examiners ; but there was certainly every addrefs to the fears of individuals, to extract from them an acknowledgment of fomething faid or done by me. I am unwilling to mark any thing as contrary to my ideas of propriety, but declaring in all, I have feen or heard, I have nothing elfe to mark, I take the liberty of ftating as what was confidered by me as improper, *viz.* the fuggeftion that the witneffes in the courfe of the examination, that the enjoyment of the amnefty which they claimed, depended on the candour with which they gave teftimony againft others."

In page 75, the fecretary lays down his pen and interrupts Mr. Brackenridge, while he is proceeding in his teftimony, and fays, "I obferve one leading trait in your account, a difpofition to excufe the principal actors, and before we go further, I muft be candid and inform you, of the delicate fituation in which you ftand; *you are not within the amn fty ; you have not figned upon the day ;* a thing we did not know, till we came on this ground, I mean the Weftern country, and though the government may not be difpofed to act rigorcufly yet it has you in its power, and it will depend on the candour of your account, what your fate will be."

"Mr. Brackenridge anfwers. *I am not within the amnefly*, and am fenfible of the extent of the power of the government; but were the narrative to begin again, I would not change a fingle word."

Mr. Brakenridge had conducted with fuch addrefs, in a fituation which rendered it neceffary for him to temporize, that he knew he was in no danger from the ufual mode of procefs, but he alfo knew, that the power of the government, with which he was threatened, conveyed another idea. He had obferved, the innocent and the guilty, indifcrimately, in many inftances, fubjected to unufual fufferings and infults, by the power of government, as exercifed by the fecretary. If fuch powerful addreffes were made to the hopes and fears of Mr. Brickenridge, who from his profeffion was able to judge of his own fituation, what may we not expect was done with fuch ignorant people, as did not know what part of their conduct or expreffions might be deemed criminal. It is obfervable, that though the *fubpœna* for Mr. Brackenridge, came from judge Peters, yet the examination was conducted, and the terrors, &c. difpenfed by the fecretary.

———————————

CHAP. XIX.

HAVING in the tranfactions already related, introduced my own agency, as feldom as the nature of the cafe would admit, I expect the reader will not be offended at finding what I did, or fuffered, brought more frequently into view in what remains of the work, efpecially in the two fucceeding chapters. I wifh indeed that this part of it had been writen by another hand, for I do not know a more difagreeable fubject to write on, than one which involves perfonal confiderations; yet being convinced that I could not have done juflice to the general fubject, if I had kept myfelf altogether out of view, I will make no further apology, but fubmit it to the decifion of the public, whether *there is, or is not a caufe.*

When colonel Morton, Mr. Redick, and myfelf, in the character of commiffioners, waited on the fecretary, then in company with governor Mifflin,

at Bonnet's camp, he treated me with decency, and
apparent friendſhip, and when I told him, that ſome
of the juſtices of the peace had commenced profecutions againſt offenders, before the commiſſioners had
returned to Philadelphia, and that on being informed,
that the diſtrict judge and attorney were coming up
with the army, they had been adviſed to deſiſt till they
would arrive, he approved of adviſing them to deſiſt,
and adviſed us to requeſt ſome of the county judges
to come to the camp, as ſoon as the judge and attorney
ſhould arrive, (they were with the rear of that wing)
and that ſome plan would be ſettled with them, for
diſtributing the profecutions. At parting I told him,
I deſigned to ſtart for Philadelphia, in about eight or
ten days. I gave the ſame information to General Lee
at parting.

My reaſon for being particular in mentioning the
time, when I intended to leave the country was, that
it might not be ſaid, that I went out of the way to avoid
a ſcrutiny of my conduct, and my reaſon for ſtaying ſo
long, was to give a full opportunity for it; though I
was conſcious of having merited approbation, I ſuſpected the ſecretary was more diſpoſed to find fault. I
had ſeen his report to the Preſident, and obſerved the
inſidious miſrepreſentations it contained. I ought to
have attended Congreſs ſooner.

After both wings of the army had encamped in the
vicinity of Youghiogany and Monongahela rivers, two
of the judges of the court of Weſtmoreland county,
general Jack, and Mr. Baird, men of very reſpectable
characters, waited on the ſecretary and the judge, in
order to be informed what offences would be **proper**

for the state magistrates to prosecute, agreeably to the secretary's advice, which I communicated to one of them ; but instead of consulting about the distribution of the prosecutions, as was expected, they were both strictly examined as witnesses against Mr. Gallatin and myself. They were urged to testify that Mr. Gallatin had expressed himself in a treasonable manner at the first Parkison's meeting, and when they denied having heard any such expressions, the secretary asserted that he had sufficient proofs of them already ; they however persisted in asserting that he used no such expressions, that they had been very attentive to his arguments at the meeting, and they stated the substance of them, and mentioned the abilities he had displayed, and the unremitting exertions he had made, on all proper occasions, to restore order, and to convince the citizens of the necessity of submitting to the laws : That his decision, talents and perseverance, had contributed more to the restoration of order than that of, perhaps, any other person, as he had been a member of all the meetings for that purpose, and acted with decision, when several others thought it prudent in many instances to temporize or were afraid to avow their sentiments.

In the examination respecting myself, no specific fact being alleged against me, it was rather an inquisition held on my character than an examination, and the object seemed to be, to prove me to be a bad man, as well as a criminal. The questions were calculated to procure testimony, either that I alone, or in connection with Messrs. Smilie and Gallatin had originated the opposition to the excise law, excited the insurrection, were enemies to the government, wished to over-

turn it, &c. Few men in that country could have
been found, who knew my character and principles,
and the situation of the country, better than those he
now examined. They told him that the opposition
to excises was brought into the country with the settlers, many of whom inherited an averfion to them
from their fathers; that it was encreafed by their fituation ; that it was not true that I had promoted the oppofition in that country ; that I had told in their
hearing before there was any ground to apprehend
an infurrection, that the excife law could not, nor
would not, be repealed foon, and figned fatisfactory
reafons for that opinion ; that I had faid it was my
wifh that the people would fubmit to it, that in their
doing fo their petitions for fuch amendments as would
render its preffure more tolerable, would have more
weight with congrefs, and the repeal of it in due time
would the more eafily be procured. They informed
him alfo of the exertions I had made, and the arguments
I had ufed, during the infurrection, to reftore order and
promote fubmiffion to the laws.

When judge Baird related fome of the arguments
which he had heard me exprefs on one or other of thefe
occafions, judge Peters was pleafed to fay, that they
were fome of the beft he had ever heard on that fubject,
and that he could freely forgive me if I had done wrong,.
on account of having ufed them, but fecretary Hamilton
replied that he would never forgive me, becaufe I
had told or wrote lies about him.

I am obliged to judge Peters for his generofity. I
know the humanity of his nature. His difpofition to forgive is not the lefs valuable, that I ftood in no need of its

G g

exertions. I fhall fay nothing further, at this time, of the
fecretary's objecting to forgivenefs, or the fenfibility
evident in his manner of doing it, farther than that
it was not the intention of the conftitution in vefting
a Prefident of the United States with authority to call
out the militia to fupport the laws, fupprefs infurrecti-
ons, &c. nor of Congrefs in directing the mode in
which the militia fhould be called out, nor, I will add,
was it the intention of the Prefident in calling out fo
refpectable an army, or the judge of the fupreme court
in granting the certificate required by law for that purpofe, or of fo many American citizens, in making fuch
facrifices, to enable a dependant fecretary to fatiate his
unforgiving difpofition on an individual for telling or
writing lies on him, even if his affertion had not been
totally unfounded; but of this in its proper place.

In converfation with thofe gentlemen, even in
public company, he expofed himfelf to contempt,
by fpeaking of me, in a manner that difcovered a total
difregard to truth, good policy, or propriety of character. Even when he was contradicted in calling me
a bad and difhoneft man, and teftimony given of my
character having long ftood in a very different point
of view, by thofe who were intimately acquainted with
it, and whofe veracity was unimpeachable, and when
the confidence which my neighbours and others, who
were beft acquainted with me, had long repofed in
me, was given as a proof of my being an honeft man,
having a confiftent character, &c. he reluctantly admitted the force of that evidence with refpect to my private character, but afferted that I was a vain man, and
a difhoneft politician, and had a very bad heart. Mr.

Gallatin and I had been elected members of congrefs fhortly before this, and he cenfured the people feverely for electing us, and added that they would never do well, nor have any thing done properly for them, while they were reprefented by fuch men. He expreffed much furprife and indignation, at their repofing fo much confidence in foreigners, that Gallatin and I were both foreigners and therefore not to be trufted. When it was anfwered, that I had been in the country from my youth, &c. and that Mr. Gallatin had come into it very young, and had been a citizen a competent length of time, to be legally qualified for the truft, that we were both fenfible men, and had a fufficient ftake in the country, to fecure our intereft, he perfifted in faying, that we were bad hearted men and difhoneft politicians, and that I particularly had told lies on him, in a pamphlet, entitled, " Thirteen letters, by a citizen," of which he afferted I was the author. He reproved them, for not coming to congrefs themfelves, alleging that though we might as they had fuggefted, have more knowledge of public bufinefs, yet we were difhoneft and dangerous politicians.

He no doubt difcovered what was true, that the two judges were folid, fenfible men, of refpectable character, and well acquainted with public bufinefs; but how could he avoid difcovering that they and I held the fame political principles, and that if I had not held the political principles which I did, I would not have been the object of their choice. He knew that though they difapproved of the excife law in principle, yet they had done every thing which their

duty as citizens and public officers required of them,
in supporting the execution, both of the federal excife
law, and the excife of the ftate, during its continuance.
He knew from evidences examined, prior to them,
even under circumftances very unfavourable to impartial teftimony, that I had not at any time done,
nor faid, any thing to promote oppofition to the execution of the law. He knew by their teftimony, that
my language and conduct was favourable to fubmiffion
to the law, before there was any apprehenfion of an
infurrection, and that I had made every exertion in
my power, to imprefs the people that were inflamed
againft the law, with a refpect for the government,
and a difpofition to fupport the laws without exception,
and that in doing this, they themfelves, and I myfelf,
had an intimate correfpondence, and were in perfect
confidence, and that we were equally objects of refentment for fome time to the ignorant and obftinate op-
pofers of the laws. He might alfo have eafily known
that feveral of thofe perfons to whom he declaimed
againft me as a foreigner, had themfelves come into
the country fince I did.

The blunders even of wife men are fometimes
aftonifhing. However, I believe, we are not warranted in giving the appellation of wifdom to fuch perfons,
as are deftitute of honour and virtue, let their ftation
be ever fo high, their talents ever fo brilliant, or their
influence ever fo powerful. The reader will be able
to judge for himfelf, how far the fecretary's conduct
was directed by wifdom, or governed by the principles
of honour and virtue, on a review of thofe facts and
others, that will be hereafter related.

To thofe who know the fecretary's own hiftory, his objecting to a man for being a foreigner, who has been thirty three years in the ftate of Pennfylvania, near thirty years of that time a head of a family and citizen, who contributed all in his power in accomplifhing the revolution, both by his fervices in the provifional government, by committees, when the eftablifhed government was abolifhed, and in the army on the moft trying occafions, and who fince the revolution has been almoft conftantly employed either in the public councils of the ftate or of the federal government ; I fay for fecretary Hamilton to object to fuch a man as a foreigner, muft be aftonifhing to thofe who have any knowledge of his own hiftory ; Nor will it perhaps be lefs furprifing to thofe who are able to trace his conduct, to hear of his illiberality, in affuming to judge the badnefs of another perfon's heart, with whofe character and conduct he was fo little acquainted.

Various other inftances are known of his endeavouring, by improper influence, to procure teftimony againft Meffrs. Smilie, Gallatin, and myfelf, but it is not my object to fwell the book with numerous details ; a few well attefted facts are fufficient to my purpofe.

When the fecretary was on his return, while he lodged in the houfe of captain R. Dicky, within a few miles of my refidence, (I was then in Philadelphia,) after enquiring if I did not live near, he fpoke of my character in his ufual manner, and abufed the people for fending me to Congrefs, adding that I was the principal promoter of the infurrection, &c. &c. Captain Dicky vindicated my character, and informed

him of my general conduct and character, as a friend
to order, and of my exertions during the insurrection,
&c. He had been acquainted with me long before either
he or I lived in the western country, and therefore
spoke of my general character with confidence. The
secretary, full of resentment at hearing me advocated,
exclaimed that I was a bad man, and that it was in
vain to vindicate me, because he had the proofs of my
guilt in his pocket. Captain Dicky alleged that this
was not possible, but the secretary persevered in asserting it to be true, and asked Dicky if he had read
the thirteen letters. Upon his answering in the af-
firmative, the secretary swore that he believed there
was not an old woman in the country but what had
read them, that they contained lies on him, and were
written by me. Dicky offended at the secretary's scurrility against me, told him he had read them and believed the facts they contained ; and would believe them
till they were proved not to be true, let who would
have written them. Captain Dicky himself had been
one of the delegates of that township, at the Parkison
and Redstone meetings, from whence he was sent as
one of the committee to the commissioners at Pittfburgh.

General White, whose treatment of the prisoners
I have already taken notice of, abused my character in
all companies, and told the most manifest falsehoods
with respect to my conduct, when at Carlisle with the
President, and when he was told that his assertions
were not true, he gave secretary Hamilton for his author, saying that the secretary was present at the
interviews with the President. I will just mention a

few inftances of his conduct in this refpect, of which I have the moft authentic vouchers.

' At table in the houfe of Mr. Kirkpatrick in Greenf-burgh, he told in a numerous company, that I had infifted on the Prefident to fend an army into the country, and that the Prefident had anfwered, by faying, " Mr. Findley you have raifed the devil, and you may lay him again yourfelf." On this major Dunham, who was prefent, remarked, " That, fir, is very unlike the Prefident." The Reverend Mr. Powers had been alleging that his reprefentations of my conduct were not probable, when general White appealed to the Prefident's treatment of me, in confirmation of what he faid. While he remained in the fame family, and was as ufual declaiming againft me, he afferted that I had abufed the characters of the whole people in the weftern counties to the Prefident, in order to convince him of the neceffity of fending an army againft them, and that the Prefident anfwered me by faying, " Mr. Findley you have raifed the devil, but you cannot lay him again, or you may lay him again yourfelf," and that I replied, that the people in my neighbourhood were of the moft implacable and ungovernable difpofition, &c. &c. Mr. Kirkpatrick the owner of the houfe objected to this affertion, declaring that he had been acquainted with me many years fo well, that he knew that this was not my manner of fpeaking, nor a conduct fuited to my character, that I did not exprefs myfelf in the manner which he had defcribed on any occafion ; that general White being now acquainted with the country muft know that the people were not fuch as to anfwer this defcription, and that it was

highly improbable that I would give a character of
them that they did not deferve. General White anfwered that I was a damned old hypocrite, and that he
had made a point of telling the above wherever he
came, and faid I deferved no credit or popularity, and
he was determined I fhould have none.

In the fame family in the hearing of Hugh Rofs,
Efquire, and others, he afferted that I told the Prefident
that the people in the weftern counties were perverfe
and inimical to all good government, beyond concep-
tion, and fo abandoned, as that no character, however
influential, could reftrain or perfuade them, and obferved that it would have been well, if the people
had known of my having ufed that converfation before
the election, as in that cafe they would not have confided
in fuch a perfon as I was.

At the houfe of William Todd, Efquire, where he
lodged, he enquired if I lived near ; being anfwered
that I did, but was gone to Congrefs ; he faid they
might as well fend nobody, that I did not reprefent
the people at all. Being told by Mr. Baldridge (whofe
father-in-law, Mr. Todd was then attending in the ftate
Senate) that the people there knew better, and that he
could not take a readier way to infult their feelings,
than to fay fo ; he replied that I would not be heard in
Congrefs, &c. He added, that if it had not been for
my reprefentation of the people to the Prefident, he
would not have fent the army among them at all ; that
being afked by the Prefident, what fort of people the
inhabitants of the weftern counties were, I anfwered
they were the worft, and moft hardened people on

earth, and that an army was abfoluterly neceffary to reduce them to order.

Being afked if he had heard me fay fo, he faid he had not, but had it from Mr. Hamilton, the fecretary of the treafury, who heard it from my own mouth, and faid that the fecretary told him fruther that the Prefident afked me if I thought that any thing lefs than fending the army would do to pacify the minds of the people, and that I replied that nothing lefs would do. When Mr. Baldridge, to convince him how little credit could be given to his affertions, informed him how far my conduct had always been the reverfe of his ftatement of it, what great exertions I had made to preferve and reftore order, and how well I ftood with my neighbours ; he afferted or fwore, that if it had not been for Findley, Smilie, and Gallatin, there would have been no infurrection, and much more to the fame purpofe, here and elfewhere avowing it to be his object to render us unpopular, and giving the fecretary for the author of the fcandal and falfehood which he uttered againft us. Indeed in the houfe of reprefentatives of the ftate in the winter of 1794, a mifreprefentation of what I had faid to the Prefident at Carlifle was made by a very refpectable member, who had been with the army, and who pointed to the fecretary, as his author, in a manner eafily enough underftood, though he was not named. I fent a true ftatement of it in writing to Mr. Gallatin, who corrected the mifreprefentation on the floor of the houfe, and inferted my ftatement in his printed fpeech.

If the Prefident's manner of converfing had been as well known to thofe with whom General White

H h

communicated, as it appears it was to major Dunham, those affertions would not have gained any credit. Or if general White's true character had been known to the people, little respect would have been paid to his stories. Indeed his manners were such as to prevent confidence in his representations, if he had not given the fecretary for his author, but finding that even with that aid he was not credited where I was personally known, I paid no respect to his affertions until I found the falfehoods were not only circulated among people in the weftern country, who knew me only by name, but also through other ftates. Though few, even of thofe, believed him at the time, yet being fupported by the authority of the fecretary's name, and my taking no pains to contradict his affertions, nor to enable my friends to do it, gave them a currency which they could not otherwife have procured, and determined me at laft to take notice of them in this place. I had indeed determined to have treated any thing coming from general White with that filent contempt with which I ufually treat every thing which comes from a man of his character and manners. However, knowing that time is favourable to truth, I have not been hafty in defending my own caufe. This is the firft attempt I have made to vindicate my character, and I do not do it by affertions. I have ftated the whole correfpondence, which Mr. Redick and myfelf had with the Prefident at Carlifle.

It is obfervable that Mr. Redick and myfelf perfectly coincided in fentiments and conduct in converfing with the Prefident, yet nothing has been afferted againſt him ; the reaſon of the diſcrimination however is pretty obvious.

In our interview with the Preſident, it will appear that he treated us with that decency and politeneſs, which was ſuitable to the character he has always ſuſtained, and agreeably to the dictates of a policy dictated by a proper attention to the occaſion and circumſtances.

It will likewiſe appear that while we acted the part of honeſt men, in acknowledging the agitation that had prevailed, and the outrages that had been committed, which indeed would not only have been uncandid, but fooliſh to have denied, (as the truth was already known,) we at the ſame time repreſented that the majority of the people in the weſtern counties had always been well diſpoſed, and ſtated the circumſtances, and explained the reaſons, that prevented the well diſpoſed people from being ſucceſsful in their exertions to reſtore order ſooner, and why the number of thoſe who ſigned the amneſty, was not as great as could have been wiſhed.

It will appear likewiſe that we aſſured the Preſident that the well known outcries againſt the ſtate courts, wages, ſalaries, &c. the inſults offered to judges and other reſpectable citizens, the threats of burning, &c. &c. which made ſo much noiſe abroad, and kept the well diſpoſed people in ſome places in fear, for a time, was principally conducted by an ignorant and obſtinate claſs of people, who had little character or property to loſe.   That this circumſtance had convinced the citizens generally of the neceſſity of exerting themſelves in ſupport of the laws, and convinced them that their own peace and fecurity depended on the due execution of them : And we gave it as our opinion, that this circumftance alone afforded to government ground of more unequivocal confidence than fubfcribing any formal affurances, or than could even be expected from the march of an army into the country. We alfo obferved to him that judges and other refpectable citizens in the weftern counties, who had given their opinion to the commiffioners that an army was neceffary, had feen fufficient reafon to change their mind, and mentioned a letter from prefident Addifon, and the unanimous refolution of the laft Parkifon meeting, to prove this change of fentiment. In fhort, it will appear on reading the correfpondence, that we from our own knowledge gave it as our opinion unequivocally, that the laws could be executed and atonements made in all the four counties, that with refpect to the fettlements near Parkifon's Ferry where we had not perfonal knowledge, and about which we were more ftrictly examined, we gave our opinion on the affurances received from others, whom we efteemed worthy of credit. So far were we from affigning the well known folly and obftinacy of a few ignorant people, and their infulting the ftate magiftrates, or the defign againft the court of Weftmoreland, &c. that had been difcovered and prevented, as a caufe why an army fhould be fent into the country, that we made ufe of thefe circumftances as the ftrongeft ground of affurance that the march of an army was not neceffary, becaufe thefe circumftances made it the people's own intereft to preferve the peace of the country, and effectually convinced them, that if they permitted even a bad law to be oppofed, or obnoxious officers to be abufed, théy eventually deftroyed the beft fecurity for their own liberty and property, and we fuggefted that a fufficient teft had been given as foon as could have been reafonably expected, all things confidered, that the citizens were able and willing to preferve order and punifh offenders, and that fuch offenders as had not figned the amnefty in time were too few in number, and too infignificant in character, to be proper objects for the ftrong hand of government, and that even thefe would have time enough to efcape before the army could arrive.

Thefe circumftances indeed, on weighing them maturely, in our own minds, were conclufive with ourfelves, and from our own conviction, we ftated them with candour and confidence to the Prefident.   Hence it is evident that that heat and inflammation, which produced alarming diforders for a time in the weftern country, and occafioned fo much anxiety of mind to the citizens, was fo far from being ufed by us as an argument in favour of fending an army, that it was honeftly applied as the moft conclufive argument againft it.   It is alfo evident that thefe diforders were ftated to be few in number, and to have prevailed in but a few places, and conducted by fuch as could have but little influence in fettled times.   By examining the eleventh chapter, which defcribes the ftate of the country at and after the time of figning the amnefty, and the fourteenth chapter, which contains the information given by Mr. Redick and myfelf to the Prefident at Carlifle, it will be feen whether or not we underftood the ftate of the country, and whether we gave a candid account of it. It will alfo be eafily difcerned that all the information we gave was calculated to convince the Prefident, that the march of the army was not neceffary for the purpofe of procuring fubmiffion to the laws, and would not be fuccefsful in obtaining the proper fubjects for making atonement.

To thofe, who are acquainted with general White's character, and with mine, no apology will be neceffary for entering no further into a conteft with him, than merely by ftating facts to enable the citizens to judge for themfelves, what credit ought to be given to his affertions. I have always been happy in having few enemies in private life, and confider it as a confoling reflection in my advanced age, that I have never had a quarrel with a neighbour. However, if it is my lot to have enemies, though I may regret the circumftance, yet my regret will be the lefs if I have given no juft caufe of offence, and if my enemies are fuch men, as are neither refpectable for the morality of their principles, or the decency of their manners. It would give me fenfible pain to know that any conduct of mine had given caufe of offence to a good man.

Numerous other ftories have been circulated as from fecretary Hamilton and his friend general White, which as I have never taken pains to obtain vouchers to prove, I fhall pafs over in filence. The ftory, however, of the latter infulting me at Carlifle was not true. I have never yet feen him, fo as to be able to diftinguifh him from another man. I was informed, however, of his obferving me, and fpeaking of me when I was out of hearing, in fuch language as was fuitable to his character; for though I do not know his perfon, I have not been fo little converfant with the officers of the late army, and the citizens of New-Jerfey, as to be unacquainted with his fame. I need fcarcely be at the pains to deny that I went on my knees to the Prefident to befeech him to fend forward the army, for though this has been circulated to a very great diftance on the authority of general White, I prefume few fenfible people gave credit to it, and the correfpondence with the Prefident, here publifhed, is a full refutation of it. I will juft add that the report in the eaftern counties, that my fon was concerned in the riot on Webfter, the collector of excife, was abfolutely falfe, yet this was afferted with fuch confidence through Pennfylvania, that even my friends for fome time admitted it to be true, but fuppofed it to have been without my knowledge.

━━━━━━

C H A P.   XX.

.

AF T E R having given so full a view
of the insurrection, and the measures connected with
it, and of the influential secretary's virulence against
myself and others, I beg leave to call the reader's attention to a concise relation of my own conduct, respecting the excise law ; it will, however, be necessary
to preface this with an account of my conduct and principles respecting the federal government generally.
Under the confederation I always contributed what I
could to have the requisitions of the old Congress carried into effect ; but after the fatigues and risks of the
war were over, I ardently wished to have a more efficient general government, and in the state legislature
contributed to the revision of the confederation, by
voting for delegates to the general convention. When
the federal constitution became a subject of discussion,
and was submitted to the state conventions by Congress,

I had feveral exceptions to it, and wifhed amendments to the inftrument to be recommended, and an adjournment previous to ratification.   I was the more folicitous to obtain the laft, on account of fome circumftances of irritation that were unfriendly to cool difcuffion at the time ; but both were refufed.   However, when I obferved that moft of the other ftates took fufficient time to deliberate before they called their conventions, and that the conventions of the other ftates very generally recommended amendments to the confideration and adoption of the firft Congrefs, which was to meet under the government, I became convinced, that delaying in order to call another general convention, in the then ftate of things, would be highly inconvenient, and approved of the putting the government in operation.   My fentiments were well known to my friends, and it is alfo well known that no oppofition was made to putting the government into operation in any part of the weftern counties, nor were there any heats or difturbance on account of it.

I indeed, on cool reflection, became convinced, that fome of my objections to it were not well founded, and the firft Congrefs having early recommended fome of the amendments I wifhed, and which have been fince ratified, gave confidence that other amendments might be attained, when they became neceffary. I indeed embraced the government as my own and my childrens inheritance, for though I knew it had fome defects partly arifing from indifpenfible caufes, yet I believed it to be capable of being well adminiftered, and on the whole, the beft government in the world.

I i

Though from mistaken party spleen, myself and others who acted the part I did, have been called Anti-federalists, as a name of reproach, yet I do, and always did, treat the appellation with contempt. If we erred, it was from an excess of zeal for federalism, and a jealousy least the federal republican principles of the government were not sufficiently guarded, and in this we agreed with the majority of the citizens of the United States, who recommended, with the first Congress, who adopted, and with the legislatures who ratified the amendments. I never have been found among those, who opposed or embarrassed the measures of a government. Though I knew and acknowledged that the first constitution of Pennsylvania had defects, and assisted afterwards in revising it, yet I never was found among those who combined to embarrass the measures of that government, but contributed all in my power to support its operations and prevent its perversion.

I, in common with other citizens, was attentive to the operations of the federal government in its outset, and though I was pleased with many things done by it, yet before it had been two years in operation, I was surprized to observe so much of the legislative business referred to the heads of newly erected departments, and especially at the originating revenue systems being referred to the head of an executive department. This influential power being specifically vested in the House of Representatives, and of an untransferable nature, the transfering it to an executive officer seemed the more extraordinary. Indeed, people generally were surprised to observe, not only petitions, but the most.

important legiſlative buſineſs, referred to one or other
of the ſecretaries.

Being elected a member of the ſecond Congreſs,
I took my ſeat with a determination to oppoſe the reference of legiſlative buſineſs to executive officers,
otherwiſe than to call for ſuch information as they in
their official capacity might be able to give. A number of members who had acquieſced in this practice in
the beginning, became convinced of the impropriety
of it and oppoſed it in the ſecond Congreſs. My
oppoſition to it did not ariſe from any perſonal averſion to the ſecretaries to whom the buſineſs was referred, but ſolely from an opinion, that it was unconſti-
tutional and improper, and that it was really oppreſſive
to the officers themſelves, eſpecially to the ſecretary of
the treaſury, to whom the originating of all matters,
reſpecting revenue, were referred. I had recently
ſeen a ſtriking inſtance in Pennſylvania of the bad effects, both to the public and the officer, reſulting from
transferring a multiplicity of buſineſs to an executive
officer, and was ſenſible that theſe references prevented
the houſe from poſſeſſing ſo much information within
itſelf, as if the meaſures originated with committees,
and that it laid a foundation for an in and out of door
influence, to combine through a ſecretary as a center
of connection, which might biaſs the deliberations of
the houſe, and which could not ſo eaſily influence a
committee of fifteen members, choſen from each ſtate;
and that ſuch committee would have leſs inducements
to report the ſtate of the revenues in an impoſing manner, or to conceal at any time their real ſituation. I
had no apprehenſion, however, that the ſecretary of

the treafury would take umbrage at the houfe refuming the exercife of its own powers, until I was informed, that he was highly offended at the firft oppofition that was made to a reference of revenue bufinefs to him to originate, and threatened, that if this was refufed, he would refign his office. Though I exerted myfelf in that oppofition, yet I was not alone; it was fupported by a number of the moft diftinguifhed federalifts and experienced politicians in the houfe, and when the queftion was taken, it was loft by a very fmall majority.   On this occafion, not only the fecretary himfelf was alarmed, but thofe that attached themfelves to his intereft out of doors were much agitated.   A few days after the vote, I heard a refpectable revenue officer in a public company fay, that a fet of d—d fellows in Congrefs had attempted to take the originating of revenue meafures out of the hands of the fecretary, and that if they fucceeded, all confidence would be loft, and that certificates had fallen confiderably in two days, in confequence of the attempt.   This agitation with a certain defcription of people out of doors, and the extreme anxiety difcovered by his friends in the houfe, to fupport the fecretary's originating influence, changed my fears, that this undue connection of legiflative and executive bufinefs would at fome period produce an undue combination of intereft, into real fufpicions, that it had already produced this effect.

However, though the oppofition to minifterial originating of revenue fyftems, was fupported by a large minority, it did not fucceed in the fecond Congrefs, nor indeed in the third, without difficulty and delay, and when a committee of ways and means was appointed, in an advanced stage of the session, which sat in the winter and spring of 1794, a majority of the committee were so attached to their usual mode of proposing revenue measures, that a sub-committee, chosen out of the committee of ways and means, immediately referred the business to the secretary. In this way, the taxes on loaf sugar, snuff, &c. were originated. It is known, that during the next session, the secretary resigned, and that before he withdrew, he reported to the house a plan for new modifying the revenue system, in such a manner as to put the disposal or arrangement of the revenue measures, as much as possible, out of the power of future Houses of Representatives. This report was introduced, without being called for by the house. In the present Congress, no opposition has been made to the appointment of a committee of ways and means, nor has the business been referred by it to the secretary of the treasury. Though this statement may seem unconnected with the insurrection, yet it leads to the probable source of the secretary's resentments against me, as well as against Smilie and Gallatin, who are of the same sentiments with me, respecting those measures, and as general White, who appears to have been only the instrument of the secretary's vengeance, acknowledged, when he was detected in asserting falsehoods against me, for which he gave the secretary as author, that his object was to destroy the people's confidence in me ; it goes far to confirm the apprehension, that political party spleen influenced the secretary's conduct in the western expedition. On what other ground, could the secretary exprefs fo much refentment againſt the people for electing us to Congrefs.

Though an unqualified power of levying excifes was veſted in Congrefs, yet an expectation that that power would never be exercifed but in cafes of the laſt neceſſity, which had been induſtrioufly inculcated by the moſt influential advocates of the government, and fondly believed by all, had a tendency to filence objections to the government going into operation ; but when in the fecond feſſion of the firſt congrefs, the fecretary of the treafury of his own motion originated an excife bill, and laid it before Congrefs, (which however the houfe of Reprefentatives laid afide at the time) the alarm given by the appearance of an excife law in fo early a ſtage of the operations of the government, and its apparent rejection, gave fuch alternate emotions of grief and joy in the ſtate of Pennfylvania, as is more eafily imagined than defcribed. This circumſtance enabled the houfe of Reprefentatives, in the ſtate Legiſlature, to be fo unanimous in requeſting the fenate of Congrefs to reject the excife bill, in which bufinefs the city members took a lead. (See Chap III.)

When the excife law was enacted, I was fincerely grieved at the introduction of an excife fyſtem, with all its oaths and officers, and the unavoidable inequality of its preſſure. I was alfo apprehenſive that it might put the vigilance and energy of our new born government prematurely to too fevere a teſt, and abate that confidence in it with which it was fo generally embraced at its outfet, and which was fo neceſſary for its fupport, until it derived ſtrength from age and

habits of fubmiffion. I reflected that the execution
of this law might have obftacles thrown in its way in
all places, but efpecially where it would be peculiarly
oppreffive and confequently moft obnoxious. I reflected that to fecure a prompt fubmiffion to the operations of this law, the aid of a judiciary and proper executive officers fhould be extended fo as to correfpond with and fupport the officers in the execution of
the law, and protect the citizens who might be, or who
fuppofed they were, oppreffed by them. The want of
this in the federal government, I thought augured ill
to the prompt execution of a law, the operation of
which was found difficult to carry into effect in the
beft eftablifhed, and moft energetic, governments.

But did I then, as the fecretary and many of his
friends have malicioufly afferted, fet about to promote
oppofition to it? No; my conduct was the very reverfe of this.

In June 1791, the operation of the excife was
to commence, but in the weftern counties, and I prefume in many other diftricts in the union, offices we re
not provided for the entering of ftills, and the law on
experiment proved to be in fo great a meafure impracticable, that a revifion of it was immediately found
to be neceffary. An advertifement was publifhed,
inviting the citizens of the weftern counties to meet
at Redftone old Fort, to confider and give advice how
they fhould proceed with refpect to the excife law; on
hearing of the intended meeting, reflecting on the
chagrin which prevailed in the minds of the people
on account of the fo unexpected introduction of a
fyftem which they fo much abhorred, and knowing

the violent oppofition that had been given to the execution of the ftate excife law in fome parts of the country, I was confiderably alarmed, left that if only fuch people attended the meeting, that were moft violently oppofed to the excife law, meafures unfavourable to the peace of the country might be promoted. Therefore, though no correfpondence had taken place between thofe who promoted the meeting, and the people of the county in which I refide, I determined to attend it, and to take fome difcreet men with me. I never yet knew who firft promoted the meeting, but the defign was lawful and proper, it was to conduct meafures for petitioning Congrefs in order to quiet the minds of the people. Three men accompanied me to the meeting, viz. John Moore, then judge of the court of Weftmoreland, colonel John Shields and captain Samuel Manhead. I mention their names, becaufe they have always been refpectable for their love of order, and for fupporting the government and the laws. It being the harveft feafon, the meeting was not numerous, there were few from a great diftance; and no kind of diforders were attempted. After the meeting was opened, and the hardfhips, that would refult from the excife law, explained in fome addreffes to the chair, I obferved, that though the principles of the excife law, and the local oppreffive effects it would have on the weftern counties, were developed, yet the conftitutional power of Congrefs to levy it was not fufficiently explained. This induced me to addrefs the chair in a difcourfe of fome length, in which I firft afferted and explained the conftitutional authority of Congrefs to levy excifes, and faid, that they themfelves had acknowledged that

right, by adopting the government, electing reprefentatives to it, and having the ftate officers fworn to
fupport it. I next proceeded to fhew the bad effects
of violent oppofition to it, and endeavoured to convince them, that the only choice they had, was either
to pay the tax, or otherwife to refrain from ftilling, and
fuggefted that to refrain from ftilling altogether, was
a much more tolerable evil than any mode of actual
oppofition, and that in the mean time, it was their duty
to lay their grievances before Congrefs by petition,
but that as petitioning itfelf was an acknowledgment
of the authority of government, in the cafe refpecting
which they addreffed it, petitioning was therefore inconfiftent with oppofition. I concluded by pointing out
the evils in the excife law and the hardfhips peculiar
to their local fituation, to which their petitions fhould
apply, and took particular care not to invite them to
expect an immediate repeal, but encouraged them to
look for relief to be obtained by a revifion of it, as I
knew it could never be executed till it was revifed, and
informed them, that in its prefent ftate, it was impracticable.

I appeared to be heard with attention, at leaft there
was no appearance of the contrary. I was informed
however, when I fat down, that one man during the
early part of the difcourfe, flowly lifted up his ftaff to a
ftriking pofition, and the obferver was prepared to prevent the ftroke, by feizing the ftaff, but when I came
to point out the grounds to which the petitions fhould
apply, the ftaff was let down again, without being exercifed. I expected a petition had been prepared to
be offered at the meeting, but it was not. (See chap.

K k

III.) No argument was offered in my hearing, nor obfervation made that was calculated to encourage riotous
oppofition to the law.

This was the only popular meeting, either refpecting the excife or any other law, that ever I attended
or addreffed in the weftern counties, until after the infurrection took place, and I did nothing in the meeting
except making the difcourfe I have mentioned; my
avowed intention of attending it, was to pay the wages
of the militia, that had ferved on general Harmer's
campaign, many of whom refided in that part of the
country, and attended at the meeting.

In about two weeks after this meeting, I had to
attend a feffion of Affembly at Philadelphia, and did
not return till the week before the election, at which
I was chofen to reprefent the ftate in the fecond Congrefs. At the county courts, which fat the week preceding the week of the election, there appeared a publication in the Pittfburgh gazette, charging me with
being one of the authors and promoters of excifes; it
was alfo fent to the election diftricts. There was no
time left for me to reply to it, if I had been fo difpofed; it did not however prevent my being elected by
a large majority, though it no doubt made that majority
lefs. The candidate oppofed to me, was a member of
the Pittfburgh meeting, which in 1791, prepared a petition to Congrefs refpecting the excife law, and publifhed fome indifcreet refolutions againft feveral other
meafures of government. (See chapter II.) The
perfon who was the candidate oppofed to me at the
election, had been a uniform federalift and never that
I knew of difcovered any difapprobation of the excife

law, before he was a member of the Pittſburgh meeting.
I cenſured the reſolutions freely, both to the gentleman
to whom I have alluded, and to ſuch other members of that
meeting as I had an opportunity of ſeeing. I was at home,
when the meeting was held at Pittſburgh, in Auguſt 1792,
and was requeſted by general Wilkin of Pittſburgh to
be at Pittſburgh, at the time of it, not as a member,
but to have an opportunity of giving my advice againſt
intemperate reſolutions, if any ſuch ſhould be offered.
I declined attending and gave him ſuch reaſons for
doing ſo, as ſatisfied him afterwards, if not at the
time. I had always thought it improper for a meeting
convened for the expreſs purpoſe of preparing a petition or memorial to government, to avail themſelves
of that opportunity to cenſure the meaſures of government. My ſentiments on this ſubject were well known
to my friends. Mr. Brackenridge in page 22, and
ſome other places, of his incidents, ſeems to overrate the
unpopularity that was attached to perſons who advocated ſubmiſſion to the execution of the exciſe law; it
was not made a teſt of character, to my knowledge, to
the degree he mentions. I knew of no men preferred
at elections, for the ſtate legiſlature, or any other purpoſe, for oppoſing it, either by word or deed, at the
elections in which I was concerned. The moſt popular official characters in Weſtmoreland county, judges
and others, were known to be in favour of the execution of it. In Fayette county, James Findley was
known to be an advocate for ſubmiſſion to the exciſe
tax, yet he was an aſſociate judge, a ſenator and again a
judge, as it ſuited his conveniency; few indeed, how-

ever, advocated the principles of the law itself, and that will always be the cafe; but many ufed arguments in abatement of the hardfhips arifing from its operation. However, I do not difpute the truth of Mr. Brackenridge's remarks, with refpect to what fell under his own obfervation, and his book for the moft part, treats only of fuch things, as did fall under his immediate obfervation.

The infpector's houfe, with the attack on which the infurrection commenced, is faid to be about eight miles fouth weft of Pittfburgh. I live above forty miles north eaft of it, confequently, near fifty miles diftant. I never have been in the part of the country where it lays, nor had I ever been in the fettlement, where the infurrection is believed to have originated, until laft fummer, that having occafion to go to Wafhington, I took the road which paffes through Mingo Creek fettlement, when I planned to lodge a night at the houfe where general White gave fuch a difplay of his total want of the feelings of humanity. I was a perfect ftranger to the road and to the inhabitants. I had heard indeed of a number of decent refpectable people living in that fettlement, and I being fo much in public life, they had no doubt heard of me, but not one of the citizens in that fettlement, ever had a correfpondence with me even by letter. None of the inhabitants ever happened to be members of the public bodies where I was employed.

Yet the fecretary and his emiffaries have not fcrupled to affert, that I was the author of the infurrection, that I fet it a going, but had cunning enough, to keep myfelf clear, and many other fuch malicious and totally unfounded affertions. Smilie and Gallatin were ufually connected with me in the charge of promoting the infurrection, and planning to overturn the government, &c.

I did not hear of the marfhal coming up to ferve the proceffes, nor was I informed circumftantially of the attacks on the infpector's houfe till after the Braddock's field rendezvous, viz. near two weeks after the infpector's houfe was burned, my firft correct information of the bufinefs was received from a young man in the neighbourhood, who had been on a vifit to fee relations in Wafhington county, and had for curiofity attended at the Mingo Creek meeting and at Braddock's field. He called at my houfe in the morning to tell me the news, and informed me very circumftantially refpecting all the meafures, and particularly of Bradford's fpeech at Mingo Creek meeting, and his fubfequent conduct in procuring the mail to be robbed, promoting the rendezvous, &c. and of the agitation among the people and their confidence in Bradford, &c. I had fome days before feen the advertifement of the meeting intended to be held at Parkifon's ferry, and of the mail having been robbed, and had gone to Greenfburgh to enquire what the meeting was intended for, and from what fource the appointment came. I there got an indiftinct account of the burning of the infpector's houfe, but no further information about the meeting, but in confultation with with my friends there we agreed not to take any notice of the meeting, and I advifed my neighbours to the fame courfe, but on receiving circumftantial information from the young man, and learning that the outrages were occafioned by the marſhal ſerving writs, and being further informed by him that it was highly dangerous for me, or any other perſon, to enſure Bradford's meaſures I was agitated with ſuch a mixture of grief and anger, that I ſpoke of their conduct with unguarded ſeverity. He urged me in vain to be cautious, ſuggeſting that if my language came to be known it would bring me into trouble; though I knew he was my friend I paid no reſpect to his advice, and ſcarcely took it in good part, till in leſs than an hour after, one of the country commiſſioners called to inform me of the alarming news. He alſo adviſed me to ſpeak of it more cautiouſly, leſt I ſhould come to trouble, and told me that a party were gone that day from the ſouth of Weſtmoreland to attack Wells, the collector of excife, at his houſe in Fayette county. I learned through another channel that threatening letters were ſent to the next townſhip to the one in which I lived, in order to excite a party to pay an unfriendly vifit to Webſter the collector of Bedford county. It is eaſier to imagine than deſcribe my ſenſations on receiving ſuch alarming information, in ſuch rapid ſucceſſion. After compoſing my mind in order to reſolve with the greater coolneſs what was beſt to be done, I concluded that the only practicable method to ſtop the progreſs of anarchy and outrage was to procure as many diſcreet perſons as poſſible to attend as delegates at the Parkiſon's meeting. As ſoon as my mind was made up to this purpoſe, I went to the neareſt tavern on the great road, and ſent for Mr. Todd, one of the judges of the court, to meet me, in order to conſult what was beſt to be done. We agreed to hold an election for delegates, and for this purpose to warn the people, and to perfuade difcreet perfons to accept of the appointment. While I was at the tavern a meffage came to my houfe from general Jack at Greenfburgh, recommending the very plan I was purfuing. It is remarkable that the fame meafure was fuggefted by the urgency of the occafion in Fayette and Weftmoreland, and at Pittfburgh, without any correfpondence between the people of thefe different counties (See Chap. IX.)

Befides the delegates, I advifed the judges and other difcreet citizens to attend and mix with the people, alleging that every one of them might find fome man to converfe with, who might take their advice or be bettered by their information, and I went myfelf with the fame defign. It was with this view that general Jack, judge Beard, and other refpectable and influential citizens attended at Parkifon's Ferry meeting. While I was there, and before the meeting had proceeded far in its bufinefs, I received a letter by exprefs from the commiffioners, who had come in great hafte as far as Greenfburgh. In the letter they informed me that they had fent forward an exprefs to go to my houfe, but were glad to find that I was gone to the meeting to promote the very object for which they were fent by the Prefident, viz. to reftore order. They explained the nature of their miffion in their letter to me, but informed me that the fuccefs of it muft depend on meeting with correfpondent fentiments in the people, and requefted me to inform the meeting of their arrival, and to endeavour to have arrangements made for opening a correfpondence between them and the meeting, but not to read their letter to me, to the meeting. (See Chap. IX.)

In short, I attended at every meeting that was held for the purpose of reftoring order, except the fecond meeting at Parkifon's Ferry, which was convened to give affurances that order was already reftored, and I alfo attended at different worfhiping congregations, at the court, and at every place where I could get an opportunity to converfe with the people ; and where I thought it could be ufeful I addreffed them in a public manner. In the moft critical fituations, I neither temporized nor concealed my fentiments. This was indeed a new fcene to me, for I never had been accuftomed to addrefs popular meetings. I alfo travelled into different places of the country, in order to ftir up fuch as I thought were capable of inftructing their neighbours, and to affift them with the beft reafons and moft powerful arguments that I could fuggeft ; and feveral applied to me of their own accord, to affift them with fuch information and arguments as I thought could be ufeful. Indeed, from the time I engaged in the bufinefs, which was as early as I had opportunity, I took no reft, either to body or mind, and fuffered much grief and vexation on account of the diftrefs and folly of a number of people with whofe fituation and anxiety of mind I fincerely fympathized, while many of them were offended at the part I took, and treated my advices with contempt, and my affertions for fome time with difcredit; but I was always fupported and encouraged by citizens, who had in fettled times the greateft credit for underftanding and patriotifm.

The whole of my conduct was stated and proved to the secretary in stronger terms than those in which I have related it, by men of the most respectable character, who were not only eye and ear witnesses to much of it, but who were fellow labourers with me, in promoting the restoration of order and submission to the laws, and who also testified to the uniformity of my conduct and sentiments both before and after the insurrection.

But the secretary had more early and unequivocal proofs within his own knowledge of my endeavours to have the excise law well executed as long as it continued unrepealed. Early in the winter of 1792, I wrote a letter to the President, at the instance of governor Mifflin, and some time after another at the instance of the Attorney General of the United States, and the attorney of the district of Pennsylvania, relating to the case of Beer and Kerr, both of which I had reason to believe were given to the secretary; in these letters I gave my opinion that if special sessions of the court were held in the country, the courts would be protected and competent juries found to confirm this opinion. I stated in substance, that the state courts had never been insulted, nor the want of good juries complained of in cases arising under the state excise law, or other cases equally obnoxious, and at the same time suggested, that carrying people all the way to Philadelphia, was so obnoxious, that doing it might be attended with difficulty, if not with risk, and would render witnesses more difficult to procure; that supposing the persons charged to be innocent, as I was confident thofe in queftion were, the taking them to a diftance for trial, would be the more unpopular.

In the preceding feffion, when I knew the fecretary was preparing a report for the revifion of the excife law, I by letter, requefted a converfation with him on the fubject. In the confequent interview, I informed him, that though I difapproved of the excife law, I was fenfible it could not be releafed from the appropriation until we could fupply its place with another tax, which I knew Congrefs was not then difpofed to do, that therefore I wifhed by all means to give it a fair trial and have it promptly executed, and mentioned my apprehenfion of bad confequences to the government, if the execution of it was trifled with, becaufe that the credit and authority of the government were equally pledged for the execution of all its laws, fo that if one law was impracticable or oppofed with fuccefs, the authority of other laws would be alfo difregarded, and the number and magnitude of crimes would be encreafed by impunity. I recommended feveral alterations, which I thought would render the execution of the excife law more practicable; among thofe, were lowering the tax, at leaft till the people were better reconciled to the execution of the law, and eftablifhing feffions of the court in the country. On this laft I laid great weight, and lamented, that competent authority had not been vefted in the ftate courts for that purpofe.

When the report was made, few of fuch amendments were propofed as I had advifed, fome of them I endeavoured to introduce in the houfe, and fucceeded fo far as to have the tax made one cent lower than the fecretary reported, but this did not equalize it with the tax on other fpirits, in proportion to the then felling prices in the market; much lefs did it anfwer the political purpofe of reconciling the people to it.

It had become cuftomary, for the members to read the reafoning with which the fecretary always accompanied his reports, as arguments on the floor, to which I had been always oppofed; but on this occafion, I oppofed the practice with more than ufual warmth and perfeverance, rifing more frequently than I had ever done in the committee of the whole, to declare it out of order, &c. and afferting, that the members exclufively were entrufted to give information of the ftate of the country for the purpofes of taxation, and that the information given by the individual members, formed that aggregate of local knowledge, which ought to guide the difcretion of the houfe, in accommodating the laws to the circumftances of the citizens, and that the information received from the fecretary's clofet, being collected from revenue officers, or other agents who were not publicly refponfible for the information they gave, and who frequently were interefted in giving it wrong, and the fecretary himfelf not being conftitutionally qualified, nor refponfible for it, I confidered it as no authority for our conduct, and improper to be ufed for that purpofe. I do not remember, that his reports have been made ufe of on the floor, otherwife than for information refpecting his official ftatements, fince that time, but the oppofition commenced on this occafion was perfevered in, till it was finally fuccefsful, and until the houfe refumed the ex-

ercife of originating revenue fyftems. The hand I
had in this, and fome cenfures I paffed in the houfe:
on fome fyftems originated by the fecretary, no doubt
rendered me obnoxious to him, and the more fo as
the public mind teftified in favour of this change, at
the next election, but more decidedly at the election
which took place in Pennfylvania, previous to his arrival in the weftern country. This accounts for his
being fo outrageoufly offended at Gallatin and myfelf
being elected into Congrefs, and he and his friend
general White making fuch malicious exertions, and
afferting fuch mean falfehoods, to deftroy my popularity, as they expreffed it. A mighty object indeed,
for the man who affumed or had afcribed to him by his
friends, the honour of guiding the helm of ftate, both
in its legiflative and executive meafures! It alfo accounts for his officious endeavours to influence the
Virginia militia, refpecting the election then depending in that ftate; but it is beyond my purpofe to
give a ftatement of his exertions in that bufinefs.

One charge which he mentioned with great fenfibility and refentment, was, that I had wrote a pamphlet,
called "thirteen letters," which he faid, contained lies
on him; but he has neither proved me to be the author
of that pamphlet, nor pointed out any particular lie it
contained. Writing is not my profeffion, nor have
I ever engaged largely in it, nor publifhed a falfehood
to my knowledge. I never have in my life publifhed
a fentence that I would deny being the author of, if
decently called upon, nor did I ever give a piece to
a printer anonimoufly, or direct him to conceal my
name. However, if the fecretary will acknowledge

himself to be the author, if true, of a great variety of pieces, which have by public opinion, been afcribed to him, I will make a full acknowledgment of all I ever publifhed; thefe, it is true, will be few in number, but they will difcover that I have been confiftent in my principles. I am miftaken, if on examining the numerous productions afcribed to him, the author might not be quoted in oppofition to himfelf, and if fome of the moft valuable characters in the United States would not appear to have been traduced by his pen. If I were explicitly to deny a charge made in this way, he might charge me in the fame manner with writing Catullus, Maffachufitenfis, the ftate of parties, Manlius, &c. &c. and though I would acknowledge they contained untruths, I could not eafily prove that I had not wrote them, for I have fpread fome of them all, though the fecretary or fome of his friends know beft their authors. To fatisfy other citizens, however, I will affert, that I have not for feveral years publifhed a line in the Pittfburgh gazette or any other newfpaper, except in the fpring previous to the infurrection, when I fent up to the editor of the Pittfburgh gazette, a correct account of the revenue laws that had been enacted that feffion, in order to counteract the falfe reports, that I had been informed were circulated concerning them.

The fecretary was miftaken with refpect to the fpread of the thirteen letters, which he faid, had been read by every old woman in the weftern country. I have fince been particular in examining, and can difcover but a few of them to have been fpread in the weftern furvey, previous to the infurrection. I heard

of but one in the town or county of Washington; there
might have been more; but after the secretary had difcovered fo much refentment againft that pamphlet, all
that could be procured of them were difperfed, and
whatever doubts might have been entertained of the
truth of the facts fuggefled in them, the fecretary's afferting that they contained falfehoods without particu-
larizing any of them, has been confidered as a confirmation of the truth of the whole they contained.
I had put fome of them into the hands of my friends,
as I do of all political publications, and more of them
I believe were in the north of Weftmoreland, than in
all the weftern counties befides, and I have not difcovered that any perfon who read them, engaged in
the infurrection : there was not one of them known
to be in Mingo creek fettlement.   They appear chiefly
to contain a ftatement of facts, from which inferences
are drawn.   If but a few of the leading facts were
proved to be falfe, others would be difcredited and
the inferences would fall of courfe.   This would be a
more eafy and honorable method, than holding an inquifition at the head of an army.

    An apology is neceffary to the reader for engaging
his attention fo long about what relates to myfelf. I
would not have done it merely on the account of Alexander Hamilton and William Findley, but a head of
the financiering department, an influential member of
the cabinet, who not only conducted his department
in fuch a manner as to render a powerful military expedition neceffary, and moft probably with a view
to promote that event, and who in that expedition was
underftood to influence its movements and to direct

and affume the exercife of the judiciary authority, without being attached to the expedition in any known and refponfible character, and who, thus armed with the exercife of military authority, attempted to chaftife the people in one ftate for electing fuch perfons as he difapproved of, and to influence the elections of another, is a confideration of more importance to the citizens, and the knowledge of it may have greater influence on the future meafures of the executive department, than merely confidered as relating to Alexander Hamilton as a citizen. What refpects myfelf is of no other importance to the public, than that as a Reprefentative of the people, and on account of my political principles and conduct, I was marked out as a victim of minifterial vengeance. All the fecretary's exertions could have no effect on the opinion of the citizens with whom I enjoy intimate fociety, and as all my ambition is to fpend the remainder of my days in a comfortable retirement in the bofom of my family and friends, when I ceafe to reprefent them in a public capacity, this I can enjoy without having it impaired by Mr. Hamilton's virulence. Thankful indeed I am, that though no government can prevent a man of fuperior talents, dangerous principles, and malevolent temper, from being armed at times with a dangerous portion of public power, yet fuch are our government and laws that fuch men are reftrained from gratifying, though not from difcovering, what they would do if they had power.

After an inquifition accompanied with the moft illegal inducements to promote difcovery, and notwithftanding the fecretary's repeated afleverations to the

witneſſes that he was already poſſeſſed of proofs of criminality againſt Smilie, Gallatin, and me, no teſtimony was found even to lay a foundation for ſuſpicion.
The ſituations in which we lived, and the conduct of
the people around us, forbid ſuſpicion of either combination among ourſelves or connection with the inſurgents; living as we do near 30 miles from each other,
we have little or no correſpondence but when we meet
in Philadelphia, and reſiding from thirty to fifty miles
from the ſeat of the inſurrection, and having no connection or correſpondence in that part of the country,
nor perſonal acquaintance with the citizens reſiding in
the ſettlement where the outrages commenced, we had
no opportunity of influencing them either for or againſt
the exciſe law, nor of knowing that theſe citizens were
more determined in their oppoſition to it than others,
nor did we know of the exiſtence of the Mingo creek
aſſociation which is ſuppoſed to have produced the inſurrection, till we were informed of it afterwards.
Though the heat and inflammation ſpread into the counties in which we are reſident, during the progreſs of
the diſorders, yet no perſon from either of theſe counties had any part in originating the inſurrection, nor
did the official certificate from judge Wilſon, nor the
proclamation of the Preſident bottomed on that certificate, ſuggeſt that an inſurrection exiſted in theſe
counties, but confined it expreſsly to the counties of
Waſhington and Allegany. It is alſo known that
though the whole people of the county of Fayette refuſed to ſign the amneſty, and though a great proportion of the people of Weſtmoreland declined ſigning it,
or varied the form of the aſſurances, yet only three

persons were sought after or taken prisoners from these two counties. Against two of these no bills were found, and the third, whose character and fate is described in page 211, was a person of whom I had not the most distant knowledge, though he resided in the same county about twenty miles distant. Smilie and Gallatin living in Fayette county, of course did not sign the amnesty, and for particular reasons they would not have done it even if it had been produced to them for that purpose. I did not sign it on the day appointed myself, though I had laboured to promote the signing of it by others. I thought it most consistent with the station which I occupied and the part I acted, to put it out of the power of any person to say, that I had signed the amnesty to avoid a scrutiny of my conduct. That scrutiny has been made by an artful, a discerning, and revengeful enemy, and not even the semblance of exciting opposition to the execution of the law, or of enmity to the government, or of endeavouring to embarrass its measures, or even of the crime of treating an excise officer unpolitely, has been discovered. Indeed I treated the inspector with the same attention that I had done formerly, and Mr. Wells, the collector, with greater attention than I had ever formerly done. I never heard him complained of for illegal seizures or other acts of oppression, my only complaint against him was want of decision and address in the execution of the law. Nor was there any testimony found against Messrs. Smilie and Gallatin, but much was testified in their favour. It was known and testified that I had discountenanced the meetings that denounced the excise law and the officers under it, and that I censured

M m

the refolves as indifcreet and impolitic ; that in fhort I had difcountenanced every meafure except petitioning, and that I encouraged this as a direct acknowledgement of the authority of the government, and as a means of turning the attention of the people to it as the only lawful and practicable fource of relief.

Though I had never heard any perfon advocate a riotous oppofition to the excife law, yet I was always watchful to reprove any expreffions that I thought leaned that way, and to defcribe the dangerous effects that encouraging them would have on fociety. Often have I faid on fuch occafions, that to countenance riots againft the execution of any law, was like throwing the bridle on a wild horfe's neck, of whom, when he was let loofe, there was no telling what courfe he would take, or where he would ftop, and fuggefted that even liberty exercifed without a fubordination to rule would foon become allied to the worft paffions, and produce the moft arbitrary and ruinous effects, fuch fentiments as thefe were frequently introduced in converfation and in my letters to my friends, and I can appeal to all who had an opportunity of knowing, to teftify if I ever fpoke, wrote, or acted contrary to thefe fentiments.

Perhaps it will be replied that I wrote a letter to Mr. Petrikin at Carlifle during the time of the infurrection, and that as he was charged with promoting fedition, my letter to him muft have been of a feditious nature. This conclufion was induftrioufly promoted by fome, but certainly a knowledge of my conduct refpecting the infurrection would have juftified another conclufion; however I will infert the letter, and leave the original with the printer, but firſt I will ſtate the circumſtances in which it was written.

On the evening of the 1ſt of September 1794, when I had juſt returned from the Redſtone meeting, and was full of anxiety on account of the difpoſition evidenced there which occaſioned the miſcarriage of the deſign of that meeting, and the uncertainty of what might be the event, a friend who was going over the mountains to Greencaſtle and Carliſle offered to carry letters to my relations. I wrote letters to two of my brothers-in-law, the one near Greencaſtle, and the other near Carliſle, viz. John Coughran and Joſeph Junkin, both known to be well diſpoſed fenſible men. Before I went to bed I received a letter from Mr. Petrikin of Carliſle, the purport of which was to inform me of a county meeting to be held at Carliſle, and though he did not explain the intention of the meeting, yet I fuſpected that it might poſſibly be his intention to diſſuade the militia from obeying the orders of the Preſident, and though I hoped there would not be a neceſſity for the militia to march, yet I knew that reports of their refuſing to march, or appearing to join the inſurgents, would tend to defeat our endeavours to reſtore order. Under this impreſſion I immediately wrote an anſwer to Petrikin's letter. Under the ſame impreſſions and with the ſame views I would have written to any perſon exiſting, if there had been the ſame proſpect of doing good, or preventing miſchief. The only dread I had in writing it was, that the contents of the letter might ſome way or other find their way to the inſurgents, and ſubject me to trouble from them. Under

this impreffion I omitted the names of thofe who
promoted the diforders which the letter defcribes,
and gave no advice, but confined myfelf to giving a
relation of the ftate of things with us.   The defcription which I gave, I thought might have a happy
effect in preventing the citizens of Cumberland county from doing any thing in imitation of the rioters, or
that would encourage them.   However, as things took a
more favourable turn with us, the contents of the letter
could not have found their way back in time to do
me any harm, for though the impreffion of terror
was the greateft at the Redftone meeting of any inftance that had fell under my immediate obfervation,
it was the laft exertion made by thofe who directed the
robbing of the mail, and the expulfion of thofe who
wrote letters ; my letter to Mr. Petrikin indeed was
haftily wrote and rudely digefted.   However as much
has been faid about it, I fhall take the liberty of infer-
ting it.

September 1ft, 1794.

" Dear   Sir,

" Yours of the 26th ult. I have juft received, and
as a bearer ftarts early in the morning, though it is now
late, I fhall acknowledge the receipt of it before I fleep.
Our riotous oppofition to the excife law has gone the
length of expelling the excife officers from this diftrict,
but not without flagrant inftances of outrage and diforder.   Several of thofe who took a lead in this bufinefs
had been early friends to liberty,   the moft active of

them were warm federalifts. The diflike to the excife
law is general, but the leaders of the confufion do
not now ftop at this, for fome who have been zealous
friends to the federal government now declaim in favour of total difunion and independence. Such is too
generally the conduct of unprincipled men, even a good
caufe would be injured by receiving fupport from fuch *.
Though on proper occafions I have endeavoured to
inform the public mind fo as to promote a repeal of
the excife law, or more effential amendments, yet I
was always watchful againft riots or any thing that
might tend to promote any unconflitutional exertions.
When we had recourfe to thefe in the late revolution,
the object to which they were to lead the way was of
the greateft importance, and the exertions were conducted with prudence and fyftem. The difturbances
with us commenced by accident and have been conducted with diforder and extravagance, the general
diflike to the law had indeed rendered the citizens in
fome places too fufceptible of irritation and too much
difpofed to commit outrages.

"However a meeting of from two to five delegates
from each townfhip were met to confider of the beft
means of reftoring peace and order, when the commiffioners arrived from Philadelphia, avowedly for the
fame purpofe. Their arrival and errand was announ-

* When Bradford declaimed in favour of war and independence at Redftone, I
fufpected that he was encouraged by others. It appears however I was miftaken,
for a difpofition of that kind has not been traced further than that declamation, which
was probably the ravings of the moment. The difturbances were not fo much promoted by fuch as had been difappointed of offices as I had been then informed.

ced to the meeting by me, and had a good effect upon
their deliberations, but the proclamation and the orders to the militia arrived next morning and produced a contrary effect, and excited a high degree of irritation among those characters that were most inflammatory. I must acknowledge that the commissioners
do not offer terms with exceptions of persons or by
halves, as the British did at the late revolution. They
propose a full indemnity to all offenders, and for all
offences, and a remittance of the excise for the time
past, and also conditionally to refrain from calling the
people out of the counties for trial, on condition of a
promised submission to the laws. This is indeed all
the President could do on his part, and it is necessary
on the part of the people, even if it had no other advantage than to open the way for petitions to Congress
in order to obtain a repeal of the excise law, or reasonable amendments. It is also necessary on account
of the disorders and threats of violence of the people
in opposition. Two committees have agreed to the
terms with a reference to the approbation of the people, the obtaining of which from all the people is
doubtful ; and there is great dread of internal disorders and violence ; freedom of speaking and writing has
been for some time suppressed, but this evil is wor-
king its own cure, by rousing and uniting the well disposed to exert themselves in restoring order. *I am, &c.*

This is the letter, which has been represented as so
criminal in me, not so much on account of its contents as
of the person to whom it was directed. He has informed
me that he never read the letter to any person, but told

some sentences out of it perhaps pretty fairly. I did not intend it to be kept a secret. I with difficulty procured it from Mr. Petrikin, and not till I had to promise to return it to him, if necessary for his defence, before he would part with it ; through the haste in which this letter was wrote it is not perfectly accurate, however the liberality of the terms offered in behalf of the President is somewhat exaggerated, and the armed party appearing at, and overawing the Redstone meeting, from which I had returned, omitted with design. I knew liberty poles had been erected at Carlisle, and though I did not know that William Petrikin had any hand in erecting them, yet from what I knew of his character I was afraid he might take a warm part at the meeting, and therefore stated the conduct of government and of the insurgents in such a manner, as to give him no ground to complain of the one, or encouragement to imitate the other, and mentioned my own dislike to the excise law, to shew that the outrageous opposition that was made to it was calculated to prevent and not to promote its repeal. William Petrikin's letter to me contained nothing injurious, and it was the first and only letter he had ever wrote to myself or any other person in the western country to my knowledge And notwithstanding the mischievous rapidity with which inflammatory news was spread through the western country that summer, I could not trace it letters; but one of that sort was discovered, and it was not signed by the author.

I knew that it was reported in the army, and circulated even among the members of Congress, when I took my seat, in November 1794, that I had corresponded with Bradford, and that such of my letters

were found among his papers, as would prove me to
have been at the bottom of the insurrection. It will
be remembered, that the secretary on his return to
Philadelphia told Captain Dicky, that he had sufficient proof of my guilt in his pocket. It was told in
the city, as a secret which soon was heard by every
body, that proofs were, obtained against Smilie, Gallatin and myself, that we were deeply concerned in and
promoted the insurrection. I traced some of those
stories, to sources from which I did not expect they
would have come, and I called on the late attorney
general and the attorney of the district, who assured me
there was no proof of criminality of any kind against
us. The district attorney acknowledged, however,
that a scrutiny had been made, and promised when
he had leisure, to select the places where my name was
mentioned for my perusal. I then designed, to have
procured and published a certificate from him, but
on second thoughts declined doing it. I knew the attorney general advocated my conduct from what he had
observed, and was informed of it when he was com-
missioner in the western counties. He and judge
Yates had sufficiently expressed their confidence in me
on their arrival in that country, by sending to me first,
explaining the object of their mission in a confidential
letter, and employing me to procure the means of cor-
responding with the meeting. The last time I ever
saw the late attorney general, he asked me to take a walk
with him at the state house, and after consulting me,
with respect to a subject which he thought of importance
for the peace and happiness of Pennsylvania, and par-

ticularly of the weſtern counties*, he took an opportunity of expreſſing his diſapprobation of the liberties that had been taken with my character, and aſſured me he had always been my advocate. He had long known me; our firſt acquaintance was at the camp at Amboy, in the year 1776.

The truth is, letters had never at any time paſſed between me and any perſon concerned in promoting the inſurrection, except colonel Marſhal; with him I had correſponded ſeveral times, but not for two years previous to the inſurrection, except one in anſwer to a letter reſpecting his ſon, then reſiding in the city, who was about going into a new line of buſineſs. There were few men indeed, in whom I would have had more confidence, and none engaged in the inſurrection at whoſe conduct I was ſo much ſurpriſed. I never ſaw Mr. Bradford's hand writing, nor to my knowledge did he ever ſee mine.

I have near relations living in three of the four weſtern counties, and though I had no opportunity of adviſing thoſe of them who lived in enſnaring ſituations, yet I had the ſatisfaction to find, that every one of them had been uniformly oppoſed to the diſorders, and that no friend, with whom I had ever been intimate in any of the counties, was concerned in promoting the diſturbances, except colonel Marſhal, and he withdrew as ſoon perhaps as he durſt. It might have been otherwiſe, and I not to blame.

N n

* It was about the propriety of Congreſs at its next ſeſſion, preparing a previous plan for dividing ſtates ſo as to prevent the parts to be ſeparated from becoming enemies to each other, in a conteſt about the diviſion. At his requeſt, I promiſed to conſider of it, but aſſured him, that the ſenſible citizens in the weſtern counties did not deſire it.

A few days after I arrived in the city, and before the secretary returned, a respectable gentleman high in office, asked me, with apparent anxiety, if any thing at all was found against me. I answered, that there was not; he asked me if I was certain of that. I told him I was certain there was nothing to be found against me. He then asked me, if I was sure that none could be procured to perjure themselves against me. I said, I knew nothing about that, and asked him with surprise how he came to suspect such a design. He said, he knew that no means would be left untried to injure or ruin me.

Until I was informed on the road coming down, of the secretary's conversation with some of the citizens on his way to Potowmac, and had this information in the city, I did not suspect that even malice itself could have suggested a suspicion of my conduct; but while all regard to morality and decency was sacrificed in order to injure such as had done all in their power, first to prevent and then to allay the disturbances, such as had administered fewel to the flame were in some instances considered and treated as good citizens.

C H A P. XXI,

I H A V E frequently mentioned the of-
ficial report made by the fecretary of the treafury to
the Prefident of the United States previous to the
iffuing of his proclamation, and I have had recourfe
to it as an authority refpecting the riots committed
againft revenue officers, not having ever heard of feveral of thefe riots through any other channel; at the
fame time, however, I have fuggefted that the candour
of the report was doubtful, and produced fome ftriking
inftances of mifreprefentation. (See Chap. viii.)
I fhall now affign fome further inftances of the fecretary's want of candour in this report.

In page 118 of the executive proceedings, he mentions the hoftility of the ftate officers, and particularly
of one high official character, to the execution of the laws,
as one of the moft ferious obftacles to their operation,
and in a letter to governor Mifflin, which is now before me, in anfwer to a demand made by him for an

explanation of this infinuation, he afferts that Albert
Gallatin, then a member of Affembly, was of the committee which met at Pittfburgh in September 1791.
This is not true, Albert Gallatin and myfelf were attending the Affembly of Pennfylvania, then in feffion.
In this explanatory letter he ftates charges againft feveral characters who have been uniformly friends to government; in his charges againft Mr. Addifon Prefident
of the courts in that diftrict, the arts of mifreprefentation are carried to a confiderable height. I fhall
briefly detail them. The judge refufed to act as deputy out of the line of his official duty in certain inftances for the fupervifor of the diftrict, though he at the
fame time affured that officer of ample protection and
every neceffary affiftance to enable him to do the duty
of his ftation himfelf; his not having treated the excife
officers with proper marks of attention, in two inftances,
is another charge; one of the inftances was his telling
the tavern keeper, with whom he lodged, that the man
who was then a collector of excife was not an acceptable companion in the lodging. The fecretary did not
reflect that that officer might not have been an acceptable companion for the judge, previous to his being an
excife officer, and that the honours attached to that office were not fufficient to elevate his character. I will
refer him to the judges of the fupreme court of Pennfylvania for the truth of this remark; they are acquainted with the collector. With refpect to the infpector
not receiving the marked attention of the Prefident of
the court, the fecretary fhould have enquired whether
there did not exift perfonal caufes abftracted from his
holding the office, or whether there were not fuch

caufes exifting with fome other of the judges on whom the President had no right to impofe ; for this great crime which was confidered as a matter of fuch importance by the fecretary, was nothing more than the President's neglecting to invite the infpector to a feat on the bench during the feffion of the court, though he had invited a relation of his. None of thefe inftances happened in the county where I refide, and the firft I heard of it was from the fecretary's official information. I have, however, enquired into them fince. With fuch charges as thefe the fecretary's explanation to the governor of that general fuggeftion in his report abounds. Why were not real crimes punifhed in due time? And why were things of no moment or criminality magnified into real offences?

Prefident Addifon was early in his endeavours to promote the execution of the excife law. For this purpofe he wrote in the newspapers in the fummer of 1791, and for the fame purpofe he attended at Redftone old fort on the 2;th of July, on the day when it was refolved by the meeting at that place to petition Congrefs. Though he took no part in the meeting, he was ready to give his advice, or to exert his authority if neceffary in favour of the laws. I converfed with him on the occafion and found he was in favour of fubmiffion, for which reafon fome thought him too friendly to the excife. In his charges to the grand juries, he uniformly reprehended the attacks on excife officers, and recommended a ftrict cognizance of the offences, and in all his converfation on this fubject he teftified againft the oppofition to the law. In the winter previous to the infurrection an animated pub-

fication in the Pittsburgh gazette exhorting the people
to a compliance with the law, was afcribed to him, and
he promoted an agreement among a number of the
moſt reſpectable diſtillers to enter their ſtills, on condition of having officers appointed whoſe deportment
would be reſpectable (See Chap. v.) I always accounted it a misfortune that he was in Philadelphia
when the inſurrection commenced; his advice and
authority might have been of great advantage; he was
very uſeful in reſtoring order when he returned; he
was threatened by the inſurgents before he returned,
but this did not prevent him from doing his duty with
ſuccefs. At the ſame time that he was obnoxious to
the inſurgents, he was the object of the ſecretary's
reſentment; in this, however, he was not ſingular.
Others, who exerted themſelves to the utmoſt in preventing outrages and reſtoring order, were the peculiar
objects of miniſterial perſecution. After all the ſcrutiny that could be made and all the exertions to extort
teſtimony, the character of the Preſident and the ſix-
teen aſſociate judges of the four weſtern counties ſtood
unimpeached, except we call the ſecretary's charge
of want of politenefs in two inſtances to exciſe officers
a ſufficient cauſe of impeachment. The truth is, that
judges and other friends of order were offended at theſe
officers for not making more vigilant exertions in the
execution of their truſt, and for treating the people
rudely, when conciliating manners might have engaged
reſpect and promoted ſubmiſſion. Certain it is, that
when general Wilkin, who purchaſed whiſkey for the
army, though his refuſing to purchaſe any that had not
paid the exciſe tax made him partake of the odium at-

tached to the law, yet by his good fenfe in reafoning,
with the people, and by his conciliating manners, he
induced many to enter their ftills in June 1794, and
was morally certain of procuring a general acquiefcence at the next opportunity of entering ftills.
The apprehenfion of want of vigilance and conciliating manners in the excife officers difcouraged thofe
who wifhed the law to be executed from making exertions. Such citizens did not chufe to be knight-errants
in fupporting a law, the execution of which was fo much
neglected by thofe whofe duty it was to enforce obedience to it. However, from the fecretary's report to
the Prefident, and his explanation of it to the governor,
it is evident that the revenue officers were vigilant
fpies, not only on the conduct, but the language of the
citizens, and very minute in reporting the fmalleft expreffions of difrefpect to themfelves or the law, unconnected with the circumftances of provocation on their
part to the fecretary; and that though he was not
attentive to punifh real crimes in the ordinary courfe
of law, yet he was very attentive to record incidents
of little importance, and arrange them in the moft criminal drefs fuited to his defign, when the crifis arrived
which he probably defired and promoted. But the
information, though minute, was not accurate. This
is ufual with the information of fpies in all countries.
The report contains feveral other inftances of mifreprefentation with refpect to incidents too trifling to
be inveftigated, which I fhall pafs unnoticed; one contained in the laft paragraph of it, however, is of too
much importance to efcape remark. His words are:
" There is too juft caufe to believe that this is connected

with an indifpofition, too general in that quarter, to
fhare in the common burthens of the community, and
with a wifh among fome perfons of influence, to embarrafs the government. It is affirmed by well informed perfons to be a fact of notoriety, that the revenue
laws of the ftate itfelf have *always* either been refifted,
or very defectively complied with in the fame quarter."

  This is fo palpable a mifreprefentation, as to require but little examination to refute. I appeal to
the records of the ftate treafury ; there it will appear
that notwithftanding the almoft ceafelefs diftreffes of
the weftern counties, fome of them have always been
the foremoft in paying their ftate taxes of any counties
in the commonwealth, and none of them the moft
backward, and that if there are any arrears remaining
due it is on the unfeated lands, the property of people
in the city or other parts of the ftate, the collecting of
which has been prevented by fpecial interpofitions of
the legiflature. If he had defired to be well informed,
it would have been eafy for him to have confulted the
treafury department of the ftate, and if he had applied
to the land office, he would have found that the efficient
revenue produced by it has been more promptly paid
by the people of the weftern counties, than by many
in more favourable fituations. If he had been in purfuit of truth he would have applied to the proper four-
ces to obtain it. Another object however was in view.
It was neceffary to load the whole people of the weftern
country, with every defcription of odium. God
knows, too many of them were blameable indeed, but
that the revenue laws of the ftate have been *always*

either refifted or defectively complied with, and that this was promoted by a wifh of fome perfons of influence to embarrafs the government, or as he expreffes it, (Report p. 110) the enmity which certain active defigning leaders had induftrioufly infufed into a large proportion of the inhabitants, not againft particular laws only, but of more ancient date, againft the government of the United States, are charges abfolutely void of truth.

I never heard a perfon either in public or private in that country exprefs a fentiment againft the government of the United States fince it was ratified, except what fell from Bradford at the Redftone meeting, and fo far from having old enmity, he was a moft zealous federalift. There were none engaged in the infurrection that ever poffeffed extenfive influence in that country, except colonel Marfhal, and he had never been diftinguifhed for political fervor.

Why did not the fecretary name the perfons and ftate the facts. If he knew that fuch influential perfons had induftrioufly infufed enmity againft the government into a large proportion of the inhabitants, he muft have known who they were, and what induftry they ufed. Indeed the whole of thefe fuggeftions are mere fabrications, publifhed at a critical period for the moft nefarious purpofes. No teftimony to this purpofe could be procured by all the influence which was exerted even under all the terrors of an armed force, neither could any proofs of it be obtained on the moft careful and judicious fcrutiny, made under the di-

O o

rection of the circuit courts. It exifted no where but
in the fruitful invention of the ex-fecretary himfelf.

Before I leave the fecretary's report, I will make
one other quotation form it page 117, where he fays:
" It is not to be doubted that the different ftages of this
bufinefs were regularly notified to the malcontents,
and that a conviction of the tendency of the amendments contemplated to effectuate the execution of the
law, had matured the refolution to bring matters to a
violent crifis. "

This infidious affertion was no donbt levelled
againft Mr. Smilie, and myfelf, then in Congrefs.
There were no others from the weftern country in the
city who had an opportunity ; and the fecretary's numerous declarations that we were at the bottom of all
the difturbances, and that he had proofs againft Mr.
Gallatin and us already, his illegal endeavours to
extort teftimony againft us in the weftern country, his
infulting the people there for electing us into Congrefs,
and employing his friend general White to fpread
falfehoods againft us, particularly againft myfelf, was
fufficiently explanatory of his intention in the paragraph juft quoted.   I have already ftated that I never
was acquainted in the part of the country where the
difturbances originated, nor had correfponded even by
letter with any perfon who had been concerned either
in promoting or countenancing the difturbances, except
James Marfhal a confiderable time before. I am authorifed to make the fame declaration refpecting Mr.
Smilie. Mr. Gallatin was not then in Philadelphia. I
had correfpondents in Wafhington county, whofe

friendfhip I value, and whofe conduct during the difturbances and previous to their commencement does
them honour.

I remember to have received letters from three
diftillers that fpring, and anfwering them ; that thefe
diftillers were not concerned in the infurrection, except
in oppofing it, is a fufficient juftification of my corre-
pondence ; they were William Todd, Efquire, a judge
of the court, Mr. John Dennifton, and my brother
John Findley. Indeed I had no ufeful information
refpecting the excife law to write : the bill to which
the fecretary alludes, he acknowledges was not enacted
till the fifth of June, and until the laft reading in the
Houfe. I was induced by information from the treafury
department to believe, that the excife would be turned into a direct tax on ftills, and an amendment to
that purpofe was tranfmitted from the treafury department to the chairman of the committee which brought
in the bill, while it was under difcuffion in the Houfe,
but he did not fee caufe to move for its adoption. If I
had correfponded with the people who unfortunately
commenced the infurrection, I flatter myfelf that I
would have contributed by removing their miftakes to
have prevented their exceffes. I am fure all with whom
I have correfponded will bear witnefs that that would
have been my endeavour.

When we reflect that the law in queftion authorifed the ftate courts to take cognizance of offences againft
the United States, that long before it was enacted the fecretary had procured writs to be iffued out of the diftrict
court to compel the appearance of delinquent diftillers at Philadelphia, and delayed to have thefe writs

executed until harveft, after the people had been gratified with the reafonable expectations of having their fuppofed delinquency examined in the vicinity of their refidence, and that thefe writs, the execution of which produced the infurrection, were made returnable in a manner or at a time which rendered them of no effect ; I fay when thefe circumftances are candidly reflected on, the reader will be able to decide for himfelf, whether there is not as folid ground, as the nature of the cafe can be fuppofed to admit, to conclude that the fecretary himfelf at this period contemplated and planned to promote the violent crifis which took place. By his own account we find he was regularly informed by his fpies of the moft minute circumftances of the clandeftine outrages, and conducted his plan in a manner the beft calculated to excite an open rupture. If this was not his defign, why did he not ufe the proper means of reftraining offences in feafon, and why did he not caufe the procefs to be ferved fooner, and at a more convenient feafon, or otherwife make an experiment of the fuccefs of the ftate courts ?

The great error among the people was an opinion, that an immoral law might be oppofed and yet the government refpected, and all the other laws obeyed, and they firmly believed that the excife law was an immoral one. This theory became with many a religious principle, in defence of which they reafoned with confiderable addrefs. In endeavouring to reftore order, and fubmiffion to the laws, the moft arduous

talk with people otherwife of good morals was to convince them of the error of this principle. As no riots
that I knew of were attempted in the county where
I refide, or by the people of it previous to the infurrection, and as I had never heard any perfon threaten
any other kind of oppofition than laying afide their
ftills, I confequently knew nothing of this principle
being entertained till the infurrection took place; but
I then found it to be one of the greateft obftacles to
people even of good under ftanding figning fuch affurances as might imply an approbation of the law. Indeed
I defpair that people, refiding in fituations where excifes, applying directly to agriculture, demand
two or three times the quantum of tax in proportion to the
price in the market for the produce of their farm, that
the farmers in more favourable fituations have to pay,
can ever be brought to approve of fuch a law by any
methods in the power of government. Their objections are obvious and eafily comprehended, and
address themfelves powerfully to their interefts; whereas the arguments arifing from the unequal preffure
of impofts on the inhabitants of towns, and people
generally who manufacture little themfelves, and confequently confume much of foreign manufactures or
luxuries, not coming under their obfervation, are not
underftood nor admitted in abatement of their own
complaints ; confequently the citizens in fituations remote from market are advocates for direct taxes, pro-
portioned to the value of property, and always pay
them without complaint. To explain the operation

of other taxes, which tended to an abatement of the preſſure of the excife tax, and the inequality which would ariſe from apportioning direct taxes according to the conſtitutional rule, was the great object of thoſe who endeavoured to reconcile the people to the ex-cife law. There were circumſtances however which could not be accomodated to the principles of juſtice. Theſe were balanced with political conſiderations.

━━━━━━━━━━━

C H A P XXII.

T W O important queſtions have agita-
ted the public mind, which the facts ſtated in this
work, by beingjudicioufly compared, will affiſt the reader in determining.   The firſt is, whether or not the
inſurrection was the reſult of a previous combination
or preconcerted plan.   The ſecond is, whether or not
the march of an army into the country was neceſſary
for procuring ſubmiſſion to the laws, protection to the
revenue officers, and obtaining proper ſubjects for
atonement.   About theſe there has been a great variety of opinion.

   With reſpect to the firſt, the ſecretary, in his report
and otherwife, has taken fo much pains to imprefs
the public mind with an opinion that ſtate officers
ufed the weight of their official influence in promoting
combinations and hoſtility againſt the laws, that even
members of Congrefs had been employed in maturing
the reſolution to bring matters to a *violent criſis*, and

this opinion has been so industriously promoted in the army and throughout the United States by various means, that notwithstanding it has not been supported by a single well attested fact, the impression that has been made by it is not yet fully removed.   By the relation I have given, however, it will appear, that the insurrection commenced without any preconcert among the people, and arose from an event which they could not have foreseen; that even those, whose names afterwards made the greatest figure in the insurrection, were not privy to its commencement; that if the marshal had served the remaining writ without waiting to go to Pittsburgh and bring the inspector along with him, he would have met with no interruption in the discharge of his duty, and the distillers would have entered for their appearance at Philadelphia, however. distressing and unexpected such a journey might have. been to them.   It is evident that if he had conducted in this manner, the last writ might have been served before the evening on which the militia were rendezvoused at the appeal, and that if the inspector had not come out with the marshal and put himself unnecessarily in the way, the attack on him would not have happened; and that if he had not rashly first attacked the party of young fellows, who came the first morning to his house, and killed and wounded a number of them, the second and most formidable attempt would not have been made; and further, that if even on the second attempt the papers had been given up, or the house had been permitted to have been searched for them by a few men selected for that purpose, the party would have dispersed, the subsequent meetings would not have taken place, and the rioters would have been profecuted individually with fuccefs before the ftate courts, as they had been for the riot committed on the ftate excifemen.

So far were the judges of the county courts, or the prefiding judge of the diftrict, from being in a combination againft the execution of the law, that on a fcrutiny, no doubt the more fevere, that the former fupervifor and the fecretary of the treafury had prejudged their character, it appeared to full conviction that they were without exception friendly to the execution of the laws. It is certain that a profecution never failed for want of fufficient zeal in the courts ; the difficulty was to find evidence. It will appear furprifing that when the revenue officers could give fuch minute and circumftantial information to the fecretary, which he details in his report, and more minutely in his explanatory letter to the governor, that thefe fame officers could never produce teftimony to the ftate courts to enable them to punifh breaches of the peace againft themfelves ; and that even the teftimony which they produced to fupport profecutions in the federal court was either evidently fabricated or doubtful. It is acknowledged that the teftimony they procured againft Kerr and Beer, was abfolutely falfe. It is not lefs certain that the teftimony given againft Robert Smilie was unfounded, and it is the general opinion that the teftimony produced againft M'Culloch and fome others was equally unworthy of credit.

If the infurrection had been the refult of a preconcerted plan, fome difcovery of it would have been found by the commiffioners of the United States and of the ftate of Pennfylvania, while in the weftern country, but fo far was this from being the cafe that the commiffioners fent by the Prefident of the United States to the weftern country, in their report, which, though concife, gives an intelligent and candid account of the temper and fituation of the country until the day of figning the amnefty, and a relation of many of the grievances of which the people complained, yet does not give the leaft countenance to the opinion that the infurrection was the refult of a preconcerted plan, or that the ftate courts had been defective in their duty, or the judges, &c. oppofed to the execution of the laws, and it was on the information given in this report that the army was ordered to rendezvous. It is printed in the proceedings of the executive, and perfectly agrees with the preceding relation as far as it enters into the fubject.

The Report of the ftate commiffioners, who acted in concert with the commiffioners of the United States, is not printed, but I have an authenticated copy of it before me. It is contained in a feries of letters written from the weftern country to the governor, and preferved on files in the fecretary's office. As it is not in print I will give fome extracts from it. In page 2, the commiffioners give the following ftatement.

" The marfhal of the diftrict of Pennfylvania had procefs to ferve on divers perfons refiding in the counties of Fayette and Allegany, and executed them all (above thirty) without moleftation or difficulty, excepting one which was againft a Mr. Shaw. He or fome other perfon went to the place where doctor Beard, the brigade infpector for Wafhington county was hearing appeals made by fome of a battallion which had been called upon for its proportion of the eighty thoufand men required to be in readinefs agreeably to an act of congrefs. There were upwards of fifty there with their fire-arms, to whom it was related that the federal fheriff, (as they ftyled the marfhal) had been ferving writs in Allegany county and carrying the people to Philadelphia, for not complying with the excife laws, and that he was at general Nevil's houfe. It was in the night of the——of laft month; between thirty and forty flew inftantly to their arms, and marched towards Mr. Nevil's above twelve miles diftant, where they appeared early next morning.——— The delinquents againft whom the Marfhal had procefs told him that they would enter their ftills, and pay him the excife together with the coft of fuit. Major Lenox applauded their prudent conduct, and told them that though he had not authority to comply with their wifhes, yet, if they would enter their ftills with the infpector, and procure his certificate, and fend it to Philadelphia, upon payment of the money due with the cofts he was perfuaded all further profecution would be ftayed. If this detail is true, it is evident that the outrages committed at Mr. Nevil's houfe were not owing to deliberate preconcerted meafures, but originated in an unbridled guft of paffion artfully raifed among young men, who may have been at the time too much heated with ftrong drink."

In their third letter the commiffioners, ftating the difappointment of their expectations from the meeting at Redftone old Fort, occafioned by an armed party, and the outrageous behaviour of Mr. Bradford, thus express themselves : " From our best conjecture the people of Washington if governed by what appears to be the majority, will prefer a civil war to a submission to the excise laws, so infatuated and frantic are their leaders in opposition; a great majority, however, of the other three counties, are friends to peace and order."

To explain this character of Washington county, it is to be remarked that it was believed that the armed party whose presence and behaviour terrified the meeting came there from Washington county, in concert with Bradford, for that purpose. I was present, and believed this to be the case, until afterwards that it was fully proved that the company in arms knew nothing of the meeting being held there, till they were near the ground, and that their whole object was to pay an unfriendly visit to Mr. Jackson. I heard the man, who I am since informed was the leader of the party, censure Bradford's harrangue while he was delivering it to the meeting ; yet it is certain the spirit of opposition was stronger in a part of that county then in any other place.

In their fourth and last letter, written from Bedford when the commissioners were on their return, they say "Upon the whole we entertain a reasonable hope that the great mass of the people will comply with the terms proposed, and be dutiful citizens in future, and that their example and influence will in a few days prevail on most of the residue to do the same. However it must not be concealed that there are several unruly and turbulent spirits, who will require correction and punishment, and these men having little or no property to lose, may possibly create new disturbances.

Should our opinion prove to be well founded, it is probable the ordinary course of judicial powers may be sufficient to reduce them to submission and order, without military aid."

The commissioners of the Union and of the state, concurred in their consultations and measures ; as far as there was any difference, the chief justice was the most severe ; he wanted to have the committees to sign assurances individually at the first, and to have the power of the civil magistrate, put to the test without delay. Though this was complained of at the time, as too severe, the people were afterwards convinced that he was for their good ; in one instance, he urged a justice of the peace to exert his authority, and he did it with success.

The result of the scrutiny made by the judiciary, aided by the terrors of the army, the dispensing power of the commander in chief, and the artful and arbitrary conduct of the secretary, and also the examinations of numerous witnesses before the circuit court held at Philadelphia and York, agree in proving to a demonstration, the truth of the opinion given by the commissioners, that *the outrages committed at Mr. Nevil's house, were not owing to deliberate preconcerted measures, but originated in an unbridled gust of passion, &c.*

With respect to the second question, viz. whether the march of an army into the western country was necessary, &c. I have already expressed my own opinion that it was not necessary for the objects proposed, and in this I was supported by that of well informed persons who knew the state of the country better than I did myself. I have been particular in my

enquiries of the same and other well informed persons, a
year since the insurrection, and though it is the opinion
of some individuals, that the submission to the laws
by some of the most obstinate people south of the
Monongahela, was sooner accomplished and rendered
more compleat by the march of the army into the
country, than it would otherwise have been ; yet it is
agreed by all, with whom I have conversed on the subject, that in all other parts of the country the submission would have been compleat without it.   The greater number of well informed persons, however, believe that it would have been compleat in all the
counties, but this fact cannot now be ascertained with
precision.   It is certain, that the state courts were at
no time interrupted, and that they have since senten-
ced to correction and punishment such as they thought
deserved it for offences committed during the disturbances, with as little difficulty as at any other time,
indeed, I never knew of a process from a justice of the
peace resisted even in the time of the insurrection, and
the magistrates had in many places proceeded against
offenders without resistance, before the army left Carlisle.   In the places where the disturbances prevailed,
the alarm and terror was so great as to render it imprudent, if not impracticable, to execute the laws of the
state, until the agitation would subside, and till the
friends of order could know and put confidence in each
other.

But after all, I do not conclude that it was improper in the President to order the army to advance into
the country.   I have no doubt, but that if he had received the same assurances before the different divisions

of the army had rendezvoused, which he did at Carlifle, he would not have ordered the army to march; but he muft have judged the affurance; to have been in a higher degree unequivocal, than could be procured in fo fhort a time, to have convinced him of the propriety of putting a ftop to the expedition when it was fo far advanced; for however confident Mr. Redick and myfelf were, who drew our information from our own obfervations, and the obfervations of others in whom we had perfect confidence, taken on the fpot, yet as the Prefident had not the opportunity of making obfervations for himfelf, we could not expect his confidence to be fo compleat or fo firmly eftablifhed as ours.

The difficulty that had been experienced in raifing the army at the fift, and the eagernefs difcovered by the officers and others at Carlifle to march into the weftern counties, muft have had its weight with the Prefident in determining him to carry forward the expedition. He might reafonably conclude, that bad confequences in future might refult from difgufting them, by what thofe of greateft influence might think a premature difcharge. As he mixed every day with the army, in order to imprefs it with a proper fenfe of the importance of fubordination to the laws, it is not to be doubted, but that he availed himfelf of this opportunity of difcovering its difpofition, and that his determination was in fome meafure influenced by that difpofition; nor is it to be doubted, but that the advice of fecretary Hamilton, and his influence with the army, were exerted in favour of carrying on the expedition.

His information and advice were calculated to promote that object from the first.

The President, however, did not consider the number of the army, nor its advance into the western country, as destined exclusively for restoring submission to the laws, or coercing offenders in that quarter ; the flame had caught in other places, and discontents prevailed and liberty poles were erected, through a great extent of country, on the east side of the mountains, and a rising had actually taken place in the state of Maryland.   It was these untoward circumstances which prevented the President from giving longer time for the people in the western counties to restore order by their own efforts ; for further information on this subject, the chapters which describe the temper of the army at Carlisle, and the communications of the President to the commissioners from the Parkison ferry meeting, may be examined.

I have suggested oftener than once, that the head of the revenue department conducted the execution of the law in the western district, in a manner that was calculated to promote the event that happened.   To support a suggestion of this nature, positive proof cannot be obtained ; to me, however, it appears better established than could reasonably have been expected ; from the means I had used to promote a due execution of the law, and the observations I had made on the manner in which it was conducted, I had suspected his design, and for some time looked forward to the event with dread ; but in the spring of 1794, when competent powers were vested in the state courts, my prospects brightened, and I blamed myfelf for my fufpicions. But the mine was ready to be fprung, when I had flattered myfelf that the danger was over. I will not however, recapitulate the grounds upon which my opinion was founded, but leave the reader to examine and compare the facts for himfelf, and judge of the refult. The facts are truly ftated.

Q q

A P P E N D I X.

WHEN the Prefident received the infor-
mation of the daring outrage committed at the houfe of the
Infpector, he held a conference with the heads of the departments of the federal government, and the governor and law
officers of the ftate of Pennfylvania, and though no record is
preferved of the fentiments expreffed on that occafion, yet it
is known, that the chief juftice of the ftate, gave it as his
opinion, that the power of the judiciary fhould be further
exerted, and have a full and fair trial, before it would be proper to employ a military force, and that the governor and
law officers of the ftate, and the fecretary of ftate of the United
States, concurred with him in that opinion. In fupport of
this opinion, the governor made a communication to the Prefident in writing, dated the 5th of Auguft, 1794. The correfpondence which commenced with this letter, is to be found
in the executive proceedings, from page 58 to 98.

In this communication, after ftating the outrages that had
taken place, together with their fpecial circumftances, the governor proceeds to remark " that whatever conftruction may be
given on the part of the United States, to the facts that have
been recited, I cannot hefitate to declare, on the part of Pennfylvania, that the incompetency of the judiciary department

of her government, to vindicate the violated laws, has not at this period been sufficiently apparent, and that the military power of the government ought not to be employed until its judiciary authority, after a fair experiment, has proved incompetent to enforce obedience, or to punish infractions of the laws."

After stating the principles on which the military force can with propriety be called forth, in aid of the civil authority, he proceeds to say : " Experience furnishes the strongest inducements to my mind, for persevering in this lenient course. Riots have heretofore been committed in opposition to the laws of Pennsylvania, but the rioters have invariably been punished by our courts of justice. In opposition to the laws of the United States, in opposition to the very laws now opposed, and in the very counties supposed to be combined in the present opposition, riots have likewise occurred, but in every instance, supported by legal proof, the offenders have been indicted, convicted and punished before the tribunals of the state. This result does not announce a defect of jurisdiction, a want of judicial power, or disposition to punish infractions of the law ; a necessity of an appeal from the political to the physical strength of the nation.

" But another principle of policy deserves some consideration. In a free country it must be expedient to convince the citizens of the necessity that shall at any time induce the government to employ the coercive authority with which it is invested. To convince them, that it is necessary to call forth the military power, for the purpose of executing the laws, it must be shown, that the judicial power has in vain attempted to punish those who violate them, and therefore thinking, as I do, that the incompetency of the power of Pennsylvania has not been sufficiently ascertained, I remarked in the course of our late conference, that I did not think it would be an easy task to embody the militia on the present occasion."

In the conference, the governor had been called on to order out the militia of the state, in pursuance of a law of the state, which was supposed to exist, but which, on examination, was found to be repealed. The propriety of ordering out a military force was then suggested to him, in consequence of his general power to enforce the due execution of the laws. The discussion of this principle produced the correspondence, from which I have made these quotations.

The secretary of state of the United States, in his reply to the governor's first letter, does not so much object to the principles advanced by the governor, as to his opinion respecting the existing circumstances, and after stating the facts and reciting the certificate from the judge, which had been newly obtained, he says, "Thus then, is it unequivocally and in due form ascertained in reference to the government of the United States, that the judiciary authority, after a fair and full experiment, has proved incompetent to enforce obedience to, or to punish infractions of, the laws—that the strength and audacity of certain lawless combinations have baffled and destroyed the efforts of the judiciary authority, to recover penalties or inflict punishments, and that this authority by a regular notification of this state of things, has in the last resort, as an auxiliary of the civil authority, claimed the intervention of the military power of the United States," &c.

In the progress of this correspondence, the secretary of state of the United States informs the governor, that the question unequivocally was, if he as the executive of the state has power to put the militia in motion, previous to a requisition from the President under the laws of the United States, if it should be thought advisable so to do, &c. This question being thus explicitly stated in the last letter to the governor, and the actual requisition of the militia rendering a reply unnecessary and calling the governor's attention from the subject, we have to regret the want of his answer to it. But if I understand him rightly in the preceding letters, he did not conceive that he was justified by the constitutional power vested in him, in calling out the militia, unless he was convinced in his own judgment that the judiciary authority was incompetent to vindicate the violated laws, or was called on to do so by a formal requisition from the Prefident of the United States. In vindication of that opinion, he fuggefts, that the Prefident's refponfibility is fhielded by the interpofition of the opinion of a judge of the fupreme court, certified according to law, which the governor's is not.

The governor fays, that it is certain that at the time of the conference there was no fatisfactory evidence of the incompetency of the judicial authority, to vindicate the violated laws, and that therefore he could not as the executive magiftrate proceed to a military plan.

The fecretary in behalf of the Prefident difclaims his being under an obligation to judge of the validity of the teftimony himfelf, and manifefts his determination to depend on the decifion made by the proper authority, viz. the opinion of a diftrict or affociate judge, to whofe refponfibility he folely referred the competency of the teftimony. Judge Wilfon who gave the official certificate which made it lawful for the Prefident to aid the judicial authority by military force, did fo on his own opinion of the validity of the teftimony that was laid before him by the executive. There were no witneffes examined, nor depofitions tranfmitted; fome private letters containing information of the facts and the general notoriety of the outrages were confidered as fufficient vouchers on which to ground the judge's certificate, and this certificate was the authority which warranted the military expedition.

It muft be admitted, that in times of public confufion and danger the obtaining of legal teftimony would fometimes be attended with too much delay, and that in fuch cafes the notoriety of the facts fuperfedes the neceffity of legal forms; ftill however, there is danger of miftakes, and it is certain, that the Prefident and affociate judge, were impofed on with refpect to fome material facts refpecting the riots, until a fcrutiny was made by the circuit court. Some of thefe impofitions were too deeply impreffed on the public mind by the report of the fecretary of the treafury, in which they were fanctioned by his official authority, but exprefsly contradicted by unexceptionable teftimony taken before the court.

The chief juftice with the concurrence of the other law officers of Pennfylvania, at the conference, firft fuggefted the plan of fending commiffioners to the weftern counties, and in aquiefcence with this advice, h: and general Irwin were appointed by the governor to that fervice. Though in a letter by the fecretary of the 7th Auguft, the Prefident objects to the governor's opinion, that a further trial of the power of the judiciary fhould be made, before the aid of the military force was required, yet he fays, "that to manifeft his attention to the principle that a firm and energetic conduct does not preclude the exercife of prudent and humane policy he has (as the governor has been alfo advifed) concluded on the meafure of fending commiffioners to the difcontented counties to make one more experiment of a conciliatory appeal to the reafon, virtue, and patriotifm of their inhabitants, and has alfo fignified to you how agreeable would be to him your co-operation in the fame expedient, which you have been pleafed to afford."

This interefting correfpondence chiefly embraces two fubjects of controverfy, viz. the refponfibility of the executives of the union and of the commonwealth, and the incompetency of the judicial authority, which is affirmed in behalf of the Prefident, and objected to by the governor. Without deciding pofitively betwixt the two opinions, it is worth obferving, that though the law firft provided for fending fpecial feffions of the court into the delinquent country, and afterwards vefted the authority in the ftate courts, yet the competency of neither one nor the other of thefe methods prefcribed by law was ever put to the teft, and that all the trial that had been made of the competency of the judicial authority was by the marfhal ferving the proceffes, which gave rife to the infurrection, and that even in this cafe, that officer ferved thirty nine writs without moleftation, to thirty four of which at leaft a proper fubmiffion was teftified, and that refiftance was offered only in one cafe out of forty, and not till the obnoxious infpector affifted with his prefence, and till the laft cafe. It is true, a deputy marfhal was

fent two years before, but influenced by the advice of the infpector and his own fears, he did not attempt to exercife his
authority; a fheriff of the county, or probably a marfhal of
good character refiding in the country, could at any time have
executed writs; it has been obferved, that fheriff Hamilton
propofed to do it even in the time of the infurrection. The
reader will judge, whether this was a fair and full trial of the
incompetency of the judiciary, as afferted in the name of the
Prefident.

If the judiciary authority had been exercifed agreeably to
the provifions made by law, I am confident no infurrection,
nor refiflance would ever have happened, and if in addition to
fending commiffioners the governor had fo far rifked his refponfibility, as to have embodied a fquadron of light horfe and
marched into the weftern counties, order would have been reftored without the aid of any other force ; this would have
been a center for thofe who were timid and well difpofed to
rally round, and would fooner have produced a difcrimation of
parties; it would alfo have afforded protection and given confidence to the civil magiftrate, in places where the fpirit of oppofition had the afcendant, and encouraged the orderly citizens
in all parts of the country. I will not affert that the governor
had competent authority for this purpofe, but I cannot refrain
from expreffing a wifh that he had conftrued his powers to have
extended fo far, and trufted fomething to the difcretion of the
legiflature afterwards.

However, it muft be admitted in behalf of the governor,
that he had little time for reflection ; for the decifive certificate
was procured from the affociate judge the next day after the
conference, at which it was propofed to the governor to call
out the militia under his own authority.

The citizens of Ohio and Monongahela counties in Virginia had been earneftly folicited by circular letters from Mr.
Bradford, who believed he had influence among them, to join
in the infurrection, or at all events to attend the Parkifon
meeting, and give their advice. He no doubt expected them

to ftrengthen his party at that meeting in order to form a combination againft the authority of the government. Three delegates attended from Ohio county at this and at the Redftone
meeting, but I have not been informed what part they acted;
it appears, they waited on the commiffioners at Pittfburgh,
along with the firft committee of twelve. The commiffioners
informed them that they had no authority out of the fourth
furvey of Pennfylvania, but at the fame time encouraged them
to expect no further trouble for indictable offences, if they gave
affurances of fubmiffion to the laws for themfelves, and in
behalf of thofe by whom they had been delegated. They feem
to have been fent but by a few people, and I do not find, that
any thing further was done refpecting them. There had been
but one riot committed there; the collector of the revenue appears to have given up his papers to the rioters without refiftance; therefore, there were no inftances of flagrant outrage.
The averfion poffeffed by the citizens of thofe counties of Virginia to the government and laws of Pennfylvania, and to the
people of it near them, occafioned by the territorial conteft,
had a good effect in preventing a union in the prefent oppofition.

Before the army left the weftern country, a feparate corps
confifting of not more than 2,500 was raifed for a term, not
exceeding three months. They encamped near the Monongahela on the fouth fide, under the command of general Morgan. This meafure was fanctioned by a law, dated November
29th, 1794. The object of continuing this force in the country was *to caufe the laws to be duly executed*, they were partly
raifed out of the corps that were employed in the expedition,
and partly inlifted in the country; many of the laft were faid
to have been the moft troublefome of the infurgents: I was not
acquainted with any of them, and as they encamped near forty
miles from where I refide, though they remained a confiderable time in the country after I returned from Congrefs, I heare
more of them than if they had not been in the country,

The people in that part of the country, however, complain, that many of them for some time at first, demanded free quarters and such things as they stood in need of without pay, and that some of the officers committed indictable offences; but when the persons, against whom the offences were committed, commenced prosecutions, they settled the disputes amicably, and behaved well for the future. And when the people took courage to refuse to submit to impositions, the soldiers ceased to demand free quarters or to be otherwise troublesome.

Before the army left the country, the commander in chief prescribed the form of an oath which he required the justices of the peace to administer to the citizens, whom he commanded to appear indiscriminately before the magistrates for that purpose. It was taken by a number of people in Pittsburgh, and I am informed by a few in some other places. How general Lee came to assume the high legislative authority, necessary for enacting an oath of allegiance and requiring the magistrates to administer and the people to swear it, I never have been informed; it is not contained in the President's instructions to him, nor had the constitution vested the President with authority of that kind. General Lee must have known, that a magistrate had no authority to administer an oath, that the law did not prescribe. The people generally through the counties, however, paid no respect to these orders.

Previous to the return of the army, he issued a proclamation agreeably to the President's instructions, to stop all prosecutions against the insurgents, except certain persons therein named. Several of the excepted persons afterwards gave themselves up to general Morgan and stood their trial, and were acquitted. Bradford and a few others left the country, and have not to my knowledge returned again. Those from Cumberland and Northumberland counties, who were indicted for erecting liberty poles, &c. had their trial put off till the sessions of the circuit court, held at Philadelphia, in April, 1796, and then the prosecution was withdrawn by the district attorney. In some counties, on both sides of the mountain, those who erected liberty poles were heavily fined by the state courts.

Before the secretary of the treasury left the army, he made arrangements for settling with the delinquent distillers. He directed that they should be permitted to enter their stills on paying arrearages according to the capacity of the stills, for the year that commenced in June 1793, and for the current year. It was some time in December, before these arrangements were made known. Many complied with the terms and entered their stills, and some left them with the collector, not having wherewith to pay his demands. Some in Westmoreland, and perhaps in other counties, absolutely refused to pay the arrearages for 1793, but offered to pay for the current year, and enter their stills, but the money was not received and permission to enter their stills was refused. They demanded permission to enter their stills again in June 1795, and were refused. They however continued to employ their stills, and wish a decision at law ; they say, they were always willing to submit, but had not opportunity to enter their stills. All the distillers complain of being obliged to pay the arrearages of 1793, because they had not an opportunity of charging it to the owner who had his grain distilled, or laying it on the consumer according to the intention of the law. Some were making attempts to sue for the recovery of what they had paid. Those who stand out against paying the arrearages, are mostly men of information and property, and they believe the secretary had no authority by law to admit entries at any time, but that which the law prescribes; nor any legal power to refuse entries of stills, on any conditions made by his own authority. Subpoenas were served on these delinquent distillers last summer; but after they had appeared at two courts, no prosecution was commenced.

Permission to enter stills had been refused at the inspecting offices, the first or second day after the month of June expired, immediately preceding the insurrection. What a pity it was, that if the entry of stills could be admitted at the discretion of an executive officer in December, that the fame diicretion had not been exercifed early in the month of July.

As no perfon near where I refide was difturbed by the army, nor profecuted by the judiciary, there is no complaint, on their own account ; but on enquiry I find that in the parts of the country were people againft whom there was no charge were taken prifoners and dragged to Pittfburgh, and feveral of them to Philadelphia, there is much heart burning. I have converfed with fome men of influence, who were at all times the warmeft friends of government, who acknowledge that their confidence in, and love of, the government, is much abated. I mention thefe circumftances to fhew how much better it would have been to have made a feafonable and energetic ufe of the ordinary powers of government, before things came to fuch a crifis as to require fuch extraordinary remedies, as can fcarcely be fo conducted but that they will create fome new grounds of complaint. Every other means fhould be ufed to the utmoft before a militia army is raifed ; for if they are frequently called forth, or called forth on a fervice which they find not to have been abfolutely neceffary, or the neceffity of which they think might have been prevented, it will not be eafy to roufe them again when the public intereft may require it ; in this cafe a ftanding army may become neceffary, and I know a ftanding army is not the wifh of the people of the United States, and hope it will long be unneceffary.

In one year fince the infurrection the weftern furvey of Pennfylvania has remitted to the treafury about 20,000 dollars of excife tax. This amounts to one fifth of the nett revenue raifed in one year on fpirits diftilled from domeftic materials in the whole United States. It is true this includes the arrearages arifing from the preceding year. Of thefe I do not know the amount ; but when it is confidered that many left their ftills with the collector rather than pay the arrearages, and that others preferred ftanding an action which is not yet decided, the greater part muft be fet to the account of the year 1795. If other parts of the union paid in the fame pro-

.portion as to the number, without calculating on the wealth of the inhabitants, the aggregate amount would be little short of a million of dollars annually.

Whatsoever difference of opinion might have existed as to the policy of the measure when the excise law was enacted, there could be but one opinion among dispassionate citizens with respect to the impolicy of repealing it on the account of a riotous opposition in a part of one small survey, while that mode of opposition continued, and all other parts of the union professedly submitted; but now when the authority of the law is acknowledged throughout the union, it is proper to enquire into the productiveness of the revenue arising from it, and the expediency of continuing it. It is not my object to make any observations on the general principles of an excise system, its suitableness to, or practicability in, this country; but if it is true that, notwithstanding the frequent revisions of the law, this tax does not yield 100,000 dollars as net revenue,* that from some states, where it is reasonable to suppose a considerable quantity of those spirits are manufactured and consumed, after an experiment of five years, little or no revenue can be procured, though the officers receive their salaries for collecting it. If it is true that nearly one-third of this revenue is necessarily expended in the collection of it, and that the comparative quantity of spirits distilled is decreasing, and the importation and consumption of spirits and other liquors have rapidly in-

* So much of the amount of this revenue, as it is stated in the official reports, depends on estimates for which the data are not certain, and the drawbacks for that year not being fully ascertained, these statements may not be perfectly accurate; but, by the official statements for the year ending with June 1795, the produce of the excise on domestic spirits amounts to about 140,000 dollars, for the year 1797, the expence of collecting amounted to more than 41,000 dollars, exclusive of the additional expence occasioned by it in the accounting offices of the treasury department; adding this, and including the expence of new, though unproductive districts since erected, the whole expence of collecting cannot be estimated at less than 45,000 dollars per annum: taking this from 140,000 dollars, leaves 95,000 dollars to the revenue; but this being still liable to drawbacks on the revenue for exportation, stating that the expence of collection is equal to half the nett proceeds of the revenue must be pretty near the truth.

creafed, fince the commencement of the excife on domeſtic
fpirits ;" I fay if thefe things are true, it may foon be proper
for the legiflature to enquire whether fo fmall an amount of revenue is a fufficient object for the employment of fuch a number of officers, and for occafioning fo much difcontent in thöfe
parts of the union, which are increafing moſt rapidly in population.

It is proper to examine whether even this fmall amount of
revenue may not prove a fource of jealoufy, and eventually
alienate the affections and confidence of one part of the citizens
from the other. It is no unreafonable conjecture to fuppofe,
that a crifis may happen in the courfe of human events, when
this alienation may occafion very difagreeable confequences,
which by feafonable arrangements might be prevented.

A riotous oppofition to the excife law in one furvey has already colt the United States more money, than will probably be
produced by that tax from the whole United States, when it
has been ten years in operation ; and though it is to be expected
that the difplay of the power of goverament in enforcing fubmiffion to the laws in that inftance may long prevent the neceffity
of another expedition, either to protect the officers of government,
or to punifh offenders againft its laws, yet it muſt be acknowledged that this tremendous and expenfive remedy will not be
adequate to prevent evafions of the law in fo wide an extent of
territory, where the prepoffeffions againft it are general. If the
levying an excife on this, and all other manufactures in the
country, would produc a fufficient revenue to prevent the
neceffity of a direct tax, it would afford a ſtrong argument to
thofe who are oppofed to direct taxes, in favour of continuing
and extending excifes ; but when it is difcovered that fome of
them, for inſtance the excife on fnuff, will not produce perhaps as much in a year as would pay the expence of making the

---

* By the official report, it appears that from the year 1791, in which the excife
on fpirits from domeſtic materials commenced, till the year 1794, the quantity of
imported fpirits increafed from 3,673,193 gallons, to 5,693,369 gallons, an increafe of nearly two-fifths in the courfe of two years ; and that the importation of
wines, porter and beer, has increafed in a much greater proportion.

law, and that now, when a tax of 1,200,000 dollars appears to be absolutely neceffary, the greateft advocatees for excifes cannot lay their hand on fubjects for fuch taxes, it is time to enquire whether it is proper to perfift in that courfe of taxation.

It will not do for us to depend on raifing effective revenues from excifes on manufactures, as fome nations in Europe do. In thefe nations a great proportion of the wealth of the country is vefted in manufactures, and from them their exports are produced; but in our country, where manufactures are in their infancy, and but a fmall amount of capital vefted in them, and where the wealth of the inhabitants confifts chiefly in land and objects of agriculture, or is employed in a commerce which is fupported by agriculture; land itfelf with the ftock that is employed on it, and commerce, muft be the dernier refort for efficient revenues. If any aid can be drawn from manufactures, I fufpect it cannot be procured to any confiderable extent in the mode of excifes. If this circumftance had been feafonably adverted to, when the ftate debts were affumed, &c. by thofe who are moft obftinately oppofed to direct taxes, fo great an amount of revenue would not have been neceffary; but in the prefent ftate of our finances we cannot put off direct taxes much longer, and when they come, as come they muft, the writer will not avoid his fhare of the public burthens. If he ftudied only his own intereft, excifes would to him be the moft favourable mode of taxation, as the proportion, he would pay in that way, would be much lefs than would fall to his fhare by a direct tax.

N O T E [A] p. 183.

We afked Mr. M'Farlane if he would permit the office to be kept in his houfe, if general Nevil fhould be the officer;

he anfwered, that if he was the officer, he was perfonally fo
obnoxious to the people, that it would be more prudent for
him to keep it for fome time in Pittfburgh, where the garrifon
was; but that any perfon not equally obnoxious might open
an office with fafety in any part of the country.   We did not
mention general Nevil's name to the Prefident.

F I N I S.